ROMANTIC FEUDS

The Nineteenth Century Series
General Editors' Preface

The aim of the series is to reflect, develop and extend the great burgeoning of interest in the nineteenth century that has been an inevitable feature of recent years, as that former epoch has come more sharply into focus as a locus for our understanding not only of the past but of the contours of our modernity. It centres primarily upon major authors and subjects within Romantic and Victorian literature. It also includes studies of other British writers and issues, where these are matters of current debate: for example, biography and autobiography, journalism, periodical literature, travel writing, book production, gender, non-canonical writing. We are dedicated principally to publishing original monographs and symposia; our policy is to embrace a broad scope in chronology, approach and range of concern, and both to recognize and cut innovatively across such parameters as those suggested by the designations 'Romantic' and 'Victorian'. We welcome new ideas and theories, while valuing traditional scholarship. It is hoped that the world which predates yet so forcibly predicts and engages our own will emerge in parts, in the wider sweep, and in the lively streams of disputation and change that are so manifest an aspect of its intellectual, artistic and social landscape.

Vincent Newey
Joanne Shattock
University of Leicester

Romantic Feuds
Transcending the "Age of Personality"

KIM WHEATLEY
The College of William and Mary, USA

LONDON AND NEW YORK

First published 2013 by Ashgate Publisher

Published 2016 by Routledge
2 Park Square, Milton Park, Abingdon, Oxfordshire OX14 4RN
711 Third Avenue, New York, NY 10017, USA

First issued in paperback 2016

Routledge is an imprint of the Taylor & Francis Group, an informa business

Copyright © Kim Wheatley 2013

Kim Wheatley has asserted her right under the Copyright, Designs and Patents Act, 1988, to be identified as the author of this work.

All rights reserved. No part of this book may be reprinted or reproduced or utilised in any form or by any electronic, mechanical, or other means, now known or hereafter invented, including photocopying and recording, or in any information storage or retrieval system, without permission in writing from the publishers.

Notice:
Product or corporate names may be trademarks or registered trademarks, and are used only for identification and explanation without intent to infringe.

British Library Cataloguing in Publication Data
Wheatley, Kim, 1960–
Romantic feuds: transcending the 'age of personality' – (The nineteenth century series)
   1. Literary quarrels – History – 19th century. 2. Criticism – Great Britain – History – 19th century. 3. Romanticism.
   I. Title II. Series
   801.9'5'0941'09034-dc23

Library of Congress Cataloging-in-Publication Data
Wheatley, Kim, 1960–
Romantic feuds: transcending the "age of personality" / by Kim Wheatley.
   pages cm. — (The Nineteenth century series)
   Includes bibliographical references and index.
   ISBN 978-1-4094-3272-2 (hardcover: alk. paper)
   1. English literature—19th century—History and criticism. 2. Authors, English—19th century—Political and social views. 3. Romanticism—England. 4. England—Intellectual life—19th century. I. Title.
   PR447.W44 2013
   820.9'145—dc23

2013004325

ISBN 13: 978-1-138-26881-4 (pbk)
ISBN 13: 978-1-4094-3272-2 (hbk)

For Loren, Emily, and Stephen

Contents

Acknowledgements	*ix*
List of Abbreviations	*xi*
Introduction	1
1 The *Wat Tyler* Controversy: Southey Refigured	21
2 Coleridge, Jeffrey, and the *Edinburgh*: Romanticizing "Personalities"	57
3 Hunt, Hazlitt, Lady Morgan, and the *Quarterly*: Creative Reprisals	97
4 John Barrow, John Ross, and the Arctic Sublime	139
Bibliography	*175*
Index	*185*

Acknowledgements

First, I am grateful to my graduate school professor, Jerome Christensen, for suggesting that I "take a look at" Romantic-era periodicals, and for fueling my fascination with Romanticism. My intellectual indebtedness to him goes back decades, and will infuse my future scholarly endeavors.

Next, I would like to thank my friends and colleagues in the English Department at the College of William and Mary for their generous advice and support while this project took shape. In particular, Suzanne Raitt and Adam Potkay have been huge sources of inspiration and wisdom. I have also benefited from the intellectual energy and encouragement of Jack Martin, Ann Reed, Deborah Morse, Monica Potkay, Arthur Knight, Martha Howard, Liz Barnes, Jenny Putzi, Simon Joyce, Brett Wilson, Melanie Dawson, Paula Blank, Rich Lowry, and Christy Burns. Other colleagues who have kindly assisted me include Terry Meyers, Susan Donaldson, Suzanne Hagedorn, Hermine Pinson, and Chris MacGowan.

Thanks as well to the various audience members who have listened to the parts of this book presented as conference papers and talks. Many of them, especially at William and Mary and the University of St. Andrews, offered valuable feedback.

It is a privilege to belong to the wonderful global community of Romanticists. Among Romanticist colleagues at other institutions, I especially wish to thank my good friends Meg Russett and John Morillo for sharing their expertise and for the interest that they have taken in my work. Peter Manning, Stephen Behrendt, Nick Roe, and Jonathan Cutmore have also provided generous assistance for which I am grateful.

Thanks, too, to the College of William and Mary for research leaves in 2000–2001 and 2006–2007, and a summer grant in 2007, that supported this project. My colleagues in a College-sponsored grant-writing workshop, including Cindy Hahamovitch and Scott Nelson, helped me clarify my topic.

I am also indebted to the suggestions made by an anonymous reader for Ashgate Press, which enabled me to improve this book. My editor at Ashgate, Ann Donahue, has been unfailingly supportive and helpful. The rest of the editorial team, Ann Allen and Patrick Smith, efficiently answered my questions about preparing the manuscript for publication.

In addition, I would like to acknowledge the permission granted by publishers to re-use the parts of this book that first appeared elsewhere. An earlier version of the Leigh Hunt section of Chapter 3 appeared as "Conceiving Disgust: Leigh Hunt, William Gifford, and the *Quarterly Review*" in *Leigh Hunt: Life, Poetics, Politics*, ed. Nicholas Roe (London: Routledge, 2003): 180–97. A few sentences in my introduction originally appeared in my essay, "Plotting the Success of the *Quarterly Review*," in Jonathan Cutmore, ed., *Conservatism and the* Quarterly Review*: A Critical Analysis* (London: Pickering & Chatto, 2007), 19–39. More recently, an earlier version of Chapter 4 appeared as "The Arctic in the *Quarterly*

Review" in *European Romantic Review* 20: 4 (October 2009): 465–90. And I thank the Trustees of the British Museum for allowing me to use my cover image, "Art of Self Defence. Tom and Jerry receiving Instructions from Mr. Jackson, at his Rooms in Bond Street," by I. Robert Cruikshank and George Cruikshank.

Finally, special thanks go to Loren Council, for his thoughtful comments on my manuscript and more importantly for years of patience and good humor, and to our children, Emily and Stephen, for brightening the many days it has taken me to write this book.

List of Abbreviations

BL	Samuel Taylor Coleridge. *Biographia Literaria*. Ed. James Engell and W. Jackson Bate. 2 vols. Princeton: Princeton University Press, 1983.
BM	*Blackwood's Magazine*. Edinburgh: William Blackwood, 1817–1824.
CCH	J.R. de J. Jackson, ed. *Coleridge: The Critical Heritage*. London: Routledge and Kegan Paul, 1970.
CL	*Collected Letters of Samuel Taylor Coleridge*. Ed. Earl Leslie Griggs. 6 vols. Oxford: Clarendon Press, 1956–1971.
CR	*The Critical Review*. London: Archibald Hamilton, 1756–1817.
Cutmore	Jonathan Cutmore, ed. *Conservatism and the Quarterly Review: A Critical Analysis*. London: Pickering & Chatto, 2007.
E	*The Examiner*. London: John Hunt, 1808–1828.
EOT	Samuel Taylor Coleridge. *Essays on His Times*. Ed. David V. Erdman. 3 vols. Princeton: Princeton University Press, 1978.
ER	*Edinburgh Review*. Edinburgh: Archibald Constable, 1802–1929.
FM	Sydney Owenson (Lady Morgan). *Florence Macarthy: An Irish Tale*. Ed. Jenny McAuley. London: Pickering & Chatto, 2012.
Friend	Samuel Taylor Coleridge. *Collected Works: The Friend*. Ed. Barbara E. Rooke. 2 vols. Princeton: Princeton University Press, 1969.
Howe	William Hazlitt. *Works*. Ed. P.P. Howe. 21 vols. London and Toronto: J.M. Dent and Sons, 1930–34.
LC	*The Life and Correspondence of Robert Southey*. Ed. Charles Cuthbert Southey. 6 vols. London: Longman, Brown, Green and Longmans, 1850.
LM	*London Magazine*. London: Baldwin, Cradock, & Joy, 1820–29.
NL	*New Letters of Robert Southey*. Ed. Kenneth Curry. 2 vols. New York: Columbia University Press, 1965.
QR	*Quarterly Review*. London: John Murray, 1809–1967.

RR, A	Donald Reiman, ed. *The Romantics Reviewed: Contemporary Reviews of British Romantic Writers, Part A: The Lake Poets*. 2 vols. New York and London: Garland Publishing, 1972.
RR, C	Donald Reiman, ed. *The Romantics Reviewed: Contemporary Reviews of British Romantic Writers, Part C: Shelley, Keats, and London Radical Writers*. 2 vols. New York and London: Garland Publishing, 1972.
SCH	*Robert Southey: The Critical Heritage*. Ed. Lionel Madden. London and Boston: Routledge & Kegan Paul, 1972.
TLP	*The Works of Thomas Love Peacock*. Ed. H.F.B. Brett-Smith and C.E. Jones. 10 vols. London: Constable, 1924.
Wu	William Hazlitt. *Selected Writings*. Ed. Duncan Wu. 9 vols. London: Pickering & Chatto, 1998.

Introduction

Pursuing the quintessentially Romantic quest for transcendence, I find it in an unlikely location: a series of feuds involving the *Edinburgh Review* and the *Quarterly Review*, during the second and third decades of the nineteenth century. Besides the supposedly anonymous reviewers, the protagonists in these episodes of persecution include Romantic-era authors who themselves wrote for periodicals—Robert Southey, Samuel Taylor Coleridge, Leigh Hunt, and William Hazlitt—in addition to the Irish novelist and travel writer Lady Morgan (also known as Sydney Owenson) and the Arctic explorer John Ross. From its inception, the Whig *Edinburgh* (founded in 1802) had developed a reputation for "vituperative criticism";[1] its Tory rival, the *Quarterly* (founded in 1809), was soon perceived to offer more of the same, if not more so. For Coleridge, attacks by these two leading periodical works exemplified "this AGE OF PERSONALITY, this age of literary and political GOSSIPING" (*BL* 1: 41). In this context, the phrase "age of personality" signals a cultural preoccupation, frequently malicious, with the private lives of individuals in the public eye. As is well known, Coleridge and other Romantic poets and essayists often aspired to ignore fractious reviewers and rise above—or delve beneath—their deplorable emphasis on "personality." However, in recent decades, new historicist critics have revealed the extent to which Romantic literature is bound up with the print gossip and warfare of the age.[2] For many such critics, the study of "Romantic-era print culture" (a historical phenomenon) has superseded the study of what used to be known as "Romantic literature" (an aesthetic category).[3] This book, though, finds an aesthetic element even in routinely antagonistic, politicized and gossipy exchanges between writers and reviewers. Like some other critics who combine historicist excavation with close textual analysis, I see early nineteenth-century periodical culture as collaborating with, rather than resisting, the emergence of Romanticism.[4]

---

[1] Sir Walter Scott, *Letters*, ed. H.J.C. Grierson, 12 vols (London: Constable, 1932), 2: 128.

[2] See, for example, Marjorie Levinson, *Keats's Life of Allegory: The Origins of a Style* (Oxford: Basil Blackwell, 1988), Paul Magnuson, *Reading Public Romanticism* (Princeton: Princeton University Press, 1998), and Brian Goldberg, *The Lake Poets and Professional Identity* (Cambridge: Cambridge University Press, 2007).

[3] See, for example, Kevin Gilmartin, *Print Politics: The Press and Radical Opposition in Early Nineteenth-Century England* (Cambridge: Cambridge University Press, 1996), and Paul Keen, *The Crisis of Literature in the 1790s: Print Culture and the Public Sphere* (Cambridge: Cambridge University Press, 1999).

[4] Compare, for example, Jerome Christensen, who, in "The Detection of the Romantic Conspiracy in Britain," *South Atlantic Quarterly* 95 (1996): 603–27, locates a "dark Romanticism" in the "wild sarcasm" of the *Edinburgh* (625). See also Mark Schoenfield, *British Periodicals and Romantic Identity* (New York: Palgrave Macmillan, 2009).

The *Edinburgh* and the *Quarterly* have frequently been understood as anti-Romantic because of their attacks on writers traditionally associated with Romanticism: William Wordsworth, Coleridge, Percy Bysshe Shelley and John Keats.[5] However, as I have suggested elsewhere, the extravagant diction of hostile reviewers itself can be seen to register the impact of the poets' stylistic innovations.[6] My concern in this book is with content and form as much as with vocabulary. I argue that contributions to feuds involving the quarterlies unexpectedly touch on major themes of canonical Romanticism: the exploration of the "deep" self, the revitalizing of the everyday, the experience of the sublime, and even the power of the supernatural. Meanwhile, I show that certain persecutory articles in both Reviews—together with a number of the multifarious written responses that they provoked—draw on genres since associated with the major Romantics: literary biography, autobiography, lyric, and romance. As the feuds spin off into other print media—including the weekly press and monthly magazines as well as pamphlets, poems, and novels—they incorporate various other literary genres now appreciated as vital to our newly enlarged conception of Romanticism: comedy, parody, satire, and the Gothic. Approaching wars of words as multi-authored narratives, I trace how these public disputes acquire their own momentum, leaving behind their points of origin to branch off in unpredictable directions.[7] I see the feuds as behaving like works of literature, ignited and kept alive by mixtures of political, commercial, psychological, and artistic motives, as well as by the exigencies of periodical form. While inevitably inhabiting the so-called "age of personality," participants in the feuds become caught up in dramas larger than themselves, taking part—consciously or not—in Romantic stories of transfiguration. Transcendence can thus be glimpsed not only as a thematic preoccupation within the feuds but also as an effect of collaborative writing.

This book addresses a particular historical juncture—the years immediately after Waterloo—when the "sprightly"[8] rhetoric of the two major quarterlies was

---

[5] William St. Clair, in *The Reading Nation in the Romantic Period* (Cambridge: Cambridge University Press, 2004), for instance, sees the *Quarterly* as representing the "mainstream official ideology" (229).

[6] See Kim Wheatley, *Shelley and His Readers: Beyond Paranoid Politics* (Columbus: University of Missouri Press, 1999), Chapter 3. The claim can be extended to apply to Romantic poets other than Shelley, especially Keats and Hunt.

[7] In engaging with the methodological problem of what constitutes a text in the field of periodicals study, I expand the notion of what constitutes a literary text. Lyn Pykett, in "Reading the Periodical Press: Text and Context," *Victorian Periodicals Review* 22 (1989): 100–108, asks, "What is a text in [this] field …? Is it the individual essay? The issue? The volume? A run defined in some other way—say by the period of a particular editorship?" (105). For my purposes, each feud constitutes a distinct though open-ended "text." The two feuds explored in the first half of this book each extend over a few months while the intertwined feuds of Chapter 3 and the more fitful feud of Chapter 4 alike continue for years.

[8] The *Quarterly*'s publisher John Murray referred to the "sprightly pages of the Edinburgh Review" in a letter to Walter Scott dated November 15, 1808 (quoted in Cutmore, 202).

hardening into what Coleridge called a "*habit* of malignity" (*BL* 2: 109), a habit that was about to be further solidified and enlivened by the arrival on the scene of the more playful and informal monthly magazines, notably the *Edinburgh*'s Tory rival *Blackwood's*. The reviewers' rhetoric has various recognizable features. One is the reliance on so-called "personalities" or personal attacks, the era's dark form of life-writing, which, as I will show, could be perceived either as the publicizing of private lives or as expressions of seemingly private hostility. A related characteristic is the extensive use of vitriolic language and sarcasm, which tends to infect the voices of writers engaged in quarrels with the quarterlies. A third feature overlaps with these two: the practice of mocking and nitpicking criticism, extremely focused on the word choices of the texts under consideration, also often seen by its early readers as a form of personal attack. We will see that different feuds involve differing emphases on these strands of the reviewers' rhetoric, and that the reviewers' antagonists adapt and resist its strategies with varying degrees of effectiveness. By 1817, the year of the first two feuds I discuss, "personalities" had become a staple ingredient of the era's weekly newspapers, including Leigh Hunt's pro-reform *Examiner*. The revamped *Blackwood's Magazine*, beginning in the autumn of 1817, initiated the practice of more novelistic and elaborate personal attacks.

Several recent critics have stressed the conventionality of the magazine writers' slashing rhetoric, seeing it as adhering to a distinct set of rules and the product of multiple causes.[9] I contend that the reliance on convention that such critics have identified in the monthly magazines is shared or anticipated by the *Edinburgh* and the *Quarterly*, propelling the feuds that these periodicals initiated or in which they took part.[10] Despite Romantic-era writers' sense that theirs was an "age of

---

[9] Vituperation has a long history in both political and literary British culture, but critics see its use in the Romantic era as more schematic than in the eighteenth century. See, for example, Michael Allen, *Poe and the British Magazine Tradition* (New York: Oxford University Press, 1969), who claims that "journalists of the period recognized a specific and conscious convention of conflict" (41). Compare John Strachan, who, in his Introduction to Volume 6 of *Blackwood's Magazine, 1817–25: Selections from Maga's Infancy* (London: Pickering & Chatto, 2006), connects the "personal abuse" of *Blackwood's* with "the Scots tradition of flyting" (xxi), and Barton Swaim, "'Edinburgh is a Talking Town': Scottish Periodical-Writing and the Competitive Conversation," *Prose Studies* 28.3 (2006): 245–57. Swaim links the combative style of the *Edinburgh* and *Blackwood's* to a shift away from deferential politeness in the Scottish public sphere. Richard Cronin, in *Paper Pellets* (Oxford: Oxford University Press, 2011), points out that personal attacks were not "confined" to the periodical press of the period (39).

[10] Compare David Stewart, in *Romantic Magazines and Metropolitan Literary Culture* (Basingstoke: Palgrave Macmillan, 2011), on how "*Blackwood's* built on precedents" including "the slashing reviews of the Lake School in the *Edinburgh Review*" (34). See also William Christie, *The Edinburgh Review in the Literary Culture of Romantic Britain: Mammoth and Megalonyx* (London: Pickering & Chatto, 2009), on the "peculiar obsession" of *Blackwood's* "with the *Edinburgh Review* as a specular antagonist against which … it defined its own existence and its own values" (149).

personality," attacks on individuals, that is to say, did not necessarily reflect actual persons' opinions. Later in this introduction, I will expand on Coleridge's slippery definitions of personal attacks in order to address in more detail the question of the calculatedness of the reviewers' rhetoric.

Behind-the-scenes reflections by the founders of both the *Edinburgh* and the *Quarterly* seem to reveal the amount of deliberation underlying their rhetoric from the start. Francis Jeffrey, editor of the *Edinburgh*, declared that every number should contain one "tickler," meaning a nasty review.[11] The exchanges of letters between the founders of the *Quarterly* include anxious discussion of the extent to which they should imitate the "quizzing" style of the *Edinburgh* (Cutmore, 196) and its "ribaldry" (Cutmore, 200).[12] William Gifford, editor of the *Quarterly*, complained in 1810 that "the high seasoning of the Edinburgh Review has spoiled all taste for more solid and simple criticism" (Cutmore, 37). The *Quarterly*, like the *Edinburgh*, offered both—interspersing serious scholarly essays with shorter, more biting reviews—but sometimes even the most sober articles would be seasoned with what Walter Scott called "spice" (Cutmore, 26). Rising circulation figures for both quarterlies in the post-war period seemed to confirm the profitability of this formula, but to be truly entertaining, "flagellation"[13] depended on victims capable of fighting back.

Published attacks in the period almost automatically sparked reprisals, despite the problematic assumptions underlying the resort to retaliation: hence the frequency with which hostile reviews led to escalating episodes of print warfare. As a *Blackwood's* writer put it in 1820, "*give and take* is a fair motto now-a-days" (*BM* 7: 317). Accusations of "personality" were routinely used as if they would put an end to debate, when they almost invariably had the opposite effect. Coleridge voiced a commonplace of the age when he wrote to Henry Crabb Robinson in December 1817, quoting Cecil Lord Burleigh, "Calumnies suffered to pass uncontradicted are active poisons, never compleatly [sic] neutralized either by the innocence of the slandered individual or even by their own extravagance or absurdity" (*CL* 4: 785–6). This statement raises the question of whether "calumnies" can ever really be neutralized even when responded to, and it ignores the possibility that contradicting alleged slander might make matters worse, generating more "extravagance or absurdity." Like many of his contemporaries, John Ross took "the absence of any rejoinder" to signify assent.[14] Romantic-era writers' idea that an attack that is perceived to be personal

---

[11] Quoted in Strachan et al., eds, *Blackwood's Magazine, 1817–25*, 6: xv.

[12] I discuss these letters in "Plotting the Success of the *Quarterly Review*" in Cutmore, 19–39.

[13] Samuel Smiles, *A Publisher and his Friends*, 2 vols (London: John Murray, 1891), 1: 146.

[14] John Ross, *Observations on a Work, entitled, "Voyages of Discovery and Research within the Arctic Regions," by Sir John Barrow, Bart.* (Edinburgh and London: William Blackwood, 1846), 11.

automatically requires a response was frequently supplemented by their impulse to speak back on other people's behalf. Complementing what David Erdman and Paul Zall call "persecution-by-association,"[15] we will encounter in more than one feud what might be called self-defense-by-association, as well as the practice of offering reprisals for attacks on fellow-authors.

Many of these expressions of resentment, whether direct or indirect, seem problematic in the sense that efforts at self-vindication, like personal attacks, accept the (questionable) assumption that public and private lives are intertwined. Similarly, violent counterattacks blatantly ignore the option of dignified silence, while the point-by-point refutation of minute criticisms grants validity to the reviewers' fixation with small details. Reformist writers in particular faced a challenge when speaking out against a mighty institution like the *Quarterly* with its reputation as "the supposed literary organ of Government."[16] Yet like the attacks instigating them, many of the responses have an imaginative side.[17] Some of the reprisals that I will discuss appear in freestanding works of poetry, prose fiction, and satire, drawing creative inspiration from vituperation in more disposable publications. I see retaliation as crucial, because although the cycle of attacks and counterattacks may be rhetorically or politically ineffectual, with their proliferation, everybody wins in the sense that the feuds take on lives of their own. As my chosen feuds simmer in the quarterlies or drift into the weekly and monthly magazines and into other forms of print, their transmutation of the reviewers' "sprightly" rhetoric into more traditionally literary genres and concerns cuts across the authors' specific locations and leaves behind their apparent control over their choice of language and themes.[18]

---

[15] David V. Erdman and Paul M. Zall, "Coleridge and Jeffrey in Controversy," *Studies in Romanticism* 14 (1975): 75–83 (78).

[16] Lady Morgan, *Letter to the Reviewers of "Italy"* (Paris: A. and W. Galignani, 1821), 3.

[17] On the creativity of Romantic-era expressions of indignation in general, see Andrew M. Stauffer, *Anger, Revolution, and Romanticism* (Cambridge: Cambridge University Press, 2005).

[18] Following Schoenfield, David Stewart, in *"The Examiner*, Robert Southey's Print Celebrity and the Marketing of the *Quarterly Review*," *Prose Studies* 31 (April 2009): 22–39, argues that as periodicals, including the quarterlies, "became increasingly part of a post-war commercial order," publications ostensibly aimed at particular partisan readerships "performed together for [a larger] audience defined as a mass market of consumers" (25). Stewart takes this celebrity-conscious audience to be "new" in the 1810s (25). In *Romantic Magazines,* he notes that "success in the newly enlarged print market depended on controversy" (14)—success, that is, at once artistic and financial. While I do not stress economic factors as much as Schoenfield and Stewart, I share their sense that the *Edinburgh*, the *Quarterly* and other print media worked together dialogically to entertain a combined rather than a politically polarized audience.

The Convention of Anonymity

In recent decades, criticism of early nineteenth-century periodical writing has focused on its convention of anonymity with its tensions between collective discourse and individual authorship.[19] The quarterlies and other reviewing periodicals borrowed from their eighteenth-century predecessors the use of the magisterial first person plural, giving a deceptive impression of unanimity. Jon Klancher has offered an influential account of what he sees as a depersonalized corporate voice in the elite periodicals, a "transauthorial discourse" subsuming the voices of separate anonymous contributors.[20] Klancher's phrase seems especially descriptive of the *Edinburgh* and the *Quarterly* with their massive claims of cultural authority. William St. Clair has warned against applying Romantic notions of solitary authorship to the periodicals, claiming that "When reviewers employed the royal 'we,' they were implying that their views were those of the institution for which they were writing."[21] Mark Schoenfield has recently analyzed in detail the Reviews' creation of the corporate personas of the "Edinburgh Reviewer" and "the Quarterly Reviewer."[22] Other critics have sought to modify Klancher's "transauthorial" idea by unearthing the identities of particular reviewers or by pointing to the influence exerted by the editors of the periodicals.[23] Different chapters of this book give varying answers to the question of how to avoid losing sight of individual authors' voices when analyzing anonymous discourse, but they all treat the controversies under discussion as eventually independent of orchestration by either the reviewers, the reviewed, or the editors of the various periodicals involved in the feuds. My guiding presuppositions are first, that what looks like an individual voice often turns out to be a collaborative one and vice versa, and second, that the literary energy of these feuds and their escape from "personality" can be generated as much from the collective prevailing over the individual as from the other way around. Recovering individual voices does not necessarily involve reinstating the myth of solitary inspiration that is part of the Romantic legacy. None of my chosen feuds involves a straightforward

---

[19] For a survey of such criticism, see my introduction to *Romantic Periodicals and Print Culture* (London: Frank Cass, 2003). For an "ethical and aesthetic" (as opposed to "sociological") approach to the Romantic preoccupation with anonymity that coexists with the era's "enthusiasm for the autonomy of the self," see Jacques Khalip, *Anonymous Life: Romanticism and Dispossession* (Stanford: Stanford University Press, 2009), 3–4.

[20] Jon Klancher, *The Making of English Reading Audiences 1790–1832* (Madison: University of Wisconsin Press, 1987), 52.

[21] St. Clair, *Reading Nation*, 284. George Pottinger, in *Heirs of the Enlightenment: Edinburgh Reviewers and Writers 1800–1830* (Edinburgh: Scottish Academic Press, 1992), points out that Jeffrey sounded very different when reviewing Southey's *Thalaba* (1801) for the *Monthly* and when reviewing the same poem in the *Edinburgh* (86).

[22] Schoenfield, *British Periodicals and Romantic Identity*, 84 and 89.

[23] See, for example, Cutmore, and Cutmore's website the *Quarterly Review* Archive, http://www.rc.umd.edu/reference/qr/index.html [accessed August 4, 2012].

asymmetrical clash between, on the one hand, the majestic impersonal quarterlies, and on the other hand, named individuals taking responsibility only for their own opinions. My first two chapters in particular explore the paradox whereby collaborative writing generates models of autonomous Romantic selfhood, while relying on one reviewer in particular—Hazlitt—(himself a focus of Chapter 3) as a key practitioner of "personality." Even the fearless Lady Morgan (another focus of Chapter 3) partially hides herself behind her alter egos, the heroines of her novels.

Romantic-era writers themselves commented on the peculiarity whereby reviews that were deemed to include "personalities" or personal attacks were produced by writers who not only refused to reveal their own individual identity but who claimed the weight of more than one person's identity—in Morgan's sardonic phrase, the "worthy *we's*" (*FM*, 329). In the section of *Biographia Literaria* (1817) in which he condemns "personality" and gossip, Coleridge connects the "violent and undisciplined abuse" (*BL* 1: 42) of the reviewers of his day with the fact that they write anonymously. Speaking with a lofty institutionalized voice, they thus confuse "I" and "we," feeling "authorised as 'synodical individuals' to speak of themselves plurali majestatico!" (*BL* 1: 42). This false claim to a collective identity further weakens, in Coleridge's view, their critical integrity. In *The Friend* (1818), Coleridge complains of a "morbid hardness produced in the moral sense by the habit of writing anonymous criticisms, especially under the further disguise of a pretended board or association of Critics, each man expressing himself ... as a *synodical individuum*" (*Friend* 1: 183n.). As a longtime contributor to periodicals, Coleridge himself had of course written plenty of anonymous criticisms.

Arguing along the same lines, Thomas Love Peacock, in his unfinished "Essay on Fashionable Literature" (1818), attacking the *Edinburgh* and the *Quarterly* as "semi-official oracles" (*TLP* 8: 267), condemned the illusion of collective judgment created by the convention of anonymity. Of the *Edinburgh* he wrote, "Plurality is its essence. The mysterious *we* of the invisible assassin converts his poisoned dagger into a host of legitimate broadswords. Nothing, however, can be more remote from the facts" (*TLP* 8: 268). Implying that the reviewers are mere individual assassins, Peacock claims that the contributors to the *Edinburgh* do not even know each other's names and do not communicate with each other, making the *Review*'s impression of consensus an "all-pervading quackery" (*TLP* 8: 268). For Peacock, "The only point of union among them is respect for the magic circle drawn by the compasses of faction and nationality" (*TLP* 8: 269)—a standard charge that the *Edinburgh* is guilty of political bias and pro-Scottish prejudice. He goes on to assert that "The case is much the same with the *Quarterly Review* except that the contributors are more in contact, being all more or less hired slaves of the Government, and for the most part gentlemen pensioners clustering round a common centre in the tangible shape of their paymaster Mr. Gifford" (*TLP* 8: 269). As is evident from his word choices, Peacock finds the *Quarterly*'s partisanship even less to his taste.[24]

---

[24] Peacock's essay remained unpublished during his lifetime.

As this comment also suggests, the editors loomed large in the public perception of the Reviews, complicating the effects of anonymity. Whether as tangible or intangible shapes, Jeffrey and Gifford have starring roles on my stage, because their contemporaries took them to personify the *Edinburgh* and the *Quarterly*, at the risk of underestimating the Reviews' hegemonic power through shriveling collective voices into individual ones.[25] We will see, for example, that Coleridge blamed Jeffrey for the attacks on him in the *Edinburgh*, and that Leigh Hunt and Hazlitt tended to blame Gifford for the attacks on them in the *Quarterly*, despite objecting to the *Quarterly*'s own "transposition of persons" (Wu 5: 355) in its hostile review of their co-authored book *The Round Table* (1817). Both Jeffrey and Gifford were known to rewrite contributions to their respective Reviews, making them standard targets for reprisals, despite the absence of signatures. Yet according to Gifford, "Jeffrey's best articles [were] ... the result of the studies and thoughts of several friends" (Cutmore, 21). Gifford's own "Dictatorial power" (Cutmore, 191) was equally mythological. Because the authorship of reviews could be inferred but never known for certain, and because the editors tended to be held responsible for articles whether they had written them or not, anonymous reviewing dramatizes print's power to create confusion over where one person—or persona—ends and another begins.[26]

Such blurrings of agency must be set against the tendency in the period for the authorship of articles in the Reviews to be open secrets. In his (of course anonymous) *Edinburgh* attack on Southey's *Letter to William Smith* (1817, discussed in my first chapter), Jeffrey himself brought up the topic of anonymity apropos of Southey's refusal to acknowledge that he had written a particular article in the *Quarterly*. According to Jeffrey,

> If Mr Southey had not written these passages, he would have told us plainly enough. We are a little chary, it may be supposed, of this privilege of *incognito* in reviewers; and readily admit, that no one is obliged to answer impertinent questions on such a subject. Yet it is impossible to deny, that there are instances

---

[25] Compare Cronin's claim that "The great reviews were stamped with the personalities of their editors" (*Paper Pellets*, 53). See also Massimiliano Demata and Duncan Wu, eds., *British Romanticism and the* Edinburgh Review: *Bicentenary Essays* (New York: Palgrave Macmillan, 2002), an essay collection that stresses the role of Jeffrey. On the role of the editor in the monthly magazines, see Mark Parker, *Literary Magazines and British Romanticism* (Cambridge: Cambridge University Press, 2000); and Nanora Sweet, "The *New Monthly Magazine* and the Liberalism of the 1820s," in *Romantic Periodicals and Print Culture*, 147–62.

[26] Misattributions of authorship—not always involving editors—enabled perception to trump matters of fact. The most obvious example is the fact that P.B. Shelley blamed Southey for the *Quarterly*'s attacks on him (actually by John Taylor Coleridge) and on Keats (actually by John Wilson Croker), and proceeded to demonize (and immortalize) Southey in *Adonais* (1821). As we will see, Lady Morgan blamed Croker for the attacks on her in the *Quarterly* (apparently co-written by Gifford) because Croker had attacked her (also anonymously) in Irish publications earlier in her career.

in which, we suppose with the author's consent, the fact is just as notorious as if his name had been subscribed to his article. ... The truth is, that the writers of one half of the articles in a review are impatient to be known, and take effectual measures to be so. (*ER* 28: 158)

Jeffrey goes back and forth here between defending his own "privilege" and confessing that anonymity is a relative term. Although he concedes that certain writers may be "desirous of the protection" of a "mask" (*ER* 28: 158), in this case he claims Southey's authorship can be known through uncontradicted hearsay, including reports "in various newspapers" (*ER* 28: 158).

An anonymous writer in the *Monthly Review* made a similar point in bringing up Southey's attempt to "shelter himself from responsibility because [the *Quarterly*] is anonymous, and report, which may be mistaken, is the only authority by which any particular paper can be attributed to one person or another" (*SCH*, 253–4). The *Monthly* reviewer commented, "This defence we should be inclined to allow in its full force, were not the antient and established rule of secrecy in periodical criticism now so much disregarded, and the names of the contributors in question circulated with every degree of notoriety" (*SCH*, 254). For this writer, anonymity is a sham, a collective fiction belied by the "circulat[ion]" of "names," presumably in the press but perhaps also in face-to-face spoken gossip.

Anonymity, in the newspapers and magazines of the era as well as in the quarterlies, could also be belied by writers' idiosyncratic styles. Hunt and Hazlitt, for instance, wrote anonymously in the *Examiner* (though Hunt often used his trademark pointing hand signature), but as David Stewart points out, their voices were "instantly recognizable."[27] The same can be said of Coleridge's writing style in the pro-government newspaper the *Courier*. Hazlitt, for example, described the *Courier*'s essays on Southey as issuing from "the well-known pen of Mr. Coleridge" (Wu 4: 169). Hazlitt's voice is also recognizable in the articles he wrote for the *Edinburgh*, though not to the same extent. In my final chapter, I will show how the *Quarterly* reviewer John Barrow draws attention to his own act of authorship even while his lofty first person plural stands for something larger than himself.

The fact that some of the participants in my chosen feuds encountered each other in person underlines the artificiality of the reviewers' claims to impersonality. This fact reflects a historically-specific transition between a relatively contained publishing culture and the development of a more faceless literary marketplace.[28] As we will see, Southey, on a rare visit to London, goes to "the dinner of the R[oyal] Academy" in order to "meet" his attacker William Smith, M.P., "face to face, and examine his *forehead*" (*NL* 2: 156, his emphasis). Hazlitt glimpses his "old friend" Southey in the street, and passes by without a greeting (Wu 4: 193).

---

[27] Stewart, *Romantic Magazines,* 42.

[28] Compare Kenneth Curry and Robert Dedmon, "Southey's Contributions to the *Quarterly Review*," *The Wordsworth Circle* 6 (1975): 261–72: "the practice of anonymous reviewing ... seemed to protect friendships in an era when the literary world was smaller than it is today" (261).

Before attacking him in the pages of the *Edinburgh*, Jeffrey corresponds with Coleridge, visits him at Southey's house, and later strolls with Coleridge in the fields of the Lake District before dining with him at an inn. Hunt sees Gifford at a book sale in London, staring at him with "such a face!" Hunt describes the encounter in his *Autobiography*: "I met the eyes of my beholder, and saw a little man, with a warped frame and a countenance between the querulous and the angry, gazing at me with all his might."[29] At such moments supposedly impersonal hostility seems intensely personal. Hazlitt probably sets eyes on Gifford when living near him in London at the time of his feud with the *Quarterly*.[30] Lady Morgan visits the premises of her publisher Henry Colburn, and catches a "glimpse of the long leg and *ci-devant* white stocking" of the fleeing Hazlitt, who had criticized her *Life and Times of Salvator Rosa* (1824) in the *Edinburgh*.[31] The *Quarterly* reviewer and bureaucrat Barrow dines with John Ross at the home of Lord Melville of the Admiralty, and accompanies his soon-to-be enemy to John Murray's office to arrange for the publication of his first book, the same book that Barrow afterwards attacks anonymously in the *Quarterly*. At around the same time, the two men engage in what Ross calls a "personal altercation."[32] Years later, in his official capacity, Barrow is forced to correspond with his nemesis.[33]

The feuds exist in a public textual space but fairly frequently seep into private correspondence and face-to-face meetings in which physical bodies interact or pointedly refuse to do so. However, none of the participants in the feuds that I discuss engage in an actual duel or even a fistfight.[34] The "lash" wielded by the *Edinburgh* and the *Quarterly* reviewers and their opponents (*BM* 3: 161) remains metaphorical—words on the page—yet, due to the circumstance that many of the antagonists knew each other personally, capable of crossing the boundary between public and private. Actors in the feuds could be personally invested—and offended—even while performing in a spectacle for the entertainment of what Tom Mole calls "a modern audience—massive, anonymous, socially diverse and

---

[29] *The Autobiography of Leigh Hunt, with Reminiscences of Friends and Contemporaries*, 2 vols (New York: Harper and Brothers, 1850), 1: 257.

[30] Duncan Wu, *William Hazlitt: The First Modern Man* (Oxford: Oxford University Press, 2008), 490, n.93.

[31] Quoted in Lionel Stevenson, *The Wild Irish Girl: The Life of Sydney Owenson, Lady Morgan (1776–1859)* (New York: Russell and Russell, 1969; first published 1936), 238. In his review, Hazlitt does however protest against the "abuse" directed against Morgan by "some of our Tory journals" (*ER* 40: 316).

[32] Ross, *Observations on ... "Voyages of Discovery and Research within the Arctic Regions,"* 9. According to John Ross, ending a meeting at Murray's office, Barrow declared, "I'll have nothing more to do with you" (M.J. Ross, *Polar Pioneers: John Ross and James Clark Ross* [Montreal: McGill-Queen's University Press, 1994], 53).

[33] M.J. Ross, *Polar Pioneers*, 168.

[34] Coleridge, though, had to be dissuaded from challenging Jeffrey to a duel. For treatment in the context of anonymous authorship of the duel that killed John Scott, editor of the *London Magazine*, see Margaret Russett, *De Quincey's Romanticism: Canonical Minority and the Forms of Transmission* (Cambridge: Cambridge University Press, 1997), 109. See also Cronin, *Paper Pellets*, 1–17.

geographically distributed,"[35] and some of their performances seem to be aimed at more select audiences of those in the know. As they embrace and transcend politicized print warfare, their voices sometimes sound idiosyncratic, sometimes "synodical," and often somewhere between the two.

Personal Attacks

I now turn to Coleridge's discussion of "personality" in *Biographia Literaria* to illustrate the elusiveness of the term "personal" from the point of view both of textual content and intention. (I will return to the *Biographia* in Chapter 2 because part of Coleridge's feud with the *Edinburgh* is carried on within its pages.) In both the *Biographia* and the 1809 *Friend*, Coleridge bemoans the fall into what he calls "emphatically the age of personality!" (*Friend* 2: 286–7), with its investment in biographical trivia, its commercialization of literature, and its correspondingly superficial reading public. This historical development threatens the ideals in which he believes, including the power of the imagination, poetic genius, aesthetic merit, a thoughtful and learned readership, and even the spirit of Christianity. Representative of the blighted age are periodical reviewers, whom Coleridge finds guilty of both random and calculated acts of verbal violence. Coleridge's chapter in the *Biographia* on "the present mode of conducting critical journals" continues the argument, begun earlier in the book, that contemporary reviewers' lack of philosophically informed principles makes them write irrationally, with "arbitrary dictation and petulant sneers" (*BL* 1: 62).[36] According to Coleridge, the *Edinburgh Review* leads the way in its reliance on "unlicensed personality" (*BL* 2: 110). Coleridge first admits that the "damnatory style" of the *Edinburgh* is not objectionable per se "as long as the author is addressed or treated as the mere impersonation of the work then under trial" (*BL* 2: 108). The statement raises the question of what it means to treat an "author" as a "mere impersonation" of the text. Making the author a stand-in for his work might sound like standard reviewing procedure, but if "impersonation" gives a text a human face, it risks making the author himself shadowy and depersonalized.

The *Biographia*'s definitions of "personal insults" (*BL* 2: 109) show the difficulty of pinning them down either in terms of what they say, the feelings behind them or the interpretation of their rhetoric. Coleridge goes on to assert that he does object to "personal allusions" and the bringing up of "juvenile performances" since the only "motives" for the latter practice must be the attacker's "own personal malignity" (*BL* 2: 108–9). He slides here from discussing the content of the review to the emotions of the reviewer, which presumably, given the ostensible invisibility conferred by the convention of anonymity, have to be projected onto him or inferred by his readers, unless they have inside knowledge. Coleridge has

---

[35] Tom Mole, *Byron's Romantic Celebrity: Industrial Culture and the Hermeneutic of Intimacy* (New York: Palgrave Macmillan, 2007), 10.
[36] Coleridge himself, by contrast, attempts to articulate his transcendentalist philosophy before criticizing Wordsworth's poetry.

had and will have more to say on the subject of the "motives" behind personal attacks, but for the moment he brings up only one cause other than "personal malignity," one that is "still worse ... a *habit* of malignity in the form of mere wantonness" (*BL* 2: 109). "Personal allusions," it appears, can be made without "personal malignity," the products of a free-floating ill will presumably "worse" because not only dishonest but also indiscriminately applied.

Elaborating on the "damnatory style," Coleridge then switches back from what the reviewer intends to what the review says, defining a personal attack as one in which the critic betrays a "more intimate knowledge" of the author "elsewhere obtained" than from the text under consideration (*BL* 2: 109). He argues, paraphrasing "the illustrious LESSING" (*BL* 2: 110), that the display of this "more intimate knowledge" changes the meaning of the rest of the review: "his censure instantly becomes personal injury, his sarcasms personal insults" (*BL* 2: 109). The revelation of "intimate knowledge" changes the way that the reviewer's "censure" demands to be understood, but presumably the reader of the attack would need to be already familiar with the "author's publications" in order to be aware that the information was "elsewhere obtained," besides being responsible for deciding what constitutes such inadmissible knowledge. Coleridge continues his translation from Lessing to emphasize his point:

> He ceases to be a CRITIC, and takes on him the most contemptible character to which a rational creature can be degraded, that of a gossip, backbiter and pasquillant: but with this heavy aggravation, that he steals the unquiet, the deforming passions of the World into the Museum; into the very place which, next to the chapel and oratory, should be our sanctuary and secure place of refuge; offers abominations on the altar of the muses; and makes its sacred paling the very circle in which he conjures up the lying and prophane spirit. (*BL* 2: 109–10)

The melodramatic language and extreme claims invite interrogation: is a "gossip" really the "most contemptible character to which a rational creature can be degraded"? Is the writer's study or scholar's library ("Museum") really free in the first place of the "deforming passions of the world"?[37] Is the spreading of "personal insults" really an invasion of the "sacred" by the "prophane"? In a marginal note, Coleridge had called the *Quarterly*'s only review of his work—its article on his 1814 play *Remorse* (*QR* 11: 177–90)—"an instance of insolent intrusion into the sacredness of private life," apparently because it referred to his "alternations of desultory application, and nervous indolence" (*QR* 11: 190)—an allusion to his self-proclaimed lack of productivity as a writer.[38] Not everyone would see a writer's working habits as a sacred topic.

---

[37] David Erdman, in "Coleridge and the 'Review Business,'" *The Wordsworth Circle* 6: 1 (1975): 3–50, gives a negative answer to his own questions concerning Coleridge: "Would he have relished, or could he have written, reviews quite 'pure' of personality? Did he wish altogether to escape the heat of battle?" (42).

[38] James D. Wilson, in "A Note on Coleridge and the *Quarterly Review*," *The Wordsworth Circle* 6 (1975): 51–3, observes that the reviewer's "censure" is actually "rather mild" (51). Compare *CL* 3: 532.

The passage from Lessing gives the impression that the *Edinburgh* regularly exploits "intimate knowledge," but such misuse of information is not necessarily evident from Coleridge's later discussion of Jeffrey's allegedly most egregious attack, his review of Wordsworth's *Excursion* (1814). In practice, since "legitimate censure" (*BL* 2: 110) and illegitimate abuse (or persecution) can be defined by motive as well as content, and since the reviewers' lack of "general grounds or rules" (*BL* 2: 113) means that "personal malignity" can always be slotted into place as a motive, any version of the "damnatory style" becomes open to objection. By the same train of reasoning, any attack becomes as obnoxious as a personal attack. Coleridge, Wordsworth and others upset by the *Edinburgh*'s attacks despite their lack of "personal allusions" are therefore indignant not because they are not treated as a "mere impersonation" of their works but because they are: it hurts just as much to have one's work excoriated as to have one's life made public. Also, if what constitutes a personal attack is decided by the victim, there is a danger of seeing personal slurs everywhere, not only directed against oneself but against one's friends. There is no "sanctuary and secure place of refuge."

Coleridge, then, blames both "personal malignity" and a "*habit* of malignity" for the prevalence of "personalities." Coleridge's account of the motives behind the Reviews' "freedom with personal character" (*BL* 1: 43) is multi-pronged, partly because his approach to the topic is characteristically self-revising, partly because of the complex compositional history of the *Biographia*, and partly because he intertwines speculation as to the reasons why he and his friends have been verbally abused with theories concerning the causes of vituperative reviewing in general. I have already mentioned his claim that the reviewers' lack of "fixed canons of criticism" makes them write irrationally. In his discussion of the "damnatory style," he insists that "dislike or vindictive feelings" (*BL* 2: 112) come into play, but he soon foregrounds other reasons—mentioned by him only in passing previously—including "the too manifest and too frequent interference of NATIONAL PARTY" and "a cold prudential pre-determination to increase the sale of the Review by flattering the malignant passions of human nature" (*BL* 2: 112). This "cold" decision would of course be at odds with the anonymous reviewers' pretence that they work in a rarefied realm remote from monetary concerns.

Political partisanship and financial calculation may seem remote from "PERSONAL ... aversion" (*BL* 2: 111), but the end result is by implication the same. Presumably a "cold" concern for political point-scoring or financial profit might generate the "*habit* of malignity" and in turn be reinforced by it. At one point Coleridge explicitly shifts the blame to audiences, asserting that "as long as there are readers to be delighted with calumny, there will be found reviewers to calumniate" (*BL* 1: 57). An underlying assumption here is his opinion that the deluded reading public treats the reviewers like "oracles" (*BL* 1: 52). Coleridge scorns the reviewers' readers as their fitting counterparts: according to him, "the multitudinous PUBLIC, shaped into personal unity by the magic of abstraction, sits nominal despot on the throne of criticism" (*BL* 1: 59). This kind of "personal unity" promotes rather than counteracts the proliferation of fragmented versions of "real" selves. Led by its "invisible ministers" (*BL* 1: 59), this newly empowered reading public acts with the tyranny of a despotic ruler.

Adding to the multiplicity of these alleged causes of the reviewers' vitriolic language, in the part of the *Biographia* written after most of the text had been typeset, Coleridge offers a new explanation for the reviewers' reliance on personal attacks. In this section of the book he continues to stress that "a Review, in order to be a saleable article, must be *personal, sharp* and *pointed*" (*BL* 2: 157)—personal, that is, in the sense of targeting an individual rather than expressing the reviewer's own feelings. Commercial concerns come first. The context again is clearly the *Edinburgh*'s attacks on Wordsworth, but Coleridge claims to be making a wider point about the "moral system" of "anonymous critics" (*BL* 2: 157). In the same paragraph, however, Coleridge advances a different theory, asserting that the reviewers' "aggressions" can be seen as a matter of convention (*BL* 2: 156): "As we used to say at school, in reviewing they *make* being rogues: and he, who complains, is to be laughed at for his ignorance of *the game*" (*BL* 2: 157).[39]

This is the first time that Coleridge equates reviewing with a "*game*." The term implies a self-conscious set of maneuvers rather than a "*habit* of malignity," although the idea of being mocked for not knowing the rules suggests that some players serve as mere pawns in someone's else's match. Perhaps generalizing in order to soften his own attack on Jeffrey, Coleridge draws a firm distinction between private character and public participation in the sport: "With the pen out of their hand they are *honorable men*" (*BL* 2: 157). Such "men," having the "power" to "*impoverish*" authors, "knowingly" try to ruin their victims' career prospects. "But," concludes Coleridge, "this is all *in their vocation*" (*BL* 2: 158). Coleridge here has it both ways, finding reviewers guilty of consciously bad motives but at the same time letting them off the hook by suggesting that they have no choice but to act like "rogues." Hypocrisy is built into "*the game*," and, as Coleridge puts it in *The Friend*, its players "realize the lie" (*Friend* 1: 125). Coleridge's discussion of "personality" thus indirectly registers the blurred line between personal and impersonal. Where he and other writers of the period are concerned, the "personal" emerges as less a matter of the content of vituperative writing or even the intentions behind it than a trigger for response to what is perceived as an attack. In the course of this book I explore some of the implications of this reception-oriented theory of "personality."

The Literariness of the Feuds

Why these particular feuds? The controversies involving the *Edinburgh* and the *Quarterly* that I have chosen to focus on have been relatively under-explored in recent criticism, yet all offer rich materials for close reading. As Kevin Gilmartin

---

[39] The recent reception of his own and others' work—including Southey's *Wat Tyler* (1817)—may have given Coleridge a new sense that in writing with venom the reviewers are constrained by—or embracing—a set of conventions.

points out, critics have tended "to privilege a few canonical episodes of judgment and commentary" such as Jeffrey's attacks on Wordsworth and the *Quarterly*'s attacks on Keats.[40] Despite the quarterlies' cultural prominence in the early nineteenth century, Romanticists studying periodicals have concentrated more on feuds involving the monthly magazines, especially the campaign against the Cockney School in *Blackwood's*, perhaps because of the quarterlies' reputation for stodginess in comparison with the liveliness of the monthlies. Gilmartin, for example, refers to the *Quarterly* as "ponderous."[41] As mentioned earlier, I aim to show that the spirit of the *Edinburgh* and the *Quarterly* is closer to that of the monthly magazines, as well as closer to canonical Romantic writing, than has previously been thought. But I also stress how feuds originating in the quarterlies spill over into other publishing venues, inspiring further attacks, counterattacks, and reprisals. Although similar arguments might well apply to other feuds in the period, each of my chapters traces a unique narrative involving multiple layers of commentary that succeed in different ways, if only momentarily, in breaking free from the routine cut and thrust of print gossip.

Two recent critics in particular, both writing on the monthly magazines, have foregrounded the connection between the prevalence of "personalities" in Romantic-era print culture and the literariness of periodicals. Richard Cronin draws attention to the apparent paradox whereby "Personality was at once the most widely deprecated resource of those engaged in political and literary controversy and the most valued characteristic of modern writing."[42] The term yokes inappropriately personal attacks with the treasuring of individuality (in lyric poetry and the familiar essay, for example). Discussing how material and transcendent selves are closer than they seem, Cronin insists on "the connection between the twin senses in the period of the word 'personality,' as a word signifying at once an attack on private character and a word naming a distinctive identity that exists prior to and independent of any particular example of behaviour."[43] However, writers in the era less often used the word in the second, more modern

---

[40] Kevin Gilmartin, *Writing Against Revolution: Literary Conservatism in Britain, 1790–1832* (Cambridge: Cambridge University Press, 2007), 97.

[41] Gilmartin, *Writing Against Revolution*, 115. Gilmartin notes, however, that even the much-discussed "Cockney School" articles in *Blackwood's* "derived from [its] contest with the *Edinburgh*" (125).

[42] Cronin, *Paper Pellets*, 53. Cronin stresses that personal attacks in the period could also refer to "attacks on physical appearance" (39). Attacks on "persons" in the sense of looks are relatively rare in the quarterlies, but not so rare in the monthly and weekly press. Compare Peter T. Murphy, who, in "Impersonation and Authorship in Romantic Britain," *ELH* 59 (1992): 625–49, also lingers over the "double role" of the term "personalities": "persons have a part that is theirs alone, and decency requires that we leave personalities to their owners. A 'personality,' in other words, ... does violence to persons by rudely exposing to public view privately held, personal things" (631–2). Murphy adds, "'Personalities' undermine personality" (632).

[43] Cronin, *Paper Pellets*, 57.

sense, although the term "personalities" could sometimes be used disparagingly of eulogy as well as defamation. *Blackwood's*, for example, in an 1819 attack on Hunt, asserted that "We are sick of the *personalities* of this man—of his vituperative personalities concerning others, and his commendatory personalities concerning himself" (*BM* 5: 98). In this quotation, the "commendatory personalities" are just as inauthentic as the "vituperative" ones. David Stewart concentrates more on "print personality" in the sense of what Hazlitt calls "conscious individuality" (Howe 1: 36), but in emphasizing the "literary writing" of the magazines, like Cronin he takes a materialist approach to the aesthetic turn in the periodicals.[44]

My own approach is closer to that of Peter Manning, who argues that Charles Lamb's personal identity transcends its original expression in the *London Magazine*.[45] Writing under his pseudonym Elia in the *London Magazine* in 1821, Lamb jokingly complained that his real "identity" was thought to be not Elia's but that of a "Mr. L—b": "They call this the age of personality: but surely this spirit of anti-personality (if I may so express it) is something worse" (*LM* 3: 266). Elia, the persona, seems to be objecting to being identified with the shadowy "Mr. L—b"—a mysterious individual who only partially overlaps with the "I" who writes. Like Manning, I am intrigued by rhetorical maneuvers that defy "the accounts of materialist explanation."[46] I seek to combine a historicist awareness of the circumstances of production and the vagaries of reception with careful attention to the formal strategies of the reviewers' surprisingly imaginative prose as well as to the rhetorical maneuvers of the other print contributions to the feuds. While some of the latter are literary in the traditional sense—such as Lord Byron's poetic satire on Southey, *The Vision of Judgment* (1822, discussed in my first chapter) and Lady Morgan's regional novel *Florence Macarthy* (1818, discussed in my third chapter)—and others less so, the collaborative bodies of writing that make up each of my separate, though occasionally overlapping feuds all extend the scope of Romantic literature in varying directions.

Chapter 1 examines the furor that erupted in 1817 over the near-simultaneous appearance of Southey's early revolutionary play, *Wat Tyler*, and the same author's virulent attack on parliamentary reform in the *Quarterly*. Responding to allegations of political apostasy, Southey in his attempted self-defense, *A Letter to William Smith*, proudly proclaims that "in an age of personality, I abstained from satire."[47] Contradicting this statement, the undignified squabble between Southey's defenders and his opponents at first sight gives the impression that he is totally enmeshed in an exchange of "personalities." Yet as the controversy unfolds in the weekly, monthly, and quarterly press, including the *Edinburgh*, Southey and others collectively address the apparent discontinuity between his past and present

---

[44] Stewart, *Romantic Magazines*, 40, 12.

[45] Peter Manning, "Detaching Lamb's Thoughts," in *Romantic Periodicals and Print Culture*, ed. Kim Wheatley (London: Frank Cass, 2003), 137–46.

[46] Manning, "Detaching Lamb's Thoughts," 143.

[47] Robert Southey, *A Letter to William Smith, Esq., M.P.* (London: John Murray, 1817), 45.

identities, figuring him as at once a seller of his own soul and an incarnation of Romantic selfhood—profound, developing, and capable of temporarily rising above the politicized literary marketplace. The chapter thus explores how personal attacks and autobiographical self-vindications can undercut yet also re-inscribe Romantic models of self-representation. Hazlitt's series of contributions to the feud exemplifies the interrogating of what Jerome McGann calls the Romantic ideology[48]—a move that demystifies Southey as a thoroughly political creature— but also the impulse to shore that ideology back up—a move that refigures Southey as the possessor of a potentially sublime "deep self." Eventually, however, as Southey's character continues to be rewritten and re-imagined by his political enemies, he undergoes a different kind of refiguring, shriveling into a comic caricature that marks the limits both of political engagement and of emerging notions of Romantic selfhood.

My second chapter explores a tangentially related feud of 1817, centered on the fraught relationship between Coleridge and Jeffrey, the *Edinburgh* editor. Coleridge's allegation in *Biographia Literaria* that Jeffrey was guilty of a breach of hospitality provoked an unprecedented signed rejoinder from Jeffrey in a footnote to Hazlitt's attack on the *Biographia* in the *Edinburgh*. At the heart of their exchange is the question of what constitutes a "personal" attack. The chapter examines the bemused public reaction to the disagreement between Coleridge and Jeffrey, culminating in a brilliantly comic attack on Jeffrey by *Blackwood's* in 1818. As in Chapter 1, the writers' reader-oriented approach to "personality" problematizes biographical and autobiographical representation by destabilizing the Romantic illusion of authentic selfhood, but again, Romantic notions of identity resurface, especially in Hazlitt's and John Wilson's artful hostile accounts of Coleridge's career. The fact that Coleridge's squabble with Jeffrey is blown out of all proportion in the press would seem to confirm that Coleridge, like his fellow Lake Poet Southey, cannot escape from what he derisively calls, in a letter to Henry Crabb Robinson, "the degrading Taste of the present Public for *personal* Gossip" (December 3, 1817; *CL* 4: 758). Nevertheless, I show how the collective—and inventive—rewriting of Coleridge's dispute with Jeffrey by hostile and supportive commentators alike finally reduces *and* enlarges Coleridge and his adversary by transforming them into characters in a comedy of manners with a tinge of the supernatural. The fictionalizing of Jeffrey by *Blackwood's* leaves behind Coleridge's attack on the *Edinburgh* editor and Jeffrey's self-vindication even as it confirms a Coleridgean understanding of "personality" as a function of reception.

Chapter 3 explores attempts by three pro-reform writers to take revenge on the *Quarterly*, partly through direct counterattacks and partly, and, more fruitfully, through more conventionally literary methods: poetry, satire, and prose fiction. First, the chapter analyzes Leigh Hunt's rather one-sided quarrel with Gifford, comparing it to Hazlitt's related feud with the Tory editor. I offer an account of

---

[48] Jerome McGann, *The Romantic Ideology: A Critical Investigation* (Chicago: University of Chicago Press, 1983).

Hunt's difficulty in circumventing the terms of the *Quarterly*, showing how the language both of his poetry and his prose becomes contaminated by the calculated acidity of the Tory reviewers. Only in his exuberant poetic satire on Gifford, *Ultra-Crepidarius* (1823), does Hunt succeed momentarily in setting aside the outworn hostilities of his war with the *Quarterly*. By contrast, in Hazlitt's vitriolic *Letter to William Gifford, Esq.* (1819), Hunt's fellow Cockney scribbler claims to rise above his enemy through his "metaphysical discovery" of an "ideal self" (Wu 5: 376–8). I argue that if, however, Hazlitt breaks free from the "age of personality" in his feud with Gifford, it is not because of his philosophical theory but because his representations of Gifford reproduce the tensions underlying Hazlitt's doctrine of the "disinterested" imagination (Wu 5: 379). The final section of the chapter turns to the bitter feud between the *Quarterly* and Lady Morgan. This feud, sparked and nourished by private hostility, misogyny, political partisanship, and nationalistic prejudice, bleeds off, like the other feuds I deal with, into proliferating strands of controversy in other periodicals. In response to the *Quarterly*'s three violent attacks on her, Morgan retaliated in various publications and was defended and assailed by other reviewers. Throughout her long career, she "court[ed]" the "malice" (*FM*, 329) of reviewers to earn publicity.[49] Most notably, in her novel *Florence Macarthy*, she delivers a spirited rejoinder in the shape of a sustained satirical portrait of her supposed *Quarterly* attacker, John Wilson Croker. However, in this work Morgan also inadvertently rises above the fray through her intriguingly contradictory self-portrait as a beleaguered woman of letters and an idealized Gothic heroine.

My final chapter finds literary elements within the *Quarterly* itself, examining a series of reviews of books on Arctic exploration by Barrow, the government official behind the Romantic-era push to discover the Northwest Passage. Masking his political influence, Barrow used the anonymity of the *Quarterly* to advance his imperialistic, nationalistic, and private agendas, conducting a feud against the explorer John Ross, whom he himself had sent out to seek the Passage. Yet Barrow's Arctic articles reveal as well as occlude his behind-the-scenes role as the Second Secretary for the British Admiralty, parading his access to inside information and even occasionally mentioning his own name. These articles thus provide an excellent opportunity to disentangle an individual voice from a corporate one, as well as to identify an unexpectedly creative element in periodical prose. Drawing on the literary genres of epic, comedy, and romance, Barrow's persecution of Ross tells an over-determined story of delusion, obsession, and eventually revenge. Ross's indignant responses, accusing Barrow of "charges and insinuations against my personal conduct and character,"[50] reflect sardonically on

---

[49] Morgan, like the other writers I deal with, believed that hostile reviews affected the sales of books, for better or worse. Andrew Franta, in *Romanticism and the Rise of the Mass Public* (Cambridge: Cambridge University Press, 2007), in contrast with St. Clair's empirical study of reading in the period, stresses the effect of "perceptions" rather than reality (9).

[50] Ross, *Observations on ... "Voyages of Discovery and Research within the Arctic Regions,"* 3.

whether the bureaucrat and a certain *Quarterly* reviewer are "one and the same person."[51] Barrow's emergence from the pretence of anonymity in his 1846 book on the Arctic belatedly gave Ross the opportunity to indulge in some "personalities" of his own. Nevertheless, I show that the *Quarterly*'s heavily mediated encounter with the Arctic ice also yields existential questioning and a sense of the sublime, making this story the most Romantic of all.

One objection to my argument might be that these feuds' major exchanges, even though they treat Romantic themes and enact forms of transcendence, still seem detached on a local level from what William St Clair calls the "emerging romantic aesthetic."[52] Yet each feud contains explicit allusions either to works by or to the reputations of Romantic-era poets. As we will see, in one of his attacks on Southey, Hazlitt quotes from Wordsworth's lyric "My heart leaps up" (1807), and in another draws on "Lines Written a Few Miles above Tintern Abbey" (1798). *Blackwood's* unsurprisingly invokes Coleridge's *Christabel* (1816) in its review of the *Biographia*, and the "Rime of the Ancient Mariner" (1798) in its response to the *Edinburgh*'s attack on the *Biographia*; the latter article also brings up Scott's *Lady of the Lake* (1810). Hunt's own poem, *Ultra-Crepidarius*, a centerpiece of my third chapter, does not itself aspire to qualify as canonical poetry (rather the reverse), but the Cockney poet's feud with Gifford briefly features fictional representations of Byron and Shelley. Lady Morgan's *Florence Macarthy*, the novel in which she tries to take her revenge on her enemy Croker, includes a chapter epigraph from Wordsworth's "Characteristics of a Child Three Years Old" (1815). It also contains a rather Shelleyan portrait of Byron in the character of the lesser of its two heroes. Finally, even one of the Arctic exploration narratives reviewed by Barrow makes a passing allusion to Southey's *Madoc* (1805). While these explicit allusions reveal a shared awareness of writers later considered central to the era, my discussion of these particular feuds more fundamentally examines how they at once broaden and deepen the territory of Romanticism.

It might seem as if my choice of material is unduly weighted towards the *Quarterly*, but each of the feuds that I explore directly or indirectly involves both of the major Reviews. In Chapter 1, the *Wat Tyler* controversy is provoked by Southey's "Parliamentary Reform" essay in the *Quarterly* and carried on in the pages of other weekly, monthly and quarterly periodicals, but the *Edinburgh* later joins the fray by reviewing *Wat Tyler* and Southey's *Letter to William Smith*. Chapter 2 focuses on Coleridge's relationship with the *Edinburgh*, but Coleridge's disdainful attitude to reviewers was influenced by the *Quarterly*'s failure to come to his defense. In Chapter 3, the *Quarterly*'s hostility to Hunt is intensified by the relative tolerance of the *Edinburgh*. Moreover, the *Quarterly*'s antipathy to Hazlitt partly has to do with the fact that he is an *Edinburgh* reviewer. Lady Morgan's feud with the *Quarterly* seems heightened by the *Edinburgh*'s mostly silent treatment

---

[51] [John Ross], *A Letter to John Barrow, Esq. F.R.S. on the Late Extraordinary and Unexpected Hyperborean Discoveries* (London: W. Pople, 1826), 3.

[52] St. Clair, *The Reading Nation in the Romantic Period*, 286.

of her. Chapter 4 concentrates on the topic of Arctic exploration in the *Quarterly* but discusses some articles on the same topic in the *Edinburgh* as well; here, the contrast between the attitudes of the two rival periodicals reveals the liveliness as well as the irrationality of Barrow's vendetta against Ross. Barrow himself published his final article on Arctic exploration in the *Edinburgh* (in 1843) rather than in the *Quarterly*. In general, however, I am more concerned to show how each feud fans out from the major quarterlies into a variety of other forms of print, with the participants co-operating—however elusively and fitfully—upon works of imagination, the scope and directions of which they are unaware. In each case, we find both or either the *Edinburgh* and the *Quarterly* contributing indirectly to the creation of a Romantic text.

Chapter 1
The *Wat Tyler* Controversy: Southey Refigured

The story has often been told, though usually as background rather than foreground.[1] In January 1795, the 20-year-old Robert Southey visited in Newgate Prison the radical publisher James Ridgeway, to whom he had previously sent the manuscript of *Wat Tyler*, a verse drama that celebrates the peasants' poll tax revolt in the reign of Richard II. Ridgeway agreed to publish the play, but it failed to appear, and Southey did not take the trouble to recover his manuscript. Twenty-two years later, on February 13, 1817, *Wat Tyler* was finally published anonymously by the respectable firm of Sherwood, Neely, and Jones, without the permission of its author, now Poet Laureate and an outspoken supporter of the Tory government. The publication of *Wat Tyler* coincided with the anonymous appearance of one of Southey's most aggressively reactionary articles, an attack on parliamentary reform, in the *Quarterly Review*.[2] On March 14, 1817, William Smith, a Whig Member of Parliament, spoke during a debate in the House of Commons on Southey's shift from the republican sentiments of *Wat Tyler* to the intolerance of the essay on parliamentary reform. Southey took out an injunction against the unauthorized publication of his play, but Lord Eldon denied it on the grounds that Southey had not "established his right to the property," property that in any case, as a seditious work, would lose its claim to copyright.[3] Various radical publishers gleefully seized the opportunity provided by this legal ruling, and pirated editions

---

[1] See Frank Taliaferro Hoadley, "The Controversy over Southey's *Wat Tyler*," *Studies in Philology* 38 (1941): 81–96.

[2] I discuss this essay (*QR* 16: 225–79) in *Shelley and His Readers: Beyond Paranoid Politics* (Columbia: University of Missouri Press, 1999), 23–7, as a prime example of the "paranoid style" (26).

[3] Quoted from W.W. Speck, *Robert Southey: Entire Man of Letters* (New Haven and London: Yale University Press, 2006), 171. According to Speck, while the seditious nature of the play is "sometimes taken to be the basis on which [Lord Eldon] refused an injunction," the denial rests on a more "abstruse legal point" (280, n.13) in that "one William Winterbottam" had falsely claimed to own the work's copyright (171). See also Ralph A. Manogue, "Southey and William Winterbotham [sic]: New Light on an Old Quarrel," *The Charles Lamb Bulletin* 38 (1982): 105–14. Nevertheless, pirate editions of *Wat Tyler*, as with pirate editions of Shelley's *Queen Mab* (1821) and Byron's *The Vision of Judgment*, exploited the loophole in the law whereby an illegal publication loses its claim to copyright. William St. Clair calls the publication of *Wat Tyler* the "most decisive single event in shaping the reading of the romantic period" because the piracies enabled the play to reach a mass audience (*The Reading Nation in the Romantic Period* [Cambridge: Cambridge University Press, 2004], 316).

of *Wat Tyler* proliferated. The flood of responses in print included spirited attacks on Southey—notably by Hazlitt—and indignant defenses of Southey—notably by Coleridge. Southey then tried to defend himself in a pamphlet, *A Letter to William Smith, Esq., M.P.*, which extended the controversy by provoking more reviews, among them memorable attacks by Leigh Hunt in the *Examiner* and Francis Jeffrey in the *Edinburgh Review*.

Like the feud later the same year between Coleridge and Jeffrey that will be explored in my next chapter, this furor branches off into a multi-authored self-generating text. A number of central concerns emerge in the course of the reception of *Wat Tyler*: the connection between political apostasy and literary authority; the relationships between anonymity, temporary celebrity, and lasting fame; the political and historicist interpretation of literary texts; the rhetorical effectiveness of reprisals; and what constitutes a personal attack (a pressing concern in the "age of personality," as I have already discussed in my introduction). My analysis of the controversy will touch on all of these issues, but I will focus particularly on how attacks aimed at discrediting an individual—and their flip-side, efforts at self-vindication—in this case both unsettle and reinstate what we have long considered to be Romantic models of self-representation. Robert Lapp, in his study of the *Wat Tyler* episode, argues that Hazlitt's responses to Coleridge reject "the cult of transcendent genius, insisting instead on the inseparability of literary and political—and hence ideological—practice."[4] The reception of *Wat Tyler* certainly exemplifies what Lapp calls the "interpenetration of literary and political discourse" (116). However, I will argue that as the *Wat Tyler* controversy unfolds, Romantic notions of selfhood—involving growth, depth, and a capacity for transcendence—resurface even as they are challenged. Contributors to the controversy together create an increasingly complex portrait of Southey's "genius." Eventually, though, as Southey's supporters and opponents feud over his reputation, they turn him into a comic figure more notable for its entertainment value than either its Romantic idealism or its political significance.[5]

Coleridge, in one of his attempts to defend Southey, saw the unauthorized and anonymous publication of *Wat Tyler* as itself an "attack" on the poet's "character,"

---

[4] Robert K. Lapp, *Contest for Cultural Authority: Hazlitt, Coleridge, and the Distresses of the Regency* (Detroit: Wayne State University Press, 1999), 114. Further references in parentheses. On the later elaboration of Romantic notions of genius in periodicals, see David Higgins, *Romantic Genius and the Literary Magazine: Biography, Celebrity and Politics* (London: Routledge, 2005).

[5] Compare David Stewart, who, in "*The Examiner*, Robert Southey's Print Celebrity and the Marketing of the *Quarterly Review*," *Prose Studies* 31 (April 2009): 22–39, analyzes the *Wat Tyler* controversy in terms of its entertainment value in what he calls "a celebrity consumer culture" (28), situating the "spectacle" (10) in the context of Southey's political writings in the *Quarterly*. Stewart claims that in the act of writing anonymously and vitriolically in the *Quarterly*, paradoxically "Southey was making himself into a personality" (31). While Stewart's work in general helps to confirm my view that periodical discourse can be understood in aesthetic terms, in this essay he perceives Southey's "vituperative style" as more individual than cultural (28).

an attack that by definition requires a response (*EOT* 2: 453). As mentioned in my introduction, the practice of replying to supposedly *ad hominem* attacks was routine in early nineteenth-century print warfare. Southey's main effort to clear his name after what he considered to be a personal attack on him in Parliament, the *Letter to William Smith*, inevitably sparked an escalation of hostilities, but this escalation can be seen as having a positive as well as a negative side. Charles Mahoney, who interprets the *Wat Tyler* controversy as confronting Southey with his own former self risen from the grave, analyzes the *Letter* in terms of Paul de Man's notion of autobiography as at once defacing and restoring a past self.[6] I suggest that the reception of *Wat Tyler* and the *Letter* by Coleridge, Hazlitt, Hunt, and others can alike be read as disfiguring and refiguring Southey, with the disfiguring lining up with what Lapp calls "interrogating the Romantic ideology,"[7] and the refiguring at least momentarily associating the poet with a deep and potentially transcendent self. In the case of this beleaguered Poet Laureate, self-vindication—if such a thing is possible—turns out to be a collaborative endeavor on the part of enemies as well as friends. Ultimately, as the *Wat Tyler* episode turns into a comic sideshow not wholly explicable in ideological or commercial terms, Southey is refigured in a different direction, re-losing some complexity but to some extent being freed from the partisanship endemic to the "age of personality." We will see that although Southey's "character" may not finally be salvageable, it can be amusingly fictionalized.

In this chapter I will examine the major contributions to the *Wat Tyler* affair as it developed in the spring of 1817, lingering over the issue of how Southey's past and present "character" is knocked down, built back up, and finally knocked back down again, only differently. The chapter will proceed chronologically, beginning with the early reception of *Wat Tyler* and the attacks and defenses that followed, and then turning to Southey's *Letter* and its aftermath. I will conclude by looking at Byron's rather indulgent attack on Southey in his 1822 poem, *The Vision of Judgment*, a *tour de force* that pointedly refuses to have the last laugh. The writers' fixation with the career of a particular individual occurs in a reviewing culture in which, as discussed in my introduction, attacks and counterattacks were usually anonymous,[8] but when many periodical writers could expect to be

---

[6] Charles Mahoney, *Romantics and Renegades: The Poetics of Political Reaction* (Basingstoke: Palgrave Macmillan, 2003), 123–42. Mahoney's main concern is interpreting Romantic apostasy historically as a culturally-specific phenomenon and deconstructively as an "*always already*" falling away from rather than (or as well as) a standing apart from one's previous self (37, quoting Jerome Christensen's use of the Derridean phrase). Although defining apostasy is obviously crucial to the *Wat Tyler* affair, I focus more on the problem of capturing Southey's elusive identity.

[7] I am quoting the phrase from the title of Chapter 5 of Lapp's *Contest for Cultural Authority*.

[8] The convention in this case creates the illusion that while Southey has an extra-textual life, his shadowy detractors and defenders do not. Yet Southey's reputation as a successful professional writer with an unimpeachable private life helps to give the impression that he himself has a purely textual identity.

recognized, especially when, like Hazlitt and Coleridge in this case, they were personally acquainted with the protagonist and each other.[9] The result is that their "characters" too come into play, especially, as we will see, that of Coleridge, and that at moments they seem to lose sight of a wider audience, a circumstance that heightens the self-reflexiveness of this particular feud.

The Initial Reception of *Wat Tyler*

Since his appointment as Poet Laureate in 1813, Southey had been sporadically assailed in the reformist press for apostasy—the standard allegation being that he had deserted his early radical sympathies for financial gain. The publication of *Wat Tyler* did not then initiate such allegations, but its coincidental—or calculated—appearance in the same week as Southey's "Parliamentary Reform" essay in the *Quarterly* provided a seemingly heaven-sent opportunity to renew them with fresh vigor.[10] The contrast between the anti-monarchical fervor of *Wat Tyler* and the *Quarterly*'s violent attack on political reformers as "incendiaries" (*QR* 16: 227) could not have been more blatant. Most of the print reactions to *Wat Tyler* and the "Parliamentary Reform" article in the daily and weekly press followed each other in quick succession in March and April of 1817, although the furor was not soon forgotten.

One consciously literary response to Southey's apostasy—which ridicules his *Quarterly* article at some length but which does not mention *Wat Tyler*—had however presumably been mostly composed prior to the appearance of both texts: Thomas Love Peacock's three-volume satirical novel, *Melincourt*, which appeared in March, 1817. None of the other contributions to the *Wat Tyler* controversy referred to this novel, published in an expensive edition for a highly educated audience of reformist sympathizers. But its caricatured depiction of "Mr. Feathernest"—the apostate poet—resembles the sort of attacks already made on Southey in the radical press. Mr. Feathernest is denounced as "a hollow-hearted hypocrite, a false and venal angler for pension and place" who has produced insincere "Odes to Truth and Liberty" in the past and now pens "royal lyrics" for the sake of "venison and sack" (*TLP* 2: 177–9). Towards the end of the novel, a Tory cabal including Mr. Feathernest, Mr. Vamp (William Gifford), and Mr. Anyside Antijack (George Canning) confabulate in a chapter entitled "Mainchance Villa," their cynical discourse alluding extensively to the very recently published "Parliamentary Reform" essay, to which the reader is referred in over 20 of

---

[9] The reception of *Wat Tyler* moreover took place in Parliament and the Chancery Court as well as in the press, thus involving politicians and lawyers with names if not faces, since their contributions were in turn filtered through press reports.

[10] Lapp, in *Contest for Cultural Authority*, 115, implies that *Wat Tyler* was deliberately published immediately after the "Parliamentary Reform" essay (which appeared two days earlier). Hoadley, in "The Controversy over Southey's *Wat Tyler*," by contrast, implies that the contiguity of the two texts was fortuitous (81).

Peacock's own footnotes. Peacock wittily weaves phrases from the *Quarterly* into the speeches of his characters to mock its partisan account of the war with France, its intolerant attitude to reformers and its calculatedly hysterical language.

Unlike the periodical writers who will respond to the publication of *Wat Tyler*, Peacock does not assume that the "Parliamentary Reform" essay is by Southey; he takes it to represent the collective voice of the *Quarterly*, or, as he calls it in the body of his text, the "Legitimate Review" (*TLP* 2: 196). The "Mainchance Villa" chapter thus registers the idea that the "Parliamentary Reform" essay is less the expression of one man's eccentric opinion than a cultural manifestation of the political paranoia of the establishment. Yet *Melincourt*'s condemnation of the *Quarterly*'s extremism is modified by its humorous portrayal of characters in festive settings. With the other anti-Jacobins, the self-serving Mr. Feathernest sings and dances, jostling for "a finger in the CHRISTMAS PIE" (*TLP* 2: 418). After all, Peacock does not treat him, or them, as a threat.[11] This portrayal of Southey anticipates some later figurative treatments of the poet that will shrivel him into a comic stereotype without forcibly pursuing a political agenda.

The same cannot be said of the radical journalist William Hone's first public comment on *Wat Tyler*, in his twopenny *Reformists' Register*, on February 22, 1817. Hone would soon afterwards publish his own pirate edition of the play. Seizing on the news of the play's authorship, Hone aimed to score a political point by contrasting Southey's past and present identities: "Wat Tyler is attributed by the *Morning Chronicle*, to no less a person than the Poet Laureate, one Mr. Robert Southey, a gentleman of credit and renown, and, until he became Poet Laureate, a Poet" (*SCH*, 232). The phrase "one Mr. Robert Southey" shrinks this "gentleman" into a nonentity even as Hone acknowledges his "renown." In a typical move that debunks the Romantic idealization of genius, Southey is no longer a "Poet" not only because he writes for a "pension" but also because he now supports the current regime.

Hone proceeds to draw on figurative language that does not explicitly refer to politics but instead offers a twist on poetic nostalgia concerning the loss of innocence: "His present muse … is no more like that which he formerly courted, than the black doll at an old rag shop is like Petrarch's Laura" (*SCH*, 232). This grotesque comparison incongruously conjures up the notion of Southey as a love poet who has made a perverse transfer of erotic object. Hazlitt will later more elaborately sexualize Southey's political shift. In his brief notice, Hone continues to try to degrade Southey with another disconcerting comparison: "I have no doubt, he would at this moment exchange his situation, fleshpots and all, for that of the Negro, who earns his 'daily,' by sweeping the crossing at Mr. Waithman's corner!" (*SCH*, 232). The former "Poet" is here connected with the most downtrodden member of the urban poor, forced because of his race to eke out a living in the humblest of occupations. (The reference is to "Brutus Billy," a

---

[11] Compare Gary Dyer, in *British Satire and the Politics of Style, 1789–1832* (Cambridge: Cambridge University Press, 1997) on how "comedy dissolves [Peacock's] anger" (101) even while he critiques the hegemonic power of the quarterlies (121).

Jamaican who swept the crossing outside the Fleet Street shop of Robert Waithman, a linen draper and Whig politician.)[12] The implication is that at least the "Negro" has a clear conscience. The idea of Southey "exchang[ing] his situation" with the crossing-sweeper, in metonymically associating him with the inanimate "black doll," seems to destabilize his gender as well as blackening his face. Although no other contributors to the *Wat Tyler* controversy will invoke racial difference, several of Southey's future attackers and defenders will try to weaken him by feminizing him. Hone's choice of images may not cloud his jocular excoriation of Southey, but they exemplify the impulse to transform him into someone who can be more easily pinned down.

Two days after Hone's mocking dismissal, Southey was denounced for the first time in Parliament, though at this point without reference to the contrast between *Wat Tyler* and his *Quarterly* article. On February 24, 1817, during a discussion of the Seditious Meetings Bill (an act of Parliament aimed at stamping out public agitation for political reform), the Whig Member of Parliament Henry Brougham alluded disparagingly to "the poetical gentleman (the present poet laureat [sic]), who, twenty years ago, preached up in verse the universal destruction of all property and laws."[13] Brougham did not refer to Southey by name, but the Tory newspaper the *Courier* called his allusion a "personal attack."[14] The possibility of a slur by one individual against another seems automatically to provoke commentary from its audience, as we will also see with the Coleridge–Jeffrey feud. Neither Southey nor his supporters responded to Brougham, however, perhaps because the question of the connection between the individual voice of the poet and the supposedly collective voice of the *Quarterly* had not yet been publicly raised. It was the juxtaposition of the *Quarterly*'s "Parliamentary Reform" article with Southey's play that turned fitful commentary into a flurry of persecution and (self-)defense.

More Attacks on Southey

Hazlitt, writing anonymously in the *Examiner* on March 9, 1817, set the terms of much of the ensuing controversy by contrasting *Wat Tyler* with "Parliamentary Reform" to show the extent of Southey's shift in outlook, though his review's ostensible theme is the continuity that paradoxically underlies Southey's career.[15]

---

[12] "Brutus Billy," (really Charles M'Ghee), also known as "Tim-buc-too," was later rumored to have made a small fortune. The suggestion is that he is a recognizable figure to Hone's urban readers, and that his kind of celebrity status is preferable to Southey's bad eminence. See "British History Online," http://www.british-history.ac.uk/report.aspx?compid=45024 [accessed July 2, 2012].

[13] *The Parliamentary Debates from the Year 1803 to the Present Time*, vol. 35 (London: Hansard, 1817), column 626. Further references to this volume in parentheses.

[14] *The Courier*, February 26, 1817, quoted by Hoadley, "The Controversy over Southey's *Wat Tyler*," 82.

[15] Like most of Hazlitt's later contributions to the *Wat Tyler* furor, this article was subsequently reprinted in his *Political Essays* (1819), thus acquiring the dignity of appearing in a long-lasting book, not merely an ephemeral periodical.

Hazlitt at once questions and confirms Romantic assumptions concerning the value of childhood perception, connection with nature, and the autonomy of the human mind, although he invokes the major Wordsworthian theme of psychological development more explicitly in a later article. His aim in exposing how "'fierce extremes' meet" (Wu 4: 157) seems to be to condemn the Laureate all the more as a "literary prostitute," but even in this article his sustained verbal assault also comes across as an attempt to understand and explore Southey's "senseless self-sufficiency" (Wu 4: 158). That perverse sense of self bears at moments an uncanny resemblance to what Hazlitt had previously denounced as Wordsworth's "intense intellectual egotism" (Howe 4: 113).[16]

The article on *Wat Tyler* and "On Parliamentary Reform" includes as its epigraph all but the first two lines of "The Rainbow" from Wordsworth's 1807 *Poems in Two Volumes*. In choosing these lines, Hazlitt borrows some literary respectability for his review while extending his denunciation of Southey's apostasy to his fellow Lake Poet, still a contested figure subject to attacks by Jeffrey in the *Edinburgh*.[17] Characteristically, Hazlitt misquotes, and although his alterations to Wordsworth's lines were probably not deliberate, they sharpen his critique of both Lake Poets, while hinting at the possibility of recuperating a Wordsworthian model of the self. Wordsworth's poem reads as follows:

> My heart leaps up when I behold
>   A Rainbow in the sky;
> So was it when my life began,
> So is it now I am a man,
> So be it when I shall grow old
>   Or let me die!
> The Child is Father of the Man,
> And I could wish my days to be
> Bound each to each by natural piety.[18]

This poem simplifies Wordsworth's prevalent, though conflicted, claim in his major lyrics—notably "Tintern Abbey" and the "Ode" (1807)—that psychological change is growth,[19] implying instead that the joys of childhood, rather than being

---

[16] Hazlitt's review, "Observations on Mr. Wordsworth's poem, 'The Excursion,'" appeared in the *Examiner* on August 21 and 28, 1814. Stewart, in *Romantic Magazines*, notes that "the charge of egotism that Hazlitt levels at Wordsworth could just as well be leveled at Hazlitt" (41).

[17] Compare Mark Storey, *Robert Southey: A Life* (Oxford: Oxford University Press, 1997), on how "Hazlitt's attacks on Southey" broaden to include Wordsworth and Coleridge (260).

[18] William Wordsworth, *The Major Works* (Oxford: Oxford University Press, 2000), 246. Subsequent references to Wordsworth's poetry are also from this edition.

[19] On Wordsworth's "providential economy of loss and gain," see Stephen Gill, *William Wordsworth: A Life* (Oxford: Oxford University Press, 1990), 154. This theme is of course also central to *The Prelude*, not published until 1850.

replaced by a higher adult awareness, are never lost in the first place. In his 1815 *Poems*, Wordsworth had quoted the last three lines of "The Rainbow" as his own epigraph to the (renamed) "Ode: Intimations of Immortality from Recollections of Early Childhood," as if to distract attention from the "Ode"'s counter-intuitive theme of loss and recovery.[20]

Hazlitt's epigraph, by contrast, reads:

> So was it when my life began,
> So is it now I am a man:
> So shall it be when I grow old and die.
> The child's the father of the man:
> Our years flow on
> Link'd each to each by natural piety. (Wu 4: 157)

In line with his debunking of Southey's poetic pretensions, by leaving out the first two lines of the poem, Hazlitt makes the repeated "it" refer at least potentially to political commitments rather than instinctive enjoyment of nature. The omission also replaces Wordsworth's initial celebration of renewable ecstasies with an insistence on unvarying sameness, an insistence reinforced by the somber—and lengthened—line, "So shall it be when I grow old and die." By leaving out Wordsworth's melodramatic "Or let me die!" Hazlitt makes the connection between past and present even more definite, whereas Wordsworth's short line introduces a grain of doubt: will his heart always leap up?

In addition, Hazlitt's contraction ("The child's") gives Wordsworth's central metaphor of the child fathering the adult a touch of casualness that downplays the unorthodoxy of the claim. In the prose that follows, Hazlitt will go on to demystify Wordsworth's idealism more explicitly. With the revised line, "Our years flow on," Hazlitt also removes Wordsworth's emphasis on his own agency and his hint of ambivalence about the desirability of connecting past and present: "I could wish." Yet with the word choice "Link'd" softening the poet's more coercive "Bound," the phrase "Our years flow on" makes the connection between "child" and "man" seem inevitable and natural, all the better to challenge—and seal—the connection in the body of the review. Wordsworth's lines give emotional authority to the child and extend that privilege to the young-at-heart man. Hazlitt, it will soon transpire, in his rewriting of Wordsworth, admires neither child nor adult, but in suggesting that each is worse than the other, he complicates rather than merely rejecting Wordsworth's stress on the continuity of individual identity and the power of self-determination.

The body of the *Examiner* review jumps off from Wordsworth's paradoxical formulation and anchors the generalization about the child fathering the man to a specific set of historical circumstances. After its distorting epigraph, the article proceeds with relish:

---

[20] Compare Frances Ferguson's reading of the "Ode" in *Wordsworth: Language as Counter-Spirit* (New Haven: Yale University Press, 1977), 98–9.

> According to this theory of personal continuity, the author of the Dramatic Poem, to be here noticed, is the father of Parliamentary Reform in the Quarterly Review. It is said to be a wise child that knows its own father; and we understand Mr. Southey (who is in this case reputed father and son) utterly disclaims the hypostatical union between the Quarterly Reviewer and the Dramatic Poet, and means to enter an injunction against the latter, as a bastard and impostor. Appearances are somewhat staggering against the legitimacy of the descent, yet we perceive a strong family-likeness remaining in spite of the lapse of years and alteration of circumstances. We should not, indeed, be able to predict that the author of *Wat Tyler* would ever write the article on Parliamentary Reform; nor should we, either at first or second sight, perceive that the Quarterly Reviewer had ever written a poem like that which is before us: but if we were told that both performances were literally and *bona fide* by the same person, we should have little hesitation in saying to Mr. Southey, "Thou art the man." We know no other person in whom "fierce extremes" meet with such mutual self-complacency: whose opinions change so much without any change in the author's mind; who lives so entirely in the "present ignorant thought," without the smallest "discourse of reason looking before or after." (Wu 4: 158)

The child's ability to live in the moment—celebrated by Wordsworth—is here turned into a sign of the adult's inability to develop "beyond / This ignorant present" (Hazlitt misquotes *Macbeth*, I, v, 57–8). Hazlitt satirizes Wordsworth's theme of self-connectedness by holding Southey to blame for his "change" of "opinions" while stressing that he is incapable of acting any other way: "He has not strength of mind to see the whole of any question" (Wu 4: 158). Wordsworth's "theory of personal continuity" is reworked into a badge of disgrace.

However, Hazlitt's interest in the workings of "the author's mind" prevents him from simply inverting Wordsworth's assumptions and transferring them to a political context. The allusions to Shakespeare dignify Southey as well as diminishing him, with the intriguing idea of "mutual self-complacency" helping to soften the "fierce extremes" of Southey's "self." (The allusion is to a description of hell in *Paradise Lost* [2: 599].[21]) In places, Hazlitt's diatribe verges on psychological case study rather than political indictment, especially since he toys with homophobic and misogynistic suggestions of sexual boundary-crossing. The unsettling notion of Southey as his own "bastard" son, the product of a "hypostatical" union between his two (male) selves, tinges the idea of a "strong family-likeness" with the possibility of incest. Hazlitt then sets aside this implication in favor of equating the poet with the familiar stereotype of the fallen woman: "*The woman that deliberates is lost.* So it is with the effeminate soul of Mr. Southey" (Wu 4: 158). But can Southey choose his own "soul"?

Besides distracting himself and his readers from the issue of political apostasy, in places Hazlitt's distinctively trenchant style draws attention mainly to itself rather than its content: "The author of Wat Tyler was an Ultra-jacobin; the author

---

[21] References to *Paradise Lost* are from *John Milton: Complete Poems and Major Prose*, ed. Merritt Y. Hughes (Indianapolis: Odyssey Press, 1957).

of Parliamentary Reform is an Ultra-royalist; the one was a frantic demagogue; the other is a servile court-tool: the one maintained second-hand paradoxes; the other repeats second-hand commonplaces" (Wu 4: 158). This masterful prose writer's pleasure in vituperation propels this artful sentence line after line, with "Mr. Southey" at once dissolving and expanding into a potentially endless list of contradictions. Hazlitt raises the question of how a "frantic demagogue" flipped over into a "servile court-tool" only to expose the hollowness of any political affiliation. Despite this gesture beyond mere opposition,[22] the last part of the review descends into knee-jerk partisanship, Hazlitt finding fault with Southey for being "violent" and condemning the "band of gentlemen pensioners and servile authors" associated with the *Quarterly*. Skewered and puzzled over earlier in the review for his perversity, Southey here disappears into the crowd. But Hazlitt will have plenty more to say about the "mind" of Southey the "changeling" (Wu 4: 158).

Following Hazlitt's attack, the Whig M.P. William Smith, as previously mentioned, in a parliamentary debate on March 14, 1817, contrasted the *Quarterly*'s "Parliamentary Reform" essay with *Wat Tyler*, pointedly quoting from both texts. Like Brougham's earlier parliamentary reference to Southey's play, Smith's speech occurred during ongoing discussion of the Seditious Meetings Bill; in the meantime, habeas corpus had been suspended on March 4. Smith's speech and the reply to it by the Tory M.P. Charles Wynn, a friend of Southey's, offer competing characterizations of the "prose-poet" (as Hazlitt had called him [Wu 4: 158]) that themselves possess a literary tinge and that feed into later, less clearly politicized contributions to the controversy.

Addressing the House of Commons, Smith described *Wat Tyler* as "the most seditious book that was ever written" and demanded, "Why ... had not those who thought it necessary to suspend the Habeas Corpus act taken notice of this poem?" (1091). Supporters of the suspension of habeas corpus—like Southey himself—would naturally be in favor of prosecuting the authors of "seditious" publications. Smith ended his speech by calling on the government to "punish" the Poet Laureate (1092). With a touch of melodrama, he accused Southey (whom he did not name) of "the settled, determined malignity of a renegado" (1090).

Wynn's immediate response to this speech anticipates Coleridge's defenses of Southey—and Southey's own—in romanticizing the author of *Wat Tyler* and minimizing his agency. Unlike Smith, Wynn referred to Southey by name, accusing his parliamentary colleague of "dragging him before the House, without his knowledge, and, consequently without his consent" (1093). Wynn, by contrast, attempts to reinstate Southey's character, offering a different account of *Wat Tyler*: "True it was, that the poem alluded to was written by him at the early age of nineteen. It was intended for publication; but the author had listened to the better advice of his friends, and it did not appear" (1093). Wynn thus exaggerates the youthfulness of the writer of *Wat Tyler* and misrepresents Southey's attempt

---

[22] Compare Kevin Gilmartin, *Print Politics: The Press and Radical Opposition in Early Nineteenth-Century England* (Cambridge: Cambridge University Press, 1996), on Hazlitt as a writer who offers a "radical critique of radical opposition" (232).

to get it published. He also downplays Southey's responsibility for thinking up the verse drama in the first place, characterizing his friend as swept along by forces beyond his control, writing "at an era when the heat of politics affected most men" and "betrayed into the composition of a poem which he afterwards disapproved" (1093). The speech thus foreshadows later sympathetic accounts of Southey in carrying shades of Wordsworth's self-characterization in *The Prelude* (not yet published) as unable to resist the initial magic of the French Revolution. Finally, Wynn accused Smith of making "personal reflections on an individual," a statement that provoked a "Hear, hear!" from his audience (1094). As so often in the period, the implication is that an allegation of "personality" will automatically prove to be the last word. It did not.

Smith defended himself on the spot by claiming that he had intended merely to "censure those who, having changed their opinions," use "severity of language" against "those who still adhered to their former sentiments" (1094). Wynn then accused Smith, by contrast, of "throw[ing] out severe and unjust censure on those who had receded from a particular set of opinions" (1094). The shift into the plural perhaps reflects a sense of discomfort by both speakers at having made their remarks too "personal." The question of who deserves to receive, and who reserves the right to exploit "severity of language," would be revisited in the *Wat Tyler* controversy as it intensified its exploration of Southey the "individual."

The Art of Self-Defense

Southey's initial response to Smith's attack on him was to decide to try to suppress the play;[23] at the same time he wrote a letter, dated March 17, 1817, not to William Smith himself but to the editor of the *Courier*.[24] The letter does not refer to Smith's attack, but the attack had been summarized in the pro-ministry newspaper two days previously. In his letter, Southey admits to the authorship of *Wat Tyler* but he does not refer to the "Parliamentary Reform" essay, thus side-stepping to some extent the allegation of apostasy even as he moves the prospect of self-vindication to the center of debate. In four paragraphs, he offers a narrative of his own past "life," and, with the help of some historical contextualization, a defense of the "crude opinions and warm feelings" of his "youth" (*LC* 4: 254).

As in some of Hazlitt's later contributions to the controversy, an ambivalent Romantic narrative of a fall from innocence emerges. Expressing a "desir[e] that my feelings should neither be misrepresented nor misunderstood" (*LC* 4: 253),

---

[23] Hoadley, "The Controversy over Southey's *Wat Tyler*," 84.

[24] Southey apparently wrote two letters, only one of which survives. Several critics state that the letter never appeared in the *Courier*, but the letter is reprinted in *LC* with the phrase "In Courier," and Erdman says the letter was published (*EOT* 2: 450, n.4). See Hoadley, "The Controversy," 86, Lapp (119) and Matt Hill in "The Critical Reception of Robert Southey's *Wat Tyler*," paragraph 5 in an online edition of *Wat Tyler; A Dramatic Poem* (1817), *Romantic Circles*, ed. Neil Fraistat and Steven E. Jones, http://www.rc.umd.edu/editions/wattyler/contexts/reception.html [accessed July 5, 2012].

Southey recognizes the likelihood of both possibilities even as he proclaims himself to be "a man whose life has been such that it may set slander at defiance" (*LC* 4: 254). Southey writes on the assumption that his exemplary "life" requires no further justification, while inviting the question of whether anyone can truly defy "slander." He calls the letter his "'last words' concerning Wat Tyler" (*LC* 4: 252)—ironically, given that they would be followed within weeks by the separate 45-page *Letter* addressed to Smith.

Over half way through his *Courier* letter, Southey explicitly turns from "the facts" of publication (*LC* 4: 252) to "the work itself," but this transition proves misleading because writing about the "work" involves continuing to tell his own "story." Southey's self-characterization will prove controversial. It is as if he figures himself as a Romantic poet capable of side-stepping politics only to embrace partisan conflict all the more. He portrays himself as composing *Wat Tyler* "in early youth" (the phrase implies childhood rather than young adulthood) at a time when he sincerely held "opinions of universal equality," opinions naturally "outgrown" in the "course" of "years" (*LC* 4: 254).[25] As in Wynn's parliamentary speech, Southey thus comes across as attracted, like Wordsworth in *The Prelude*, to the thrill of Jacobin politics in the 1790s. As if aware that this explanation of his shift in views might not satisfy the conservative readers of the *Courier*, Southey brings up the complicating issue of *Wat Tyler*'s "dramatic form," claiming that that caused him to state his "opinions ... more broadly" (*LC* 4: 254). He thus posits a distance between the authentic voice of the youthful author and the conventions of genre, which apparently forced him to exaggerate his radicalism.

In another distancing gesture, Southey also situates his past self historically by contrasting the political situation of the early 1790s with the "present state of things," a contrast that involves a contentious reading of then and now. He adds:

> The piece was written when such opinions, or rather such hopes and fears, were confined to a very small number of the educated classes; when those who were deemed Republicans were exposed to personal danger from the populace; and when a spirit of anti-Jacobinism prevailed, which I cannot characterize better than by saying that it was as blind and intolerant as the Jacobinism of the present day. (*LC* 4: 254)

Southey, it seems, as a young believer in "universal equality" and therefore a member of an "educated" elite, heroically endured the threat of "personal danger" from the bigoted "populace."

"The times have changed," he continues, going on to explain that if *Wat Tyler* had "been published surreptitiously under any other political circumstances," he would not have tried to suppress it (*LC* 4: 254). But, given what he perceives as the replacement of popular anti-Jacobinism with its opposite tendency, he fears actual "harm" from the dissemination of the play (*LC* 4: 254). This belief of Southey's

---

[25] Compare Mahoney, *Romantics and Renegades*, on how Southey makes his "change of opinions" seem "paradoxically ... straightforward" (133).

"make[s] it doubtful whether the publisher be not as much actuated by public mischief as by private malignity" (*LC* 4: 254). The claim takes for granted that the "publisher" of *Wat Tyler* would share Southey's perception that Jacobinism has spread to less "educated" readers likely to be inflamed by the play's assumptions—although the Sherwood edition, priced at three shillings and sixpence, unlike the less expensive pirate editions that followed Lord Eldon's ruling, was not necessarily aimed at a lower-class audience. At the same time Southey seems unwilling to believe that no "private malignity" was involved. Politically motivated "wickedness," in this account, is bound up with the attack on his "character." Correspondingly, Southey is not merely trying to defend himself but to "deserve well of his country and of mankind" (*LC* 4: 254). With this final claim, the writer submerges his "private" identity beneath his role on the political world stage, even as he uses the letter to the editor of the *Courier* to construct a quasi-Romantic narrative about the discrepancy between his past and present "life."

Coleridge's private reaction, in a letter dated March 22, 1817, to T.G. Street, the publisher of the *Courier*, was to regret the shape of his friend's narrative, presumably because of its admission that Southey had held Jacobinical views in his youth. Coleridge wrote, "What injudicious advisers must not Southey have had! it vexes me to the quick. Never yet did any human Being gain any thing by self-desertion" (*CL* 4: 713). According to Coleridge, instead of asserting his coherence, Southey is betraying his true "self," though this fault is partly shifted onto hypothetical "advisers." Coleridge added, "Southey should have rested his defence on the time, the work was written, both respecting himself and the events that happened afterwards" (*CL* 4: 713). Southey, that is to say, would have gained more respect if he had portrayed himself as entirely swayed by cultural imperatives in the past—itself a problematic claim. Downplaying the poet's responsibility for his actions, Coleridge's letter thus rejects Southey's Wordsworthian implication that change is growth.

The Sublime Poet

Coleridge's public contribution to the *Wat Tyler* controversy took the form of four articles in the *Courier*, published on March 17, March 18, March 27 and April 2, 1817.[26] Between the first two and the last two, the Lord Chancellor refused to allow the injunction to prevent the further publication of *Wat Tyler*, and his decision was reported in the newspapers, including the *Examiner*, which offered a detailed account of the case on March 23, two weeks after Hazlitt's initial review. Unstable in tone and at once contorted and digressive in style, Coleridge's four articles offer an unconvincing defense of Southey and his play. Coleridge tries to deflect attention from the question of Southey's change in political views

---

[26] Erdman points out that Sara Coleridge shortened the second two in her edition of the essays, trying to consign "the more embarrassing portions of Coleridge's tirade ... to oblivion" (*EOT* 2: 449, n.1).

by berating William Smith for his "coarse invective in the House of Commons against the Poet Laureat" and later castigating the publishers of *Wat Tyler* for circulating "political poison" (*EOT* 2: 454) to the "Swinish multitude" (*EOT* 2: 452; he borrows Edmund Burke's notorious phrase without irony). Coleridge's romanticized portrayal of Southey is particularly damaging, paving the way for more scorn and vituperation from Hazlitt, but it can also be seen as feeding into a more benignly satirical treatment of the poet by Leigh Hunt.

Coleridge's first article sarcastically thanks Smith for turning the tables: instead of journalists proving politicians wrong, now a Member of Parliament has "unmasked" a "Quarterly Reviewer" to expose his "inconsistency" (*EOT* 2: 449)! Coleridge next proceeds to rail against "Mr (*Double* U) Smith"—as he calls him at one point (*EOT* 2: 468)—for being in league with "the Hunts, Hazlitts, and Cobbetts" (*EOT* 2: 455) and for his "compleat ignorance of the whole form, growth and character of a Poet's mind" (*EOT* 2: 469). For Coleridge, "a young Poet ... lives in an *ideal* world" (*EOT* 2: 470).[27] Coleridge questions at length the tendency of Smith and other opponents to read *Wat Tyler* as an expression of Southey's early political views, protesting that it is "a *Poem*, and a *dramatic* Poem, and ... it is both unfair and absurd to attribute to the Poet, as a man all the sentiments he puts in the mouth of his characters" (*EOT* 2: 457). This point would seem self-evident, except that, as Michael Foot has noted, "a play such as this, written in 1794, could not have been anything other than a play defending Jacobinism."[28]

But even in acknowledging its historical context, Coleridge creates a sense of distance. In his words, the "very young man" who composed *Wat Tyler* saw the "evils of war and the hardships of the poor" through "slides" of a "magic lanthern" (*EOT* 2: 459). Giving a twist to this argument, Coleridge calls the play "an admirable burlesque on the pompous extravagances of the demagogues of the day," yet, modifying the idea that the text should be approached solely as a work of literature, he cautions against it as potentially inflammatory: the "book" is "silly, yet poisonous" (*EOT* 2: 453). In his effort to downplay the gulf between the sentiments of *Wat Tyler* and Southey's present views, Coleridge Wordsworthianizes the young Southey, but contradictorily he also builds up "SOUTHEY, THE MAN" at the expense of the "*stripling* Bard" (*EOT* 2: 459). "THE MAN" is figured as a "gem" outshining the "costly setting" (*EOT* 2: 459) of his public roles, as if the private human being transcends his reputation, instead of the other way around. At the same time, Coleridge tries to masculinize the young Southey, improbably claiming that his choice of topic was motivated by chivalric "indignation" on behalf of "Wat Tyler's Daughter" (*EOT* 2: 460), who in the play is threatened with sexual assault. Nonetheless dismissing *Wat Tyler* as "a school-boy dialogue in verse" (*EOT* 2: 454), Coleridge misleadingly implies that

---

[27] Lapp, in his detailed analysis of Coleridge's four articles and Hazlitt's response, calls this claim "an early formative moment in what we now call the Romantic ideology" (*Contest for Cultural Authority*, 124).

[28] Michael Foot, "William Hazlitt's Reply to Thomas McFarland or Caligula's Red Cap," *The Wordsworth Circle* 19.3 (1988): 145–50 (148).

Southey had never tried to publish the play and is therefore "morally ... innocent with regard to it" (*EOT* 2: 472). He even tries to recuperate the "virulence" with which Southey has been charged as the "natural" mark of his sincerity and earnestness (*EOT* 2: 451). The last of Coleridge's four articles ends with the misguided prediction, "Southey will never retaliate!" (*EOT* 2: 477).

Needless to say, the moral high ground occupied by Coleridge's ambiguous version of Southey will prove shaky. At least one contemporary reader was alienated by Coleridge's "open rebuttal of an open assault" as he put it (*EOT* 2: 456). Dorothy Wordsworth wrote to Catherine Clarkson on April 13, 1817, "If I were in Southey's place, I sho[uld] be far more afraid of my injudicious defen[ders] than my open enemies. Coleridge, for instance, has taken up the Cudgels; and of injudicious defenders he is surely the Master Leader. ... He does nothing in simplicity—and his praise is to me quite disgusting,—his praise of the '*Man*' Southey in contradistinction to the '*Boy*' who wrote 'Wat Tyler.'"[29]

Picking up on Coleridge's phrase, Hazlitt's first public response to his former friend's attempted defense of Southey took the form of a relatively short anonymous piece entitled "The Stripling Bard," published in the opposition *Morning Chronicle* on March 22, 1817, a few days after Coleridge's first two articles. Hazlitt's essay was soon reprinted in two of the pirate editions of *Wat Tyler*, published by Hone and John Fairburn, the latter of which also reprinted Coleridge's second article under the title, "The Stripling Bard; or the Apostate Laureate."[30] Writing in the conventional first person plural, Hazlitt insists on the participation of Southey's "friends" in misrepresenting his "character" (Wu 4: 341), but does not acknowledge that his own "expos[ure]" of the real Southey may be equally inaccurate.

Hazlitt announces, "*The Courier*, in pretended friendship to Mr Southey, will not let the errors of his youth sleep. It sends Mr Southey forth to the world, covered with a garment which does not belong to him, sure that the first man who meets him must tear it from him" (Wu 4: 341). The implication here is that the *Courier* writer, in giving Southey a flimsy disguise, invited others to "tear" it off, as if deliberately complicit in the growing vendetta against the poet. Strenuously objecting to Coleridge's attempt to rewrite Southey's past, Hazlitt devotes most of his essay to arguing that the play was not a youthful aberration, as Coleridge had implied, but that Southey had held Jacobinical views as late as the year 1800, "when the Stripling Bard was about 27" (Wu 4: 343). According to Hazlitt, this point is obvious, as "the Stripling Bard was always committing himself in a tangible shape" (Wu 4: 341). The word choice here stresses Southey's own role in defining his prior public identity.

Hazlitt mockingly presents various "specimens" from Southey's poetry of the 1790s, but of course his ultimate target is the Southey of the present day, or, as he facetiously refers to him, "the stripling of 40" (Wu 4: 343). The phrase offers

---

[29] *The Letters of William and Dorothy Wordsworth*, ed. Ernest de Selincourt; revised by Mary Moorman and Alan G. Hill, v. 3: *The Middle Years*, Part 2, 379–80.

[30] See Erdman, *EOT* 2: 460n.

an image of Southey as a youth who never grows up, despite growing older like everyone else, a prey to perpetual delusion rather than (as Romantic poets would have it) the bearer of special insight. Hazlitt concludes by saying that he does not "object" to Southey's "history" but to his hostility to radical "principles" and the "violence" of his attitude: "in short, we do not object to the weakness of the man, but to … 'the malignity of the Renegado'" (Wu 4: 343). Hazlitt thus reminds his readers of the phrase that William Smith had used in the House of Commons, but in giving so much space to quotations, he allows the fearless voice of Southey's younger self to overpower these already tired allegations. Hazlitt's article begs the question of the extent to which the "man" can be distinguished from the "Renegado," while hinting at two different answers: there is no "man" independent of these various public representations, or, alternatively, the "man"—and his "history"—inevitably surpasses any mere label and may yet surprise readers.

Hazlitt reworked his *Morning Chronicle* piece into a more elaborate attack on Coleridge and Southey, published in the *Examiner* on March 30, 1817 as "The Courier and 'The Wat Tyler,'" a piece that extends his Wordsworthian rewriting of Southey. Like his March 9 attack on Southey in the *Examiner*, this article consists of energetic vituperation that at first sight seems thoroughly political as well as absolutely incisive. It is tempting to conclude that the only reason Hazlitt refrains from obliterating Southey entirely is because he makes such a perfect punching bag. But this March 30 article also helps to transform Southey into a more complex figure capable of eluding other writers' collective grasp.

Hazlitt's treatment of Southey is inflected by private venom against Coleridge, probably strengthened by the fact that he had referred in his second *Courier* article to the "Hunts, Hazlitts, and Cobbetts" as "asinine creatures" (*EOT* 2: 455). Writing quasi-anonymously, Hazlitt defends his fellow reformist journalists but does not name himself. He begins by asking, implicitly, with friends like Coleridge, who needs enemies? He asserts, "If [Southey] can escape from the ominous patronage of that gentleman's pen, he has nothing to fear from his own" (Wu 4: 165). Hazlitt will make a similar point later in the year in his elaborate *Edinburgh* review of Coleridge's *Biographia Literaria*. His *Examiner* article proceeds to dismantle Coleridge's "maudlin methodistical casuistry" (Wu 4: 166) concerning Southey's change of opinions and then offers a point-by-point refutation of what he calls Coleridge's "flabby defence of the *Wat Tyler*" (Wu 4: 169).

Hazlitt insists disingenuously, "We have nothing to do with Mr. Southey 'the man,' or even Mr. Southey the apostate; but we have something to do with Mr. Southey the spy and informer" (Wu 4: 166). This sentence sets up firm distinctions, but of course Hazlitt will have much to say on the subjects of both "man" and "apostate," if indeed they can be distinguished. The questions that follow suggest that they cannot: "If the writer of the article on Parliamentary Reform thinks the Editor of this Paper [Leigh Hunt] 'a flagitious incendiary,' 'a palliator of murder, insurrection, and treason,' what does the Quarterly Reviewer think of the author of *Wat Tyler*? What, on the other hand, does the author of *Wat Tyler* think of the Quarterly Reviewer? What does Mr. Southey, who certainly makes a very aukward figure between the two, think of himself?" (Wu 4: 166). This final question raises a further unarticulated question, where is the real Southey?

Although "Mr. Southey" here seems to vanish momentarily into a "nonentity" (Wu 4: 173), Hazlitt revives him while challenging what he claims to be Coleridge's implication that it is better to be a turncoat than never to have turned in the first place. Though preserving (questionable) gender distinctions, Hazlitt continues his previous metonymic association of Southey with the figure of the fallen woman: "The greater the sinner the greater the saint, says *The Courier*. Mr. Southey's Muse is confessedly not a vestal; but then she is what is much better, a Magdalen" (Wu 4: 166). He adds, "A woman is more likely to prostitute her person at nineteen—a man is more likely to prostitute his understanding at forty" (Wu 4: 167). Hazlitt attempts to diminish Southey by comparing him with women who sell their bodies, but at the same time he builds him back up, partly by resisting Coleridge's claim that Southey "*was a mere boy when he wrote Wat Tyler*" (Wu 4: 169, Hazlitt's italics).

He thus continues the argument begun in his anonymous *Morning Chronicle* piece (to which he refers approvingly) that Southey held Jacobinical opinions throughout the 1790s, an allegation that makes the Southey of the past more of a force to be reckoned with. This article initiates the long-standing tradition of claiming that Wordsworth, Coleridge, and Southey wrote their best poetry when they were revolutionary sympathizers: "All the authority that they have as poets and men of genius must be thrown into the scale of Revolution and Reform" (Wu 4: 170).[31] Despite granting the Lake Poets some "authority," Hazlitt insists that Coleridge in particular is lost in the world of the imagination, transfixed by what he calls, re-using Coleridge's image, "the slides of a magic lanthorn" (Wu 4: 172).

Nevertheless, part of the way that Hazlitt makes Southey disappear and reappear is by dissolving him behind and at the same time reconstituting him through Hazlitt's own trademark patchwork of literary allusions, mostly Shakespearean, sometimes Biblical. Even while Hazlitt insists on equating the literary and the political, he divides them by himself banishing Southey to the shadowy world of the imagination. In the article's concluding diatribe, he imagines Southey outdoing "Herodias's daughter" by offering "his own head," John the Baptist-like, on a "charger," and staring sightlessly like Banquo's ghost (Wu 4: 173). "And yet," he adds, "Mr. Coleridge would persuade us that this stuffed figure, this wretched phantom, is the living man" (Wu 4: 173). Hazlitt's tone, as so often, is scathing, but his own relentless barrage of quotations, rhetorical questions and grotesque images indicates that it may not be so easy to dispose of the "living man."

A week after this attack, Hazlitt published in the *Examiner* a short follow-up piece entitled "Mr. Coleridge and Mr. Southey" that calls attention to the fact that the chief protagonists in the *Wat Tyler* affair were a small circle of people with a

---

[31] Lapp, who sees Hazlitt as offering "an alternative ideology of Romanticism" in which literature and politics are intertwined, finds in this article a "counter-mythologization of Southey's apotheosis" (*Contest for Cultural Authority*, 128).

shared past. Despite writing anonymously, most participants in the controversy probably expected their identities to be recognized. This circumstance may have made some details of their contributions opaque to readers not in the know. Writing in the first person under the signature "Vindex," Hazlitt nevertheless mocks Coleridge's use of anonymity. Alluding to Coleridge's defense of Southey, Hazlitt claims that, "This hack writer of the *Courier* has a spell upon him, which denies him the happy power of invisibility. From the forced and quaint images, the vile *puns*, the uncouth and floundering attempts at humour, the bloatedness of the eloquence, and the slang of the blackguardism, we cannot be mistaken in the writer of this effusion of disinterested generosity" (*E* 484: 211). The suggestion is that if Coleridge's style "cannot be mistaken," his "affinity of [political] sentiment" with Southey is equally unmistakable.

Betraying his own identity to certain readers (if it were not already evident from *his* style), Hazlitt then attempts to prove that Coleridge's admiration of Southey as a writer is insincere, by bringing up an incident during "a visit to Bristol" in which Coleridge ridiculed Southey's poetry. The anecdote supposedly shows the gulf between public protestations and "private" behavior, but the incident in Bristol involves Coleridge declaiming his views "*publicly*, before several strangers, and in the midst of a public library" (*E* 484: 211). The only real discrepancy turns out to be between oral assertions in the past and protestations in print now. The *Wat Tyler* outcry gives Hazlitt the opportunity to dredge up what he calls a "disgusting display of egotism and malignity" on Coleridge's part (*E* 484: 211). Hazlitt makes the most of his inside knowledge and his long-standing acquaintance with the Lake Poets, without admitting that his animosity towards them and theirs towards him may also entangle private with public motivations.[32]

The Satirized Poet

Meanwhile, in a more jocular vein, Hone had published his "New Edition" of *Wat Tyler* with a Preface "suitable to recent circumstances" and an extract from David Hume's *History of Great Britain* (1754–62) on the poll tax rebellion of 1381.[33] Showing the eagerness of Southey's critics to encapsulate him with a single image, Hone first depicts Southey in terms of a visual caricature, hypothesizing "a portrait of the Laureate, weeping for his principles, 'because they are not,' wearing a cap and bells, and writing a receipt for his next quarter's salary on the back of 'WAT TYLER'" (vi). Hone then gives a humorously allegorical account of the publication of the play, figured as a "ghost ... risen from the grave" (vi). He imagines Southey "at his retreat in Cumberland," like "one Mr. Coleridge, a person residing at Bristol," being "terrified" with "strange and marvellous" political "relations" in the *Courier* (vi), causing "the two poor gentlemen" to feed

---

[32] In Chapter 2, I briefly discuss Coleridge's private hostility to Hazlitt.

[33] Robert Southey, *Wat Tyler: 1817*, ed. Jonathan Wordsworth (Oxford: Woodstock Books, 1989), iii. Further page references in parentheses.

off "each other's alarm" (vii). Southey's political writings, that is to say, express the mutually generated paranoia of himself and his friend.

Hone adds, "Mr. ROBERT SOUTHEY having been stolen 'like a grey duck from the lake,' to write, during a paroxysm, in the Quarterly, had scarcely put down his pen, when, as in retribution, up jumped WAT TYLER" (vii). The embodiment—or rather spectralization—of *Wat Tyler* as a "spirit" transforms Southey from an idealistic poet into a fictional character in a comical narrative, the victim rather than the beneficiary of Coleridge's "lay sermons in the *Courier*" (vii). Clearly, the identity of Southey's defender in the *Courier* was an open secret. This farcical anecdote with its cynical behind-the-scenes glimpse into the power of print debunks Southey's authority by drawing attention to the way in which the seemingly endless capacity of his opponents to score points from the *Wat Tyler* episode relies on the participation of Southey's supporters. Like other contributions to the controversy, it thus becomes more of a meta-critical statement than yet another reminder of its central figure's lamentable apostasy.

The reception of *Wat Tyler* took an even more comic turn on April 13, 1817, the third Sunday in a row that the *Examiner* had responded to Coleridge's defense of Southey. This week's contribution in the *Examiner* took the form of an uneven but entertaining satirical piece entitled "Death and Funeral of the Late Mr. Southey," signed with Leigh Hunt's well-known pointing hand emblem. Two and half years later, Hunt himself would falsely be pronounced dead in the sixth attack on the Cockney School of Poetry in *Blackwood's Magazine* (*BM* 6: 70–76). Hunt's "Death and Funeral" ignores Coleridge's—and Hazlitt's—romanticizing of Southey, instead reducing him to a caricature, yet one with a liveliness that counteracts the potentially tasteless fiction that the poet has been killed off by his reformist opponents.

Hunt's narrative depicts Southey as "imitating NIMROD, who hunted men" and maniacally "gallopping after divers Reformers" whom he subjects to verbal abuse (*E* 485: 236). When these "opponents" attack him physically, "our hero" calls upon the aid of his friend, "Dr. PARACELSUS BROADHUM COLERIDGE," who accidentally "expose[s]" him to his "mortal" blow (*E* 485: 236). The piece thus heavy-handedly satirizes the backfiring of Coleridge's attempt to defend Southey. Its portrayal of Coleridge boils down to three elements: his "trick of 'encumbering with help,'" his counterproductive fixation with "old books," and a hint that he drinks too much (at the funeral, he is "supported by two Bottle-holders" [*E* 485: 237]). "Dr. PARACELSUS BROADHUM COLERIDGE" bears a little resemblance to Peacock's caricature of Coleridge in *Melincourt*, the transcendentalist Moley Mystic, in seeming out of touch with the here and now and using supposedly cryptic language like "'would not retaliate;' which being interpreted out of the Doctor's mystic phraseology, meant, that his patient had no strength or vitality left" (*E* 485: 236).

Hunt's portrayal of Southey is equally stereotyped, but the character's energetic actions and the speeches that Hunt puts into his mouth revitalize the standard allegations against the poet. Hunt pulls together Southey's attitude to "incendiaries" in the by now notorious "Parliamentary Reform" essay (which he does not even need to name), William Smith's related complaint that Southey uses "severity of language" against those with whom he formerly agreed, and the depiction of the "stripling Bard" in Coleridge's and Hazlitt's articles. Southey is described as "taking his breakfast in a very staid manner" and then, in humorous contrast with this domestic detail, setting out on his manhunt, "couching his pen in hand for a lance like DON QUIXOTE" (*E* 485: 236).

Southey's first speech wittily builds on prior treatments of the poet:

> Hallo there! You vagabonds, thieves, liars, incendiaries, and worse than housebreakers, whom I formerly agreed with,—*I* was an honest and virtuous youth, a stripling of nine and twenty, for thinking as you do; but *you* are a pack of rascals, yelping curs, bears, tygers and boars, for thinking as I did; and you, especially, who are no older than I was and only think half of what I did, are a parcel of provoking beasts, brutes, cattle, vermin, and reptiles. (*E* 485: 236)

The proliferation of animal insults has some comic exuberance, even though the idea that Southey is particularly guilty of asperity and name-calling is problematic because of the pervasiveness of vituperation in Romantic-era print discourse. The next speech that Hunt puts into Southey's mouth parodically reiterates the standard charge of inconsistency against the poet in language so condensed that it carries a note of surrealism: "I'll cut ye up there, slaughterly and Quarterly! What are ye grinning at? BOB and ST JAGO! Oh the days when I was young! King and no King! Here come two of us! Charity and Persecution for ever! Principle and Apostacy ditto! What, they agree with me, do they? And without my consent!" (*E* 485: 236). With this speech, Hunt's enjoyment in making the same joke over and over again seems to take the place of any serious political point.

His account of the Laureate's funeral is less inventive, consisting of a list of mourners that includes, for example, "Jacobins with their coats turned" and "Pall-bearers" identified as "Renegadoes from Algiers"—presumably an allusion to Renaissance-era Christian converts to Islam in North Africa. Hunt also takes the opportunity to touch on his own feud with the editor of the *Quarterly* (discussed in my third chapter) by including among the attendees "WILLIAM GIFFORD, Esq.," described as "Supported by Gentleman Pensioners, but very irritable in his grief, kicking the mud on all sides of him and on the Ladies" (*E* 485: 237)—an allusion to Gifford's verbal mistreatment of the poet Mary Robinson. Having at least momentarily turned politics into sheer entertainment, Hunt's piece sounds as if it could be the final word on Southey's apostasy. Thanks to Southey himself, however, Hunt will, before too long, bring the "dead" author of *Wat Tyler* back to life.

The *Letter to William Smith*

Less than two weeks later, on April 26, 1817, the romanticized Southey returned in *A Letter to William Smith, Esq., M.P. from Robert Southey, Esq.*, published by

John Murray as a 45-page pamphlet. Southey's "Billet Doux" to Smith (*NL* 2: 156) sold 2000 copies by the beginning of May and went into several editions.[34] As mentioned earlier, it caused a heightening of hostilities, exemplifying the likelihood of a reprisal generating further attacks. Besides excoriating Smith, Southey aims to offer a self-vindication—an attempt that fails mainly because of its conflicted accounts of Southey's past *and* present selves. As in Coleridge's reprisals, the autobiographical element of the *Letter* at times explores an interplay between sameness and difference not dissimilar to Wordsworth's and Coleridge's self-representations in key Romantic lyrics such as "Tintern Abbey" and the conversation poems. Like Coleridge, Southey thus associates himself with more profound models of the self than those explored in Wordsworth's "My heart leaps up" and Hazlitt's *Examiner* review of *Wat Tyler*. The gigantic ego that emerges at the end of the *Letter*, however, though not intentionally comical, reads like a parody of Romantic selfhood.

Southey's self-defense is damaged from the outset by the aggressiveness of his counterattack on Smith, which is only modified by a slight note of skepticism about whether Smith really did mount "so strange a criticism" of Southey, "in so unfit a place" as the Houses of Parliament.[35] As if to strengthen his case, Southey accuses Smith of planning his attack: "[it] was a premeditated thing ... you had prepared yourself for it by stowing the Quarterly Review in one pocket, and Wat Tyler in the other; and ... you deliberately stood up for the purpose of reviling an individual who was not present to vindicate himself, and in a place which afforded you protection" (1–2).[36] Protection in what sense? This last phrase insinuates that Smith was cowardly enough to want to shield himself from physical harm, even though Southey himself evidently prefers to fight with words alone. Southey several times reiterates the injustice of attacking him in the House of Commons, though he also brings up "the manner of the attack" (43)—a detail that problematically reminds his readers that Southey too has repeatedly been accused of treating his opponents in what he calls "coarse and insulting language" (9). In fact, he reviles the publisher of *Wat Tyler* as "some skulking scoundrel" (5), even though he congratulates himself on avoiding "calumny" (27): "What man's private character did I stab? Whom did I libel? Whom did I slander? Whom did I traduce?" (26–7). He reserves his own strongest language for Smith, accusing him of a "malevolent heart" (6), and of being totally "unlike" Southey (23)—though the latter allegation could perhaps be twisted into a compliment.

---

[34] Storey, *Robert Southey*, 263.

[35] Robert Southey, *A Letter to William Smith, Esq., M.P. from Robert Southey, Esq.* (London: John Murray, 1817), 1. Further references to the *Letter* in parentheses.

[36] Southey's pettiest accusation against Smith has taken on a life of its own in later accounts of the controversy. Smith's alleged use of two different pockets seems to have hardened into historical fact in later accounts of the incident. See, for example, Hoadley, "The Controversy," 83; Lapp, *Contest for Cultural Authority*, 117; Mahoney, *Romantics and Renegades*, 127–8.

Shifting between second and third person as if at once to stand back from and stand behind the force of his own rhetoric, Southey adds, "Mr. William Smith is said to have insulted me with the appellation of Renegade; and if it indeed be true that the foul aspersion past his lips, I brand him for it on the forehead with the name of SLANDERER. Salve the mark as you will, Sir, it is ineffaceable! You must bear it with you to your Grave, and the remembrance will outlast your Epitaph" (28). With these fierce words, Southey seems, like Smith, "forgetful of the decencies between man and man" (43). Southey conjures up two dubious notions: the illusion of transcending the medium of print in order to write upon the body, and the idea that a "mark" thus inflicted may be "ineffaceable." Such a flight of fancy unavoidably raises the question of whether Southey himself will carry Smith's "foul aspersion" to his own "Grave." His melodramatic scenario of persecution and revenge coexists incongruously in the text with the writer's more complex depiction of "Mr. Southey" (43), as he refers to himself.

Southey's self-characterization in the *Letter* anticipates that of Coleridge in *Biographia Literaria*—and Coleridge's account of Southey in the same text—in its mixture of self-effacement and self-aggrandizement. At the outset, he seems both eager to "speak explicitly for myself" (2) and determined not to take responsibility for his own voice. He refuses to admit to the authorship of the "Parliamentary Reform" essay, insisting that the *Quarterly* has an autonomy independent of its contributors:

> The Quarterly Review stands upon its own merits. It is not answerable for anything more than it contains. What I may have said, or thought, in any part of my life, no more concerns that Journal than it does you, or the House of Commons: and I am as little answerable for the Journal, as the Journal for me. What I may have written in it is a question which you, Sir, have no right to ask, and which certainly I will not answer. (3–4)

Contradicting this disingenuous stance, Southey uses the *Letter* to reiterate beliefs put forward in "Parliamentary Reform." In addition, apparently with more pride than reluctance, he "claim[s]" *Wat Tyler* "as my own property" (6), even though he later downplays the agency of the "boy" who wrote it (13). Despite admitting that his identity is "notorious" (2), he insists that "Few authors have obtruded themselves upon the public in their individual character less than I have done" (10). As in the Coleridge–Jeffrey feud that will follow in the summer of 1817, we find a tension between the impulse to speak back and ostensible embarrassment over indulging in autobiography.

Southey next claims the moral high ground in that he has not previously resorted to reprisals:

> None of the innumerable attacks which have been made upon [my works] has ever called forth on my part a single word of reply, triumphantly as I might have exposed my assailants, not only for their ignorance and inconsistency, but frequently for that moral turpitude which is implied in wilful and deliberate

mis-statement. The unprovoked insults which have been levelled at me both in prose and rhyme never induced me to retaliate; it will not be supposed that the ability for satire was wanting, but happily, I had long since subdued the disposition. (10–11)

Southey's sweeping language in this passage draws attention to the fact that even as he boasts that he has "never" stooped to "retaliate"—the word choice echoes Coleridge's "Southey will never retaliate!"—he is in the process of doing so. The phrases "innumerable attacks" and not "a single word of reply" smack of exaggeration. His assertion that had he chosen to wield his "ability for satire," he could have "triumphantly" crushed his "assailants" betrays an over-confident belief in his own rhetorical powers that will not go unnoticed by hostile reviewers. He continues to beg the question: "It will not therefore be imputed to any habit of egotism, or any vain desire of interesting the public in my individual concerns, if I now come forward" (11).

Southey may not practice a "habit of egotism," but the *Letter* is nothing if not an attempt to engage "the public" in "individual concerns." Having insisted that he is "now" forced to "come forward," he continues with a blend of self-pity and self-elevation: "my name has served in London for the very shuttle-cock of discussion" (12). He adds,

> My celebrity has for a time eclipsed that of Mr. Hunt the Orator, and may perhaps have impeded the rising reputation of Toby, the Sapient Pig. I have reigned in the newspapers as paramount as Joanna Southcott during the last month of her tympany. Nay, columns have been devoted to Mr. Southey and Wat Tyler which would otherwise have been employed in bewailing the forlorn condition of the Emperor Napoleon. (12)

The allusion to "Toby, the Sapient Pig" (an animal exhibited by an illusionist of the era) unexpectedly betrays the glimmer of a sense of humor, as does the sardonic allusion to radicals' sympathy for the "forlorn" Napoleon Bonaparte, but the complaint about the massive press coverage that he has attracted suggests more grandiosity than self-mockery.

Having thus provided questionable insight into the *Wat Tyler* controversy—it has given its central figure unwanted fame—Southey sets out "to inform the world" what his opinions "really have been, and what they are" (13). He here conjures up the fantasy of giving a true account of himself that would redeem his own "character" (11) in the eyes of the "world." He then gives a description of himself strongly inflected by Coleridge's defense in the *Courier*, at once positing a gulf between the "stripling" and the "man" (15) and, ironically given Hazlitt's prior attack, asserting a fundamental likeness between them. He dismisses *Wat Tyler* as the "verses of a boy, of which he thought no more than of his school-exercises" (13), written "when my heart was full of poetry and romance" (14). The word choice, like that in Coleridge's *Courier* articles, resonates with Wordsworth's reference in the still-unpublished *Prelude* to revolutionary politics as possessing the "attraction of a Country in Romance" (1805 *Prelude* 10: 696). According to Southey, as "a youth of twenty," he "fell into the political opinions which the French Revolution was then scattering throughout Europe" (14). Who could blame such a fall?

Besides, "to select passages from a dramatic poem, and ascribe the whole force of the sentiments to the writer as if he himself held them, without the slightest qualification, is a mode of criticism manifestly absurd and unjust" (16). Southey thus repeats his own and Coleridge's momentary reliance on the distancing effect of dramatic form, but with an air of being over-anxious to remove himself from his past "feelings" (8). Revisiting his "enthusiastic love of liberty" (18), he brings up his circle's abortive Pantisocracy project of the 1790s, but refuses further discussion of this "fact" by stressing that "I am not writing my own memoirs" (20). Nevertheless, he tries to pull together past and present by emphasizing that "in all his writings there breathed the same abhorrence of oppression and immorality, the same spirit of devotion, and the same ardent wishes for the amelioration of mankind" (44). Here we see a move resembling claims in central first-generation Romantic poems such as Wordsworth's "Ode" that continuities within the self outweigh discontinuities and loss. Southey even claims that future readers will recognize this capacity to rise above partisan politics, assigning himself a symbolic immortality.

In context, however, the self ascribed to "Mr. Southey" is ultimately more monstrous than transcendent. At the end of the *Letter*, with what some will see as breathtaking arrogance, he projects his own posthumous fame. He insists that his "name ... will certainly not perish" (44) and, shifting to the third person again, confidently asserts that "Some account of his life will always be prefixed to his works, and transferred to literary histories, and to the biographical dictionaries, not only of this, but of other countries. There it will be related, that he lived in the bosom of his family, in absolute retirement" (44). Evidently even the uneventful nature of Southey's private life will "always" be the subject of research.[37]

With no apparent irony, Southey goes on to predict future evaluations of his work: "It will be said of him, that in an age of personality, he abstained from satire" (45). Southey, that is, stands apart from his "age"—or so he would have his readers believe. He then pre-empts future judgments of the *Letter*: "it will be said, that he vindicated himself, as it became him to do, and treated his calumniator with just and memorable severity" (45). Mahoney, who reads the *Letter* in de Manian terms as a "discourse of self-restoration" (139), sees this conclusion as Southey's own "epitaph" that risks "prematurely condemning [him]self to the silence of the grave" (142). Regardless, readers of the *Letter* will have plenty to say, killing

---

[37] This declaration provides an obvious example of what Vincent Newey and Philip Shaw call the autobiographer's investment in the future: the written "I" is bound up with the "promise of a public recollection." See Newey and Shaw, eds, *Mortal Pages, Literary Lives: Studies in Nineteenth-century Autobiography* (Aldershot: Scolar Press, 1996), 2. Andrew Bennett, in *Romantic Poets and the Culture of Posterity* (Cambridge: Cambridge University Press, 1999), sees this idea as "determining force in cultural production" in the Romantic era (2).

Southey off all over again and bringing him back from the grave, livelier than before. In doing so, they will continue the process of de-romanticizing and re-romanticizing Southey, containing and setting him free again, only to return him into a figure of fun.[38]

The Reception of the *Letter*

Positive reactions to the *Letter* were mostly private ones by Southey's friends and acquaintances. Even these do not offer unqualified praise. Walter Scott, in a letter to Southey, referred to his "triumphant answer to that coarse-minded scoundrel William Smith."[39] Southey himself wrote, "Never had any man a compleater triumph,—congratulations have poured in upon me from all quarters, nor could I have wished for a better opportunity of trampling upon my enemies than this Slander-Smith has afforded me."[40] Henry Crabb Robinson recorded in his diary on April 28, 1817, "I read Southey's *Letter to W. Smith*—a spirited little pamphlet. Southey vindicates his change of opinion successfully but does not plead to the charge of illiberality in abusing the present race of democrats."[41] Robinson's entry for May 2, 1817, recounts a conversation with Southey about *Wat Tyler* and the *Letter*, "of which I thought and spoke favourably." Perhaps the "charge of illiberality" did not come up on this occasion.[42] Wordsworth also had an objection to the *Letter*. He described it as "completely triumphant," but said that Southey's "statement of his own opinions" made him look like "a *Tool of Power*."[43]

In contrast with this modified expression of approval, at least two public comments on the *Letter* were entirely favorable.[44] The *Courier* reviewed it on the day of its publication, quoting so much of it that Southey complained about the effect on potential profits (*NL* 2: 156). The *New Monthly Magazine* referred to the *Letter* in its June 1817 issue, claiming that "The *argumentum ad hominem* was never more successfully applied than in this admirable epistle, and upon the whole the public may be grateful to the Member for Norwich for having been

---

[38] Compare Arthur Bradley and Alan Rawes, eds, who, in *Romantic Biography* (Burlington: Ashgate, 2003), offer "a call to both de-Romanticize and re-Romanticize Romantic life writing" (xiv).

[39] H.J.C. Grierson, ed., *Letters of Sir Walter Scott*, 12 vols (London: Constable, 1933), 4: 445.

[40] Quoted from Storey, *Robert Southey*, 263.

[41] Henry Crabb Robinson, *On Books and Their Writers*, ed. Edith J. Morley, 3 vols (London: J.M. Dent, 1938), 1: 206. The next quotation is from the same page.

[42] Southey was in London from April 24 to May 9, 1817, on his way to travel on the Continent partly in the hope of distracting himself from the death of his adored nine-year-old son Herbert the previous year.

[43] Wordsworth to Henry Crabb Robinson, June 24, 1817 (*Middle Years* vol. 3, Part 2: 393).

[44] Hoadley, in "The Controversy over Southey's *Wat Tyler*," summarizes the reception of the *Letter* in newspapers (89–91).

the occasion for so spirited an exposition. The poet-laureat has satisfactorily vindicated himself from the illiberal charges of apostacy" (*SCH*, 255). Southey's old enemies were not inclined to agree.

Hazlitt's scathing review of the *Letter to William Smith* is a major assault on Southey's self-characterization that extends the Romantic rewriting of the Laureate, this time by associating him explicitly with Wordsworth's "Tintern Abbey," the quintessential Romantic lyric concerning recovery from loss, the power of memory, the interaction of mind and nature, and "a sense sublime / Of something far more deeply interfused" (ll. 96–7). The review appeared in the *Examiner* in three parts, on May 4, May 11, and May 18, 1817. Reviews appearing over more than one Sunday were not uncommon in the *Examiner*, but in this case the length of Hazlitt's excoriation seems to be a symptom of his investment in Southey as well as a political strategy. At one point he tries to justify the repetitiveness of his accusations: "'Dost thou think, because thou art virtuous, there shall be no more cakes and ale,' …? While he goes on writing in the 'Quarterly,' shall we give over writing in *The Examiner*?" (Wu 4: 176). Nevertheless, the attention to detail of this review—which in places borrows the nitpicking style of verbal criticism of which Hazlitt himself was a target in the Tory press—suggests that the writer is either unwilling or unable to crush Southey completely.

Southey himself wrote to Wordsworth after the first installment: "Hazlitt's scurrility is so drest up that all who are capable of understanding it must needs loath it—to the ignorant it is almost as unintelligible as Coleridge's philosophy" (*NL* 2: 156). To Southey, the elaborateness of Hazlitt's attack is self-defeating, but this judgment sounds like wishful thinking. Hazlitt's vibrant prose has the power to keep disfiguring his victim, showing that although Southey's "personal identity" (Wu 4: 175) may be a "fiction of his own making" (Wu 4: 176), that fiction can be taken out of his hands. Yet Hazlitt does not seem to recognize that negative characterizations of his enemy could potentially work to his victim's benefit. He continues to make Southey into a potentially intriguing figure, a "painful hieroglyphic of humanity" (Wu 4: 193) who threatens to baffle the understanding. For him, Southey is a monster, "a *beau ideal* of moral and political egotism" (Wu 4: 188), but this description elevates Southey as well as diminishing him. At the same time however, perhaps because its "scurrility" is so "drest up" or perhaps because Hazlitt is personally acquainted with Southey—as he acknowledges at the end of the review—the article itself has a certain opacity that reinforces the mysteriousness of this unfortunate "Letter-writer" (Wu 4: 182).

Loaded with insults and dripping with sarcasm, Hazlitt's review of the *Letter* makes a number of predictable moves. Mocking Southey for refusing to admit to authorship of the "Parliamentary Reform" essay, Hazlitt lingers over the relevant passage from the *Letter*, taking the opportunity to expose Southey's inconsistency: "In the very paragraph before the one in which he skulks from the responsibility of the 'Quarterly Review,' and with pert vapid assurance repels every insinuation implying a breach of his inviolability as an anonymous writer, he makes an impudent, unqualified, and virulent attack on Mr. Brougham as an

Edinburgh Reviewer" (Wu 4: 177). Using such forceful language throughout the review, Hazlitt himself seems to have a double standard in sarcastically referring to Southey's "characteristic delicacy and moderation in the use of epithets" and in rebuking him for "putting a false statement into epigrammatic phraseology" (Wu 4: 178). Hazlitt himself, needless to say, is a master of epigrammatic phraseology if not of false statements.

Exposing Southey's "loss of character" (Wu 4: 187), as in previous attacks this writer tries to belittle him by associating him with disreputable women and questionable sexual practices. He refers to a struggle between Southey's "hoyden Jacobin mistress" and "the old bawd Legitimacy," depicting the former as "furiously scratching the face or cruelly tearing off the hair of the said pimping old lady, who would never let her alone, night or day" (Wu 4: 180). Southey is imagined divorcing the "virago" in favor of "the detestable old hag" and becoming "uxorious in his second matrimonial connexion" (Wu 4: 180). Hazlitt continues inexorably:

> [And] though his false Duessa has turned out a very witch, a foul, ugly witch, drunk with insolence, mad with power, a griping, rapacious wretch, bloody, luxurious, wanton, malicious, not sparing steel, or poison, or gold, to gain her ends—bringing famine, pestilence and death in her train—infecting the air with her thoughts, killing the beholders with her looks, claiming mankind as her property, and using them as her slaves—driving everything before her, and playing the devil wherever she comes, Mr. Southey sticks to her in spite of every thing, and for very shame lays his head in her lap, paddles with the palms of her hands, inhales her hateful breath ... [and] sticks close to his filthy bargain. (Wu 4: 180)

With these misogynistic lines yoking sexual obsession, power, and violence, Hazlitt goes further than the earlier perfunctory attempts to effeminize Southey, risking alienating readers with his Juvenalian railing. Later he quotes Southey: "'What man's private character did I stab? Whom did I libel? Whom did I slander? Whom did I traduce? THESE MISCREANTS LIVE BY CALUMNY AND SEDITION: THEY ARE LIBELLERS AND LIARS BY TRADE,'" adding, "After this, *Sir Anthony Absolute's* 'Damn you, can't you be cool, like me?' will hardly pass for a joke!" (Wu 4: 189). Yet the "joke" is also on Hazlitt. After such virulence, much of the review seems anticlimactic.

Earlier, and especially in the first installment of the review, however, Hazlitt deepens his portrayal of Southey, granting his victim some complexity even as he reveals what he calls, quoting Alexander Pope, his "ruling passion" (Wu 4: 175)—his "self-love" (Wu 4: 174). Hazlitt gives an account of the *Letter* that makes it seem something more than a mere display of "egotism, vanity, ill-humour, and intolerance" (Wu 4: 175). According to him, the *Letter* is "a concentrated essence of a want of self-knowledge" (Wu 4: 175). Against this paradoxical "essence" of a lack of "self-knowledge," Hazlitt opposes his own relentless power to see and know, later adding ominously, "Mr. Southey does not know himself so well as we do" (Wu 4: 186). Hazlitt calls the *Letter* "'a psychological curiosity;' a study of human infirmity. As some persons bequeath their bodies to the surgeons to be dissected after their death, Mr. Southey publicly exposes his mind to be anatomized while he is living" (Wu 4: 175). The allusion is probably to Coleridge's use of the phrase "psychological curiosity" in the prefatory note to *Kubla Khan* (published the previous year).

Hazlitt thus once again associates Southey with Romantic themes of self-exploration and self-representation. According to him, the writer of the *Letter* "lays open his character to the scalping-knife, [and] guides the philosophic hand in its painful researches" (Wu 4: 175). The result of such "researches" is presented bathetically as "the organ of vanity" but even Hazlitt's overloaded description of this undignified "organ" gives it some weight: "sleek, smooth, round, perfect, polished, honed, and shining, as it were in a transparency" (Wu 4: 175). As if unable to move past the anatomization of "character" even while implying that it is scarcely worth the exercise of the "philosophic hand," Hazlitt goes on to declare, "This is the handle of his intellect, the index of his mind; 'the guide, the anchor of his purest thoughts, and soul of all his moral being'" (Wu 4: 175). This time his (mis)quotation is from "Tintern Abbey," and on the surface Hazlitt is making a demystifying move, substituting the littleness of "vanity" for the grandeur of Wordsworth's emotional and moral foundation, nature. Yet even in invoking "Tintern Abbey," Hazlitt seems to be associating Southey temporarily with the profundity of Wordsworth's attempt to pull together love of nature, love of humanity, and the achievement of transcendence. As I have shown, that impression does not persist throughout the review.

The third and last installment ends, however, with a self-consciously poignant vignette that destabilizes the more directly condemnatory sections of the article, even though Hazlitt claims that purchasing the *Letter* "put an end to our sentimentality" (Wu 4: 194). He concludes by mentioning a personal encounter with the Laureate: "We met him unexpectedly the other day in St. Giles's, (it was odd we should meet *him* there) were sorry we had passed him without speaking to an old friend, turned and looked after him for some time, as to a tale of other times—sighing, as we walked on, *Alas poor Southey!*" (Wu 4: 193). Hazlitt here "unexpectedly" reveals himself to be an "old friend" of Southey's, troubled by his own rudeness at not greeting him in the street, despite all the virulence of the review, and momentarily taken aback by the Lake Poet's ghost-like reappearance in an urban setting. The reviewer's act of "look[ing] after him for some time, as to a tale of other times," expresses sympathy, regret and nostalgia not present elsewhere in this article. It thus anticipates Hazlitt's later ambivalent celebration of the Lake School in "My First Acquaintance with Poets" (1823).

The anecdote raises the possibility that part of the virulence of the review, as well as Hazlitt's ascription to Southey of a more complex personality than he seems willing to give him credit for, might reflect the writers' shared past, and perhaps Hazlitt's private feelings of betrayal. The brevity and belatedness of this acknowledgment that Southey is "an old friend" seem to indicate discomfort about whether political loyalties are as straightforward as Hazlitt implies. This detail gives the impression that long as the review is, there is more to Southey than meets the eye.

The most high-profile review of the *Letter*, Jeffrey's 24-page attack in the *Edinburgh*, dated March 1817 though published in May because the quarterlies tended to lag behind schedule, carried the running head, "Wat Tyler and Mr. Southey," as if to indicate that the article is more about the author than his writings, and its success in lambasting the poet's "exquisite performance" (*ER* 28: 151) takes the disfigurement of Southey to a higher level. Jeffrey reviews Southey's play as well as the *Letter*, but, as he himself points out, he gives considerably more space to the prose text, calling it "in our poor judgment, the most poetical and dramatic of the two" (*ER* 28: 152). Jeffrey however, brings out a "poetical" element in the *Letter* in the sense that he collaborates with Southey himself on what I earlier described as his parody of Romantic selfhood. At one point in the article Jeffrey distinguishes between "raillery" or ridicule, and mere "railing," finding Southey guilty of the latter and observing that "we are afraid he has not temper enough for a satirist—nor a sufficient familiarity with the language of polite life" (*ER* 28: 164). The distinction is problematic, however, since so much of Jeffrey's article consists of decidedly impolite railing. Vitriolic criticism was of course the *Edinburgh*'s trademark, but this article seems to offer what Hazlitt calls a "concentrated essence" of the genre. Jeffrey's vituperation rises to a climax when he addresses Southey's self-presentation in the *Letter*. Although Southey himself may lack a "talent for satire" (*ER* 28: 164), Jeffrey in this review moves his to the foreground.[45]

Before turning to the *Letter*, Jeffrey attacks *Wat Tyler* in terms that anticipate his sustained assault on its author. His account of the play shows no restraint. Dismissing it as "insane" (*ER* 28: 151), he accuses it of "most consummate arrogance and delightful self-complacency" (*ER* 28: 153)—phrases that sound more like possible descriptions of its author than of the play itself. Putting a slight twist on earlier attempts by Hazlitt and others to feminize Southey, Jeffrey claims that "A more pitiful piece of puling indeed was never indited by a young girl at a boarding-school" (*ER* 28: 153). He adds, "so far from being what was to be expected from a well educated young man of twenty-one, we are quite sure, that there are many patriotic misses of fourteen, who could produce something much more spirited and sensible as a holiday exercise" (*ER* 28: 161). These particular insults, carrying no sexual charge or connotations of violence, do not match the impact of Hazlitt's contrast between Southey's "Jacobin mistress" and the "bawd Legitimacy." They sound more like the kind of insults *Blackwood's* will direct towards Leigh Hunt in the attacks on the Cockney School.

Jeffrey saves his harshest language for the *Letter*. His more general descriptions of the pamphlet come across as reflections on its author: it is "irresistibly ludicrous" (*ER* 28: 152), "vituperative and self-extolling" (*ER* 28: 157), and "a more bloated

---

[45] According to Hoadley, in "The Controversy over Southey's *Wat Tyler*," Jeffrey writes "with the fiendish enthusiasm of a little child dissecting a fly he has caught" (92).

mass of self-conceit, absurdity and insolence, never fell under our view" (*ER* 28: 151–2). According to him, the *Letter* contains "about twenty pages all in a foam with self-praise and impotent anger—presenting a lamentable struggle between extreme soreness and incurable conceit—and exhibiting the humiliating picture of self-adulation, licking with fruitless affection the festering sores of wounded vanity" (*ER* 28: 162). Jeffrey here shows his own capacity for "vituperative" language. He finds Southey guilty of "not merely self-love, but self-idolatry" (*ER* 28: 166). Through his attitude of fascination, Jeffrey expands as well as punctures the monstrous ego to which he is objecting. Like Hazlitt's review of the *Letter*, this article ends anticlimactically, with an exposure of the "utter absurdity" (*ER* 28: 172) of Southey's political views. Jeffrey's tone is still scathing, but not as heightened as in his account of Southey himself. The length of his discussion of politics registers a tacit admission that in confronting the supposedly grotesque spectacle of Southey's "self-idolatry," Jeffrey had momentarily lost sight of his own political agenda and is now trying to redress the balance.

Leigh Hunt's second contribution to the controversy, another satirical piece in the *Examiner*, this one dated May 11, 1817, offers the most amusing and indulgent treatment of the *Letter*, building more elaborately on Hunt's earlier fiction that Southey is deceased.[46] Entitled "Extraordinary Case of the Late Mr. Southey," it also builds on previous attacks on the poet, intensifying their caricatured depiction of the hypocritical apostate and parodying the Romantic Southey collaborated upon by Hazlitt, Coleridge, and Southey himself. In this sense Hunt continues the familiar ideological critique of the Poet Laureate, but at times the literariness of his comic narrative—fancifully compared to "the stories in Italian romance" (*E* 489: 301)—distracts from rather than intensifies his political message. Much of the humor of the piece comes from the mock-Gothic juxtaposition of the earthly and the "supernatural," as Hunt depicts a dramatic encounter between Southey's ghost and his unfortunate publisher John Murray—also the publisher of the *Quarterly*, of course, nicknamed here and elsewhere "Murrain" (a kind of pestilence), a stand-in for "*Mister William Smith*" as Hunt's Southey calls him (*E* 489: 301).

The fact that the setting is Murray's "back parlour" (*E* 489: 301) reinforces the debunking of the Romantic Southey by reminding readers of the material conditions in which the *Quarterly* is concocted by a supposedly corrupt Tory cabal. Part of the rhetorical success of this *jeu d'esprit*—which anticipates the playfulness of *Blackwood's Magazine*—also comes from its detailed attention to the language of the *Letter* and its knowing rehearsal of the standard objections to Southey's self-defense. Hunt portrays the "didactic dust and ashes" (*E* 489: 302) as responding to multiple charges of inconsistency with a numbered list of so-called consistencies that are anything but. The implication is that Southey is even more himself dead than alive.

Hunt's "Extraordinary Case" begins by setting the scene:

---

[46] The piece follows on directly from the second installment of Hazlitt's review of the *Letter*, contrasting with Hazlitt's vitriolic tone.

Murrain's back parlour was lighted up, it seems, with some large tapers from the chapel of the Escurial, and hung with black coats curiously turned inside out … In the middle of it, the corpse was lying in state; and Murrain, with the exception of one or two private friends, was left alone with it. Mr. Canning had departed to pay his respects to Lord Castlereagh. Mr. Croker had gone home to write an account for the *Courier* of the "admirable" behaviour of the body—how tastefully it had disposed it's limbs, and what vigour there was in it's very impotence. Dr. Stothard, in a lamentably weak condition, had exclaimed he was "sick of the Times," and had been taken home to bed. Nobody knew what had taken Mr. Gifford away; only he was heard muttering as he went along something about "no patience," and was seen to lame a few apple-women with some passing kicks. As to Mr. Coleridge, he was gone to bed, having been sitting up all night consoling himself with brandy and water, proving at the same time that it was the only temperate drink, and that the undertakers (some of whom drank with him) were the only men besides himself and particular friends, who knew anything about religion and politics. (*E* 489: 301)

Hunt's throwaway jibes at Southey's associates are fairly rote. As we will see in Chapter 3, his complaints about Gifford's bad temper and misogyny are standard fare. The reference to "Dr. Stothard" is to John Stoddart—later nicknamed "Dr. Slop"—a journalist who had recently broken with the *Times* newspaper. Hunt's image of Coleridge, as in his "Death and Funeral" piece, perhaps owes something to Peacock. But the characterization of Murray in this piece is more elaborate. Despite being "much agitated," "Murrain" responds to the "public mourners" and at first to the speeches of the corpse "with all the pithy and quick indifference yet submission of a coffee-house waiter, 'Yes, Sir'" (*E* 489: 301). The "Murrain," it seems, as if there were any doubt, is the ready tool of power. However, he then starts to seem unconvinced by the arguments of the "eminent corpse," first "ventur[ing] to look a little sceptical" (*E* 489: 301), then "shrugg[ing] his shoulders," and later "almost jump[ing]" with surprise before experiencing "a sort of lethargy," putting "his hand to his head" (*E* 489: 302). Even Southey's efficient and obsequious publisher, it seems, cannot assent to all the bizarre propositions of the *Letter*. Held captive by the supernatural Southey, "Murrain" finally falls into a deep sleep.

Hunt humorously expands upon and twists the key points from Southey's *Letter* to cast its writer in an absurd light. Southey himself is characterized as tetchy and self-righteous, farcically demanding, "What, Sir, a Member of Parliament put books in his pocket!" (*E* 489: 301). In several sections of his speech, the "dead body of Mr. Southey" (*E* 489: 301) addresses his refusal to admit to the authorship of the *Quarterly* article: "Mister William Smith," he complains, "you come forward in your own name,—which is very atrocious;—whereas what I write in the *Quarterly Review* is anonymous, which of course ought to be as great a shield *against*, as it is a weapon *for*, personalities" (*E* 489: 301). Unlike Jeffrey, Hunt does not acknowledge that he is on somewhat shaky ground here, given that he too is writing anonymously.

In the longest section of his speech, Southey's ghost rehearses the *Letter*'s claims concerning the Romantic enthusiasm of his youthful political opinions and the contrast between past and present Jacobinism:

> Consistency 7.—That book, Mister William Smith, was written when I was a boy, and a very excellent boy too. (I was also—see my Poems—a very pretty boy; but let that rest.) The book is full of errors, I allow; but in *me*, such errors "bear no indication of an ungenerous spirit or of a malevolent heart." It was written when such opinions exposed people "to personal danger"—which in *me* was true boldness. It was written "in disregard of all worldly considerations"—which in *me* was amiable and noble, not riotous desperation. It was written "when republicanism was confined to a very small number of the educated classes"—which, together with my subsequent conduct, shewed *my* selectness of taste and eternal freedom from vulgarity.—Finally, Mister William, it was written "when a spirit of antijacobinism was predominant, which I cannot characterize more truly than by saying, that it was as unjust and intolerant, though not quite as ferocious as the jacobinism of the *present* day." This is manifest upon the bare mention of a few names. At that time, jacobinism, besides myself and friends, was confined to Danton, Marat, Robespierre, and a few other over-zealous people;—it denounced kings in the lump, particularly certain kings (see my friend Landor's poem)—it preached open sedition, rebellion, and total changes;—wished to decapitate whole assemblies here, and actually did it in France;—all which shews that it acted from real zeal, though misguided;—but in the present day, there are scarcely any but contemptible half-jacobins, fellows, forsooth, who tattle about their legal rights, mere anarchists in secret, skulking knaves from whom it is difficult to muster up a single desperado, and then only among the naked and the hungry. Are we, the old, well-educated, daring jacobins, who followed the opinions of the French Revolution "with ardour, wherever they led," to be compared with constitutional dastards like these!" (Here Murrain, as the phrase is, was dumb-founded.) (*E* 489: 302)

The reference to "Landor's poem" is to Walter Savage Landor's Jacobin epic *Gebir* (1798). Hunt repudiates the idealization of the young Southey and makes a serious political point about the inaccuracy of Southey's reading of pre- and post-war political dynamics. Yet he seems more intent on squeezing as much comic mileage as possible out of the *Letter*. The last paragraph of the ghost's speech plays on the self-aggrandizing conclusion of the *Letter*, as the speaker alludes to all the "indexes, catalogues, lists, references, quotations, extracts, choice flowers, and other reminiscences of infinite sorts," in which he expects to be immortalized, "both here, hereafter, and every where" (*E* 489: 303). He adds: "There it will be related also, among other excellent traits, that I lived in the bosom of my family, (which of course nobody else does), and 'in absolute retirement' (which is a merit in me, though not in others)" (*E* 489: 303). Even Southey's passing mention of his private life is made to seem ridiculously self-elevating. Southey's biographer Mark Storey contends that "in Hazlitt, Southey had more than met his match,"[47]

---

[47] Storey, *Robert Southey*, 258.

and the "Extraordinary Case" shows that he was no match for Hunt either. Hunt shows decisively that Southey's reputation is not salvageable.[48] Yet the amused tolerance of this piece sets it apart from the attacks by Hazlitt, Jeffrey and other hostile reviewers such as an anonymous writer in the *Monthly Review*.[49] Hunt even concludes, with some irony but more flippancy, after relating how "the posthumous orator returned majestically to his bier," "Peace be to his shade" (*E* 489: 303). In a sense, the artfulness of this piece is a tribute to the literary if not the political importance of Southey.

Lord Byron's *Vision*

It is tempting to treat Hunt's "Extraordinary Case" as the last word, especially since the outcry over the publication of *Wat Tyler* was dying down by mid-May 1817. But attacks on Southey as an apostate and hypocrite predictably continued to be made and fended off. As Lapp points out, Coleridge's next defense of Southey, published in the *Biographia* in the summer of 1817 but composed two years earlier, was seen as another contribution to the feud.[50] I discuss this defense, and Hazlitt's biting response, in my next chapter. But in this chapter I shall give the last word instead to Lord Byron, who extends the comic refiguring of Southey by transforming him into a slightly more human, but even less stereotypically Romantic character in a literary text—his satirical poem *The Vision of Judgment*, first published in the *Liberal* in 1822 as a rejoinder to Southey's official poetic tribute to the dead King George III, *A Vision of Judgement* (1821). Byron's poem paradoxically combines "politics as usual" complaints about the Laureate's apostasy with a lordly attitude of indulgence. *The Vision of Judgment* also continues the process whereby the *Wat Tyler* controversy becomes as much about Southey's enemies and friends as about the "rancorous Renegado" himself (Preface, 940).[51] Byron does Southey a huge favor by choosing to immortalize him in his brilliant parody, while more decisively immortalizing himself in his self-mocking portrait as the charismatic Lucifer. Byron grants Southey no complexity or depth and has plenty of fun at his expense. But unlike Hunt's May 1817 piece in the *Examiner*, Byron's poem eventually restores Southey to the real world.

As contributions to the *Wat Tyler* feud, Byron's attacks seem belated. They were provoked first by the rumor that Southey, after touring the Continent in the

---

[48] Compare David M. Craig, "Subservient Talents? Robert Southey as a Public Moralist," in Lynda Pratt, ed., *Robert Southey and the Contexts of English Romanticism* (Aldershot: Ashgate, 2006), 101–14. Craig argues that Southey's reputation was permanently damaged by the *Wat Tyler* controversy (114).

[49] The *Monthly Review* complained that the "concluding passage [of the *Letter*] ... forms a climax of self-conceit that has no parallel" (*SCH*, 254).

[50] Lapp, *Contest for Cultural Authority*, 132.

[51] Quotations are from Jerome McGann, ed., *Byron: The Oxford Authors* (Oxford: Oxford University Press, 1986).

summer of 1817, had accused Byron, Shelley, Mary Godwin and her step-sister Claire Clairmont of a "League of Incest," and second by Southey's attack on the "Satanic School" in the Preface to his 1821 *Vision*. Southey's denunciation of the Satanic School had been responding to the first two cantos of Byron's *Don Juan*, which had been published in 1819 without the now famous Dedication in which Byron addresses Southey as "my Epic Renegade" (l. 2), but with the instantly notorious parody of the Ten Commandments instructing readers not to worship Wordsworth, Coleridge and Southey. Before writing *The Vision of Judgment*, Byron also composed "Some observations upon an article in *Blackwood's Magazine*, no. xxix, August, 1819," in which he mentions Southey's "League of Incest" allegation and excoriates the writer of *Wat Tyler* in standard, perhaps Hazlitt-inflected terms as "licking the hands that smote him, eating the bread of his enemies, and internally writhing beneath his own contempt" (*SCH*, 267). Byron also poured scorn on "this pitiful renegado" (*SCH,* 291) in a note to *The Two Foscari* (1821).

Despite the lapse of time, Byron's Preface to his *Vision of Judgment*, not published with the poem when it appeared in 1822, shows that he remained preoccupied with Southey's apostastical shift from the sentiments of *Wat Tyler*.[52] In the Preface he demands, as the first of a numbered list of questions, "Is Mr Southey the author of Wat Tyler?" (940), as if the answer "yes" is itself sufficient to discredit Southey entirely. He also figures Southey as a mockery of transcendence: "The gross flattery, the dull impudence, the renegado intolerance and impious cant of the poem by the author of 'Wat Tyler,' are something so stupendous as to form the sublime of himself—containing the quintessence of his own attributes" (939).

Byron's treatment of Southey in the poem however, is more humorous, and more tolerant—very self-consciously so, since Byron boasts about his tolerance in the Preface. Southey appears as the only non-supernatural (because alive not dead) character in the poem. As the powers of heaven and hell quarrel over the final destination of George III's soul, Southey is brought as a witness to testify, in accordance with his *Vision of Judgement*, that the dead monarch does indeed deserve to end up in heaven. In his fast-moving ottava rima,[53] Byron recapitulates the contradictions that make up the "Renegado" (l. 681):

> He had written praises of a regicide:
>   He had written praises of all kings whatever;
> He had written for republics far and wide;
>   And then against them bitterer than ever;
> For pantisocracy he once had cried
>   Aloud, a scheme less moral than 'twas clever;

---

[52] The omission of the Preface from the version in the *Liberal* makes the poem seem more an attack on the dead king than on Southey, and the early reception of the poem was more concerned with its alleged blasphemy and sedition than its depiction of the Laureate.

[53] Part of Byron's triumph over Southey is formal—the gulf between his lively verse form and Southey's "spavin'd dactyls" (l. 721).

> Then grew a hearty anti-Jacobin—
> Had turn'd his coat—and would have turn'd his skin.
>
> He had sung against all battles, and again
>   In their high praise and glory; he had call'd
> Reviewing "the ungentle craft," and then
>   Become as base a critic as e'er crawl'd—
> Fed, paid, and pamper'd by the very men
>   By whom his muse and morals had been maul'd:
> He had written much blank verse, and blanker prose,
> And more of both than any body knows. (ll. 769–84)

In these lines Byron puts into exuberant verse what Hazlitt, Jeffrey and others had already said in prose. Other aspects of Byron's attack on Southey, though, are slyer and more nuanced. Before the rehearsal of Southey's inconsistencies, the poet conjures up the dismayed reactions of the "angels" (l. 731) and "ghosts" (l. 733) and the dead king himself to the prospect of listening to Southey's poetry. While laughing at Southey, Byron also laughs at himself by imagining a "throng / Which seem'd to hold all verse in detestation" (ll. 729–30).

Byron then slows down and lingers over the appearance of the "Bard" (l. 713):

> The varlet was not an ill-favour'd knave;
>   A good deal like a vulture in the face,
> With a hook nose and a hawk's eye, which gave
>   A smart and sharper looking sort of grace
> To his whole aspect, which, though rather grave,
>   Was by no means so ugly as his case;
> But that indeed was hopeless as can be,
> Quite a poetic felony "de se." (ll. 744–51)

Byron's pleasure in playing with readers' expectations can be seen in this stanza's various twists and turns. The stanza's concluding couplet, asserting that Southey's "case" is irredeemable, at first sight undercuts the hints of sympathy in the preceding lines, including the oxymoronic notion of a "smart and sharper looking sort of grace"—but the amount of ambivalent detail in the sentence cannot be canceled out entirely.

Moreover, once Southey begins to recite his poem to the assembled supernatural agents, the extravagance of their response suggests that his *Vision* is indeed "sublime" in its own way:

> The angels stopp'd their ears and plied their pinions;
>   The devils ran howling, deafen'd, down to hell;
>   The ghosts fled, gibbering, for their own dominions—
>   (For 'tis not yet decided where they dwell,
>   And I leave every man to his opinions);
>   Michael took refuge in his trump—but, lo!
> His teeth were set on edge, he could not blow! (ll. 818–24)

In these lines the statement in parentheses draws attention to Byron's refusal to write coercively. But he also jokingly assigns Southey's poem a magical power to make its audience disappear, a gesture that concedes the contingencies of reception.

Byron's amused rather than hostile treatment of Southey is even more evident in the final stanzas.[54] Saint Peter, unable to stand the sound of Southey's lines, knocks him down so that he tumbles back to the Lake District, falling

> like Phaeton, but more at ease,
> Into his lake, for there he did not drown;
>   A different web being by the Destinies
> Woven for the Laureate's final wreath, whene'er
> Reform shall happen either here or there. (ll. 828–30)

Just as he lets King George into heaven despite alleging that "a weaker king never left a realm undone" (l. 62), Byron refuses to stand in judgment on the poet. He presumably wants "Reform" but doesn't seem to care if it is on earth or in heaven. Byron pointedly refuses to kill off Southey—as if he could, but chooses not to—returning him to "his lake" to continue his writing career. The penultimate stanza of the poem underlines Byron's refusal to judge:

> He first sunk to the bottom—like his works,
>   But soon rose to the surface—like himself;
> For all corrupted things are buoy'd, like corks,
>   By their own rottenness, light as an elf. (ll. 833–7)

Byron's act of throwing up his hands circles back to Peacock's humorous acceptance of "corrupted things." At once thoroughly partisan and outside politics, Byron's poem refuses even to try to have the last word in the controversy over *Wat Tyler*, granting Southey the capacity to keep on behaving, both materially and immaterially, "like himself."

---

[54] Peter Cochran, in "One Ton Per Square Foot: The Antecedents of *The Vision of Judgment*," *Keats-Shelley Review* 19 (2005): 64–75, sees Byron's treatment of Southey as more hostile.

Chapter 2
Coleridge, Jeffrey, and the *Edinburgh*: Romanticizing "Personalities"

As the *Wat Tyler* controversy unfolded in the spring and summer of 1817, some of its major combatants became embroiled in a new feud sparked by the publication of Coleridge's *Biographia Literaria* in July of the same year. In my introduction, we saw that Coleridge's discussions in the *Biographia* of hostile reviewing in the "AGE OF PERSONALITY" circle around two related issues: the problem of how to define personal attacks and the causes of the reviewers' "malignity" (*BL* 2: 109). Coleridge also, in the *Biographia* and elsewhere, stresses the ethical value of reprisals.[1] Not all of the reviewers' attacks are personal, or are they? Is it a personal attack to accuse someone else of making a personal attack? The same questions could be asked of Coleridge's own attacks on the man who for him exemplifies the evils of current reviewing practices: Francis Jeffrey, editor of the *Edinburgh Review*. In a long footnote to Chapter 3 of the *Biographia*, Coleridge accuses Jeffrey of making hypocritical jibes at himself and his fellow Lake Poets, and of abusing their hospitality during a visit to the Lake District. Jeffrey's campaign against the Lake School of poetry had begun in 1802 in the first number of the *Edinburgh* and continued into the 1820s.[2] Coleridge goes on to criticize Jeffrey (whom he never actually names) at various other points in the text. In a move that was virtually unprecedented given early nineteenth-century reviewers' convention of anonymity, Jeffrey published a signed rejoinder to some of Coleridge's allegations in a footnote to the hostile review —written by Hazlitt—of the *Biographia* in the *Edinburgh*. Other journalists eagerly commented

---

[1] Early on in the *Biographia,* after mentioning unconvincingly that "the original sin of my character consists in a careless indifference to public opinion and to the attacks of those who influence it" (*BL* 1: 44), Coleridge goes on to say, "Indignation at literary wrongs, I leave to men born under happier stars. I *cannot afford it*. But so far from condemning those who can, I deem it a writer's duty, and think it creditable to his heart, to feel and express a resentment proportioned to the grossness of the provocation and the importance of the object" (*BL* 1: 45). Despite the claim that Coleridge "*cannot afford*" such negative feelings, a psychoanalytic approach might well identify them in the *Biographia*. At any rate, this statement raises the question of how "resentment" can be duly "proportioned."

[2] David Erdman and Paul M. Zall, in "Coleridge and Jeffrey in Controversy," *Studies in Romanticism* 14 (1975): 75–83, note that "For many years the titanic confrontation between Wordsworth and Jeffrey has overshadowed the concurrent struggle of Coleridge with this formidable foe" (75). Coleridge's feud with Jeffrey overlaps with the latter's feud with Wordsworth, since both poets were affected by the *Edinburgh*'s hostile attitude towards the "Lakers."

on this exchange, treating it as an extension of the *Biographia*'s topical theme of persecutory reviewing, and offering mostly partisan judgments about which writer they considered to have won the dispute.

The amount of attention paid to this incident suggests that Coleridge and his literary life have to be seen as enmeshed in the "age of personality," caught within the politicized squabbles of the "critical machine" (*BL* 2: 111). So much for what one critic calls Coleridge's "transcendental principle of selfhood."[3] Yet like the *Wat Tyler* affair, the feud between Coleridge and Jeffrey relies on even as it unsettles essentialized notions of Romantic identity. Moreover, the collaborative work of gossip, though not exactly sharing the "synthetic and magical power" of the "imagination" (*BL* 2: 16), in this instance spins a web that, while ensnaring Coleridge, eventually turns a private encounter between two individuals into a quasi-literary text that acquires, like poetry, what Coleridge calls a "logic of its own" (*BL* 1: 9). It is possible, it turns out, to leave behind the "personal," but, as we saw in Chapter 1, one cannot necessarily do it single-handedly. The result, as with *Wat Tyler*, is another comic ending, and in this case the comedy—supplied by the new *Blackwood's Magazine*—can be seen as a form of Romantic artistic expression generated less by individual writers and more by the changing culture of periodical writing.

In offering "*Biographical Sketches*" of his literary career, a book in which "the least of what I have written concerns myself personally" (*BL* 1: 5), Coleridge supposedly holds his own life aloof from the "AGE OF PERSONALITY." Perhaps confirming this possibility, some twentieth-century critics have questioned the extent to which the unreliable narrator of the *Biographia* is Coleridge himself or a fictional persona.[4] One argument against Coleridge's construction of a persona might point to continuities between the "I" of his letters and the speaker of the *Biographia*, but on the other hand, Coleridge can be seen as posturing in his letters as much as in works intended for publication. Some critics find in the *Biographia* a psychological interplay between self-effacement and self-aggrandizement that undermines Coleridge's aspirations to impersonality.[5] Other critics see Coleridge's characteristically digressive style as creating a tension between a fragmentary decentered self and the unified consciousness that supposedly lies behind it.[6]

---

[3] James Treadwell, *Autobiographical Writing and British Literature 1783–1834* (Oxford: Oxford University Press, 2005), 153.

[4] See, for example, Donald Reiman, who—in "Coleridge and the Art of Equivocation," *Studies in Romanticism* 25 (1986): 325–50—finds in the *Biographia* a "Shandean persona" (344).

[5] See, for example, Reeve Parker, *Coleridge's Meditative Art* (Ithaca: Cornell University Press, 1975), 147. Underpinning his reading of the *Biographia* as a "work of art" (325), Reiman finds in it a psychological need for "self-abasement" (349). On "self-effacement" as itself a "strategy," see Bradford K. Mudge, "The Politics of Autobiography in the *Biographia Literaria*," *South Central Review* 3 (1986): 27–45 (42).

[6] Various twentieth-century critics address the tensions between the *Biographia*'s discontinuities and what James Engell calls its "transcendental perspective" ("*Biographia*

Deconstructive readings, anticipated in the *Biographia*, would contend that *any* form of biographical or autobiographical writing defaces the individual whom it claims to represent.

Even when treating the text as a work of art, one can hardly address the *Biographia* without contemplating the quirks of Coleridge's complex personality in the more modern sense of the term. The book is of course also vulnerable to materialist readings that would destabilize Coleridge's "I" depending on its particular cultural context.[7] In arguing that the Coleridge–Jeffrey feud and its textual afterlife ultimately resist materialist readings, I am not claiming that Coleridge possesses what Peter Manning calls "an identity beyond the words on the page."[8] But if the true self cherished by Coleridge remains a fantasy, the trivial anecdotes and details that proliferate in the "age of personality" can congeal into an ongoing work of fiction that brings to life even while obscuring the "personal character" (*BL* 1: 43) of its protagonists. A story that is indeed "insignificant" (*Friend* 2: 286) can move past as well as perpetuating the thirst for "personality."

The distinction between superficially personal and more profoundly impersonal is complicated by the content of the *Biographia* as well as by the circumstances of its composition and reception. Coleridge's comments on irritable reviewers are preoccupied with the notoriously dismissive reviews of Southey and Wordsworth in the *Edinburgh* that were assumed to have been written by its editor. In addition to the footnote on Jeffrey, Chapter 3 includes a defense of Southey that although composed prior to the *Wat Tyler* controversy, inevitably fed into it, as previously

---

Literaria" in *The Cambridge Companion to Coleridge*, ed. Lucy Newlyn [Cambridge: Cambridge University Press, 2002], 59–74 [66]). These include Kathleen M. Wheeler, *Sources, Processes and Methods in Coleridge's* Biographia Literaria (Cambridge: Cambridge University Press, 1980); Jerome Christensen, *Coleridge's Blessed Machine of Language* (Ithaca and London: Cornell University Press, 1981); Robert Maniquis, "Poetry and Barrel-Organs: The Text in the Book of the *Biographia Literaria*" in *Coleridge's Biographia: Text and Meaning*, ed. Frederick Burwick (Columbus: Ohio State University Press, 1989): 255–309; Steven Vine, "To 'Make a Bull': Autobiography, Idealism, and Writing in Coleridge's *Biographia Literaria*" in *Coleridge and the Armoury of the Human Mind*, ed. Peter J. Kitson and Thomas N. Corns (London: Frank Cass, 1991): 99–114; and Sheila M. Kearns, *Coleridge, Wordsworth, and Romantic Autobiography* (London: Associated University Presses, 1995).

[7] The fraught compositional and publishing history of the *Biographia* has affected impressions of Coleridge's intentions. Questions of timing, for example, influence readers' understanding of the "personal." One twentieth-century critic points out that much of Coleridge's analysis of the shortcomings of contemporary reviewing, composed in 1815, predated some of the harshest attacks on him—in responses to the *Christabel* volume and *The Statesman's Manual* (both published in 1816)—with the result that when the *Biographia* finally appeared in 1817, "a book meant as a serious commentary on the methods of reviewing was mistaken for a wholly personal riposte" (*CCH*, 12).

[8] Peter Manning, "Detaching Lamb's Thoughts," in *Romantic Periodicals and Print Culture*, ed. Kim Wheatley (London: Frank Cass, 2003), 137–46 (143).

mentioned.⁹ The defense of Southey includes another long footnote in which Coleridge perversely brings up a 1798 attack on himself and others by the writers of the *Anti-Jacobin*—perversely because although it confirms that they have been attacked, it revives rather than squelches scandal. As we will see however, the reviewers of the *Biographia* were more interested in Coleridge's relatively tame accusations against Jeffrey than in the poet's own alleged past transgressions.

Contributing to the status of the *Biographia* as an act of reception, Coleridge's entire discussion of Wordsworth, taking up most of Volume 2, can be read as an extended response to Jeffrey. More specifically, much of Chapter 21, "Remarks on the present mode of conducting critical journals," replies to Jeffrey's hostile review of Wordsworth's *Excursion*. Coleridge's anecdote in that chapter about two vulgar philistine Frenchmen is a comment on Jeffrey's unhealthy "state of moral feeling" (*BL* 2: 118). In a section of the *Biographia* added in 1817 to fill up the second volume, Coleridge complains about the discrepancy between Jeffrey's private and public opinions of the *Lyrical Ballads*—one of the passages that Coleridge's daughter Sara said contained "*personal* remarks."¹⁰ Further, in the final chapter of the *Biographia*, also composed in the year of publication, Coleridge comments on the "personal enmity" motivating the reviews of his recent publications (*BL* 2: 239), even though he had already described "personality" as a "*game*." In a sense, the whole of the *Biographia*, including its chapters on philosophy, can be seen as a self-vindication in response to the reviewers' attacks.¹¹ I suggest that the fact that Coleridge responds to them makes them "personal" if they were not already.

In this chapter I will linger over the Coleridge–Jeffrey exchange, beginning with Coleridge's complaints about Jeffrey in the *Biographia*. I will also look briefly at the earlier correspondence between the two writers—which confirms Coleridge's entrenchment in the literary marketplace—before returning to the *Biographia* to examine Coleridge's additional charges against the reviewers. I will show that these sections of the text further cloud his characterization of personal attacks

---

⁹ Pointing out that "the *Wat Tyler* affair ... provides an indispensable context in which to rehistoricize the *Biographia Literaria*," Robert Lapp, in *Contest for Cultural Authority* (Detroit: Wayne State University Press, 1999), argues that Coleridge's 1817 additions to the book add "increased polemical vigor" to parts composed earlier, such as the defense of Southey (132).

¹⁰ In her edition of the *Biographia*, Sara Coleridge deleted a paragraph complaining about Jeffrey, "for the same reason" as her husband Henry Nelson Coleridge had removed the footnote on Jeffrey in the first volume of the same edition: "namely this; that as those passages contain *personal* remarks, right or wrong, they were anomalies in my Father's writings" (*BL* 2: 156, quoted in n.3). But as we have already seen, "*personal* remarks, right or wrong," are not quite so easy to classify.

¹¹ William Christie, in *The Edinburgh Review in the Literary Culture of Romantic Britain: Mammoth and Megalonyx* (London: Pickering & Chatto, 2009), offers a valuable reading of the *Biographia* that stresses its response to the reviewers, seeing Jeffrey as a "figure of radical opposition or otherness" (108)—a figure, that is, representing the materialism that the *Biographia* deplores.

(already discussed in my introduction) as fluctuating between inner emotion and outer perception, arbitrary and deliberate, mysterious and over-determined. They thus theorize what the feud itself performs. I will then analyze the response by Jeffrey and Hazlitt in their review of the *Biographia* in the *Edinburgh*, a major attack on Coleridge that, like Hazlitt's attacks on Southey, at once challenges and respects Coleridge's idealized notion of freedom from "personality." As in his contributions to the *Wat Tyler* controversy, Hazlitt both resists and collaborates in the creation of the "Romantic ideology." Finally, I will turn to contributions to the feud by other reviewers and journalists on the sidelines, notably John Wilson of *Blackwood's*. In these reactions, which also interrogate the limits of the "personal," I find continuities with creative writing. This chapter gives the last word to another more comical and imaginative attack in *Blackwood's*, this one aimed at Jeffrey rather than Coleridge, which momentarily takes this feud beyond "personality" not in the sense of choice of theme but in the sense that cultural production subsumes individual motivation.

Coleridge's Attack on Jeffrey in the *Biographia*

In Chapter 3 of the *Biographia*, Coleridge contends that he has been continually targeted by "anonymous critics" (*BL* 1: 48) for "at least 17 years" (*BL* 1: 50). Coleridge thus creates the impression that he is a hapless, beleaguered individual oppressed by the impersonal institution of reviewing. Literary historians are divided over the degree to which this complaint is a paranoid exaggeration, although of course paranoia tends to be self-fulfilling, as the Coleridge–Jeffrey dispute confirms.[12] Exaggeration or not, the impression of faceless tyranny is misleading because Coleridge may have been the victim of nameless "slanderer[s]" (*BL* 1: 42), but he has at least one individual on whom to pin the blame: the editor of the *Edinburgh Review*. Coleridge's main objection to Jeffrey, in fact, is the discrepancy between his public and private behavior. Besides meeting the *Edinburgh* editor in the Lake District in 1810, he had corresponded with him two years previously. His feud with Jeffrey takes place at a historical juncture when, as mentioned in my introduction, anonymous reviewing was the norm, but the identity of the writers was often known or inferred, in certain circles at least. Spreading gossip can thus work both ways. Coleridge's most explicit attack on Jeffrey, in the footnote to

---

[12] Jackson (*CCH*, 5) and Erdman and Zall suggest that Coleridge had "ample grounds for complaining" ("Coleridge and Jeffrey in Controversy," 75); by contrast, Bate and Engell (*BL* 1: 50, n.1) and John O. Hayden, in *The Romantic Reviewers 1802–1824* (Chicago: University of Chicago Press, 1968), 103–11, imply that Coleridge is misrepresenting the truth. Critics tend to agree, however, that Coleridge understates the extent to which he has attracted notice by publishing his work. See, for example, Christie, *The Edinburgh Review*, 107. Coleridge thus makes the "cannonading" (*BL* 1: 50) that he has allegedly suffered appear more gratuitous. Christie points out that Coleridge's "reputation" had "most often" been "savaged" as one of the Lake Poets (108).

Chapter 3, accuses him both of making false claims about Coleridge himself *and* of doing so in a malignant spirit. As the self-proclaimed victim, Coleridge insists on telling his side of the story, providing details concerning their face-to-face encounter and private correspondence to support the larger imputation that "our anonymous critics" (*BL* 1: 52) are liars. The passage invites the questions of to what extent Coleridge is accusing Jeffrey of "personality" and to what extent he is guilty of it himself.

The immediate context of the footnote is the hard-to-credit claim that Coleridge had had "little ... acquaintance with literary characters" and that on the rare occasions when he met such people, he had found them friendly, thus supporting the contention that the "persecution" that he has suffered was not due to "personal" ill will (*BL* 1: 50). Yet the note itself shows that Jeffrey's friendliness is not to be trusted. Coleridge's allegations against Jeffrey are threefold. He first accuses him of betrayal (or is it just bad manners?):

> Some years ago, a gentleman, the chief writer and conductor of a celebrated review, distinguished by its hostility to Mr. Southey, spent a day or two at Keswick. That he was, without diminution on this account, treated with every hospitable attention by Mr. Southey and myself I trust I need not say. But one thing I may venture to notice; that at no period of my life do I remember to have received so many, and such high coloured compliments in so short a space of time. He was likewise circumstantially informed by what series of accidents it had happened, that Mr. Wordsworth, Mr. Southey and I had become neighbours; and how utterly unfounded was the supposition, that we considered ourselves as belonging to any common school, but that of good sense confirmed by the long-established models of the best times of Greece, Rome, Italy and England. ... Yet among the first articles which this man wrote after his return from Keswick, we were characterized as "the School of whining and hypochondriacal poets that haunt the Lakes." (*BL* 1: 50–51)

Coleridge here offers his readers a glimpse behind the mask of anonymous reviewing, except that he keeps the mask in place by refusing to name names (as if that will keep his own hands clean rather than the reverse), while identifying the accused in terms that would presumably make him recognizable to any reader of the *Biographia*. Jeffrey is not at first sight guilty of an intrusion into private life (except in the literal sense of showing up on Coleridge's doorstep). Instead, the anecdote ostensibly reveals the gulf between private and public personas: from Coleridge's point of view, it is private knowledge that shows Jeffrey the reviewer (and editor) to possess malicious feelings. Jeffrey's "high coloured compliments" smack of insincerity, but Coleridge himself protests too much. From his suspiciously elaborate disavowal that a Lake School exists, one infers that Jeffrey's preconceptions may have been reinforced instead of altered by his meeting with Coleridge.

Coleridge's second accusation against Jeffrey is that he twisted opinions that he, Coleridge, had expressed in a letter (apparently after their face-to-face meeting) into further ammunition against his "School." This information supports the implication that Jeffrey possesses (despite Coleridge's protestations to the contrary) "feelings of vindictive animosity." Yet in the light of the *Biographia*'s later point about the "*game*" of vituperation, the reader might think back and draw a different conclusion. Coleridge's third allegation emphasizes the idea of tarring with the same brush: Jeffrey, he alleges, is guilty of lumping Coleridge with his friends as well as with the dramatist Joanna Baillie:

> For that which follows, I have only ear-say evidence, but yet such as demands my belief: viz. that on being questioned concerning this apparently wanton attack, more especially with reference to Miss Bailie [sic], the writer had stated as his motives, that this lady when at Edinburgh had declined a proposal of introducing him to her; that Mr. Southey had written against him; and Mr. Wordsworth had talked contemptuously of him; but that as to *Coleridge* he had noticed him merely because the names of Southey and Wordsworth and Coleridge always went together. (*BL* 1: 52)

By reserving this point until last, Coleridge gives the impression that this is Jeffrey's chief offence, arbitrarily transferring his malignity from one name to another, either malevolently or playfully. Coleridge himself sounds threatened rather than amused, as if being treated as a member of a school diminishes his individuality.[13] Yet if these allegations themselves constitute a personal attack (as the *Biographia*'s reviewers and later Coleridge's son-in-law and Jeffrey's biographer[14] seemed to assume), what is striking is the mildness of the accusations. Jeffrey's behavior may have been rude, but it is scarcely on a par with the allegation against Coleridge that surfaces in the *Biographia*'s footnote on Southey. It is the fact that Jeffrey responds that magnifies a footnote into a feud.

Coleridge's Earlier Correspondence with Jeffrey

As one might expect, Coleridge's correspondence with Jeffrey—which took place two years before the writers met in the Lake District—gives a somewhat different impression of Coleridge's relationship with the *Edinburgh* editor from that offered in the *Biographia*. The confidential tone of the letters and their focus on matters of business are both at odds with Coleridge's sporadic self-characterization in the *Biographia* as aloof from the world of journalism and publishing—in Donald

---

[13] Compare Jeffrey N. Cox, "Leigh Hunt's Cockney School: The Lakers' 'Other,'" *Romanticism on the Net* 14 (May 1999), paragraph 5, on Coleridge's anxiety to prove his "uniqueness and originality" (http://www.erudit.org/revue/ron/1999/v/n14/index.html [accessed August 1, 2012]).

[14] Lord Cockburn, in his *Life of Lord Jeffrey, with a Selection from his Correspondence*, 2 vols (Philadelphia: Lippincott, Grambo & Co., 1852), called the passage "a very unhandsome personal attack" (1: 199). Cockburn added that "the personal matter has now become insignificant. The parties are all dead" (1: 199).

Reiman's phrase, "unbought."[15] In 1809, foreshadowing his claims in Chapter 3 of the *Biographia*, Coleridge complained in a letter to the publisher Thomas Longman that "now for *no* poems at all but only for my acquaintanceships, I am abused in every Review & Magazine" (*CL* 3: 203). Despite this note of paranoia, Coleridge added with guarded optimism, "I have however some reason to believe that Jeffray [sic] is well inclined to make me the amende honorable (at least, if I may believe his own letters)" (*CL* 3: 203). Deirdre Coleman claims that "This was wishful thinking on Coleridge's part," because Jeffrey had continued to refer slightingly to the Lake Poets in the *Edinburgh*, and to treat them as a "*firm*," as he put it in his first letter to Coleridge.[16] As Coleman points out, the occasion for the correspondence between Jeffrey and Coleridge was the latter's offer to review a book for the *Edinburgh*: Thomas Clarkson's *History of the Abolition of the Slave Trade* (1808).[17] Coleman describes Coleridge's "long-standing grievance at being lumped together with Wordsworth and Southey" as "another, more personal motive" (39). For Coleridge however, this "personal motive" of course has professional ramifications.

Of the correspondence, eight letters survive, four by Coleridge and four by Jeffrey, all written in 1808. In his first letter to Jeffrey, dated May 23, 1808, Coleridge objects to the "charges" (*CL* 3: 117) leveled against him by the editor of the *Edinburgh*, asking, "What harm have I ever done you, dear Sir—by act or word?" (*CL* 3: 117).[18] Jeffrey's reply, after denying that he has attacked Coleridge to any great extent, gives a disingenuous reason for continuing to class the Lake Poets together: "Your name was undoubtedly the most conspicuous in this *firm* at its first institution—and if you have since abandoned the concern—you have *not advertised out* of it" (41). Implying that only a public disclaimer by Coleridge will suffice to make him mend his ways, Jeffrey here cynically gives himself an excuse for perpetuating the trend that he himself had helped to set in motion. Needless to say, Coleridge's eventual lengthy advertisement of his distance from the "*firm*"—the *Biographia*—would not get the *Edinburgh* off his back. Not having yet received this reply, in his second letter to Jeffrey, Coleridge returned to the subject of "attacks," claiming that in his case, "The ass's Skin is almost scourge-proof" (*CL* 3: 118). This assertion is particularly unconvincing because the rest of the letter is concerned with the "entwin[ing]" of "the Author's feelings [Clarkson's] ... with his own character, as a *man*" (*CL* 3: 119).

---

[15] Reiman, "Coleridge and the Art of Equivocation," 345.

[16] Deirdre Coleman, "Jeffrey and Coleridge: Four Unpublished Letters," *The Wordsworth Circle* 18 (1987), 39–45 (40). Further references in parentheses.

[17] In his attacks on the immorality of anonymous reviewing, Coleridge ignores the fact that he himself had, this one time, served as an *Edinburgh* reviewer, besides having written anonymous reviews for other periodicals.

[18] Jeffrey had just brought up Coleridge's name in his April 1808 review of George Crabbe's 1807 *Poems*. Jeffrey's language in this most recent attack expands the three Lake Poets into a bustling crowd of zealots: he refers to "the Wordsworths, and the Southeys and Coleridges, and all that misguided fraternity" (*ER* 12: 133).

The rest of Coleridge's correspondence with Jeffrey circles back to the issue of writers' individual autonomy or lack thereof. Jeffrey's second letter to Coleridge makes a sly allusion to the poet's private life: "I am glad you are so near us as Keswick and wish you could be persuaded to come up [to Scotland]—It would be edifying to some of the *genus irritable* to see me living amicably with Scott—but that is a lesson which *you* need not come for it seems" (43). Jeffrey's insinuation is that if Coleridge really were "living amicably" with his friends, he would not be so worried about being grouped with them.

In his final surviving letter to Jeffrey, dated December 14, 1808, Coleridge admits the editor's right to revise contributions to the *Edinburgh*, but protests that in the case of his Clarkson review, the contradictions "betrayed a co-presence of two writers in one article" (*CL* 3: 148). Coleridge understands that periodical discourse tends to be collaborative but seems to believe that editors should preserve the fiction that each individual article is the product of a single voice. In his reply, Jeffrey did not take the trouble to comment on Coleridge's objection, instead offering criticisms of Coleridge's prospectus for *The Friend* with the attitude of what Coleman calls a "perfect worldling" (39). Educating readers, according to Jeffrey, "is a pretty vision but no project of a waking man" (44).

Meanwhile, contrasting with his polite letters to Jeffrey, a letter from Coleridge to Humphry Davy dated December 7, 1808, emphasized his low opinion of the *Edinburgh*'s editor. Coleridge refers to a recent attack on Davy in the *Edinburgh* as "the grossest and most disgusting KECK-UP of Envy, that has deformed even the E. R." (*CL* 3:135). He informed Davy that he had written a "spirited and close reasoned Letter to Mr Jeffray [sic]" (*CL* 3:135). The letter, however, was not sent and does not survive. In his letter to Davy, Coleridge added, "It is high Time, that the spear of Ithuriel should touch this Toad at the ear of the Public" (*CL* 3: 136). Perhaps Coleridge hoped that the *Biographia* would serve as such a "spear."

"Personality" in the *Biographia*

While Coleridge's first letter to Jeffrey foreshadows the issue of "persecution-by-association"[19] addressed in his footnote on Jeffrey in the *Biographia*, Coleridge's discussion in Chapter 3 of the *Biographia* of why he has been targeted leads to an exercise in self-defense-by-association. Coleridge "account[s]" for the "attacks" on him by asserting, "The solution may seem to have been given, or at least suggested, in a note to a preceding page. *I was in habits of intimacy with Mr Wordsworth and Mr Southey!*" (*BL* 1: 55). Coleridge offers this theory as a "solution" to the question of why he has been criticized so harshly and for so long, yet immediately concedes, "This, however, transfers rather than removes the difficulty" (*BL* 1: 55). The theory transfers rather than removes the difficulty in the sense of obliging Coleridge to offer motives for the "abuse" (*BL* 1: 63) heaped on his friends. It also implausibly suggests that *all* the alleged attacks on Coleridge for the past 17 years have been for the same reason.

---

[19] Erdman and Zall, "Coleridge and Jeffrey in Controversy," 78.

Apropos of his soaking by the "water-fall of criticism" Coleridge then asks "how came the torrent to descend upon [Wordsworth and Southey]?" (*BL* 1: 55), only to segue into fulsome praise of Southey. If the footnote on Jeffrey implies that there is no escape from "personality," the defense of Southey tries to take a stand against that possibility, but ends up reinforcing it. The discussion of Southey interrupts and is itself twice interrupted by Coleridge's meditation on the causes of the reviewers' "irascibility" (*BL* 1: 43), so that rather than confirming that the attacks on himself are inexplicable, Coleridge insinuates that the problem is part of a larger phenomenon in that the "abuse" of reviewers is by definition excessive, although he also implies that Southey like himself has been singled out for obloquy.

The passage is problematic in a number of ways, not least because it takes for granted that public attacks can be counteracted with private information. First, while editors of the *Biographia* note that Coleridge's praise of Southey conflicts with his "private view" of Southey's poetic achievements,[20] the praise itself is undercut by his failure to account fully for the "abuse and indefatigable hostility of his anonymous critics" (*BL* 1: 63). Even while Coleridge emphasizes the "extent of [Southey's] acquirements," he imagines a "future biographer" (*BL* 1: 63) of Southey adding to an edition of his works "an excerpta of all the passages in which his writings, name and character have been attacked" (*BL* 1: 57), implying that a huge amount of negative material should be preserved for posterity. The conventional compliment of the appeal to future fame could be seen as a move that figuratively kills off a rival poet. Coleridge claims that since Southey has been publicly "reviled," Coleridge "therefore" has a "duty" to praise his private life (*BL* 1: 65). Hazlitt, in his review of the *Biographia*, will have much to say on this subject. Contradicting the assumption underlying Coleridge's later complaints about reviewers' "intrusions into the sacredness of private life" (*BL* 2: 111), the defense implies that personal attacks can be counteracted with appeals to domestic virtues.

Finally, Coleridge ends his account of Southey with the footnote in which he brings up the 1798 attack on himself in the *Anti-Jacobin* for abandoning his wife and children. Here, one might think, is proof of an unmistakable personal attack (in the sense of spreading scandal) but the phrasing leaves open the possibility that Coleridge really had "*left his poor children fatherless, and his wife destitute*" (*BL* 1: 67). The anonymous writer had dragged in the names of Coleridge's friends—not Southey and Wordsworth but Southey and Charles Lamb. The charge is so egregious that Coleridge's act of reviving the allegation seems self-destructive, especially since its throwaway placement at the end of the chapter gives the impression that he is less offended by it than by Jeffrey's behavior. Moreover, Coleridge presents the story as if to confirm that Southey has been unjustly attacked (hence the attacks on Coleridge), but it actually shows not that Coleridge was attacked because his name was linked with Southey's but that Southey was attacked because his name

---

[20] Coleridge, *Biographia Literaria*, ed. George Watson (London: Dent, 1975), 38. Compare also Bate and Engell, *BL* 1: 65, n.1.

was linked with Coleridge's, as Coleridge himself acknowledges by calling his defense of Southey "a debt of justice to the man, whose name has been so often connected with mine, for evil to which he is a stranger" (*BL* 1: 67). It may not be that easy to counter the contagiousness of "evil."

Coleridge ends the footnote with a controversial political point:

> With severest truth it may be asserted, that it would not be easy to select two men more exemplary in their domestic affections, than those whose names were thus printed at full length as in the same rank of morals with a denounced infidel and fugitive, who had left his children *fatherless and his wife destitute!* Is it surprising, that many good men remained longer than perhaps they otherwise would have done, adverse to a party, which encouraged and openly rewarded the authors of such atrocious calumnies? (*BL* 1: 67)

By attacking the Tories of the past, the rhetorical question, as Hazlitt's review later recognizes, sounds like a contorted apology for Coleridge's earlier radicalism. The common theme of treating Coleridge and his fellow Lakers as interchangeable sets up an uneasy connection between this footnote and the footnote on Jeffrey, giving the impression that Jeffrey's misdemeanors resemble those of the *Anti-Jacobin* writers, despite the seemingly obvious discrepancy between Jeffrey's relatively minor infringements of professional decorum and the Tories' "atrocious calumnies." On a political level, Coleridge may be trying to displace his anger against his former enemies onto the editor of the Whig *Edinburgh*. At any rate, Coleridge's sarcastic use of italics implies that the allegation about his abandonment of his wife and children is self-evidently absurd and that the implication that Southey was "in the same rank of morals" even more so. Perhaps the reader is supposed to infer that the mere act of repeating the attack constitutes refutation.

Having both re-emphasized and weakened his complaints about Jeffrey with his discussion of Southey, later in the book Coleridge levels more charges against the *Edinburgh*'s editor. The first of these proceeds circuitously. In Chapter 21, after discussing the tendency of the *Edinburgh*'s "censure" to become "personal injury" (*BL* 2: 109), Coleridge turns to its "arbitrary and sometimes petulant verdicts" (*BL* 2: 113), presenting as his example its attack on the *Excursion* and accusing the unnamed reviewer—Jeffrey, of course—of concluding "with a strain of rudest contempt evidently grounded in the distempered state of his own moral associations" (*BL* 2: 115). Perhaps Coleridge would justify such strong language on the grounds that he is retaliating on his friend's behalf, but this claim reduces the reviewers' nastiness to a matter of one man's ill will and lack of good taste.

Coleridge then relates an anecdote about viewing Michelangelo's "stupendous statue" of Moses and overhearing two "officers of distinction and rank" who, apparently because they were French, were unable to appreciate the whole for the parts and "immediately" connected the statue's horns with adultery. He concludes the chapter by asserting that given Jeffrey's nitpicking attention to the accoutrements of the peddler in Wordsworth's poem, "this critic in my opinion cannot be thought to possess a much higher or much healthier state of moral feeling than the FRENCHMEN above recorded" (*BL* 2: 118). The persuasiveness of this attempt to discredit Jeffrey is diminished by the anecdote's stereotyping of Frenchmen (displaced from Coleridge himself onto "a Prussian artist, a man of genius" [*BL* 2: 116] and further displaced by the suggestion that these men are constitutionally incapable of seeing the wood for the trees, rather than obsessed with sexual impropriety). One might also object that the anecdote is tainted by self-elevation (unlike the philistine Frenchmen, Coleridge and his Prussian friend admire the statue appropriately). As a story foregrounding national traits, social class, art appreciation, and foreign travel, it may distract from rather than strengthen Coleridge's condemnation of Jeffrey.

Moreover, the ending of the next chapter of the *Biographia* contradictorily suggests that Jeffrey's taste may not be so bad after all. Coleridge's next overt attack on the editor of the *Edinburgh* occurs in one of the sections added closer to the time of publication. The context again is what Coleridge calls "the wantonness and the systematic and malignant perseverance of the aggressions" against Wordsworth (*BL* 2: 156). Evidently recalling his meeting with Jeffrey in the Lake District, Coleridge asserts,

> I myself heard the commander-in-chief of this unmanly warfare make a boast of his private admiration of Wordsworth's genius. I have heard him declare, that whoever came into his room would probably find the Lyrical Ballads lying open on his table, and that (speaking exclusively of those written by Mr Wordsworth himself,) he could nearly repeat the whole of them by heart. (*BL* 2: 156–7)[21]

This is certainly a "personal" attack both in the sense of singling out an individual and in the sense of using "intimate knowledge, elsewhere obtained" than from the text under consideration—the text in this case being Jeffrey's reviews of Wordsworth. In November 1810, Coleridge had told some of his friends about Jeffrey's private declaration. Henry Crabb Robinson noted in his diary, "He related to us that Jeffrey, the editor of the *Edinburgh Review*, had lately called on him, and assured him that he was a great admirer of Wordsworth's poetry, that the Lyrical Ballads were always on his table, and that Wordsworth had been attacked in the Review simply because the errors of men of genius ought to be exposed. Towards me, Coleridge added, Jeffrey was even flattering. He was like a schoolboy, who, having tried his man and been thrashed, becomes contentedly a fag."[22] David Erdman comments, "Jeffrey was nobody's 'fag.'"[23]

---

[21] A letter by Jeffrey dated March 21, 1799 corroborates this information. Jeffrey describes himself as "enchanted" by the *Lyrical Ballads* and praises the "true poetical horror" of "The Rime of the Ancient Mariner" (quoted by Jackson, *CCH*, 60). Compare Coleridge in a July 1825 letter to Daniel Stuart: "I give you my honor, that Jeffray [sic] himself told me, that *he* was himself an enthusiastic Admirer of Wordsworth's Poetry—but it was necessary that a Review should have a character" (*CL* 5: 475).

[22] Thomas Sadler, ed., *Diary, Reminiscences, and Correspondence of Henry Crabb Robinson*, 2 vols (London and New York: Macmillan, 1872), 1: 159.

[23] Erdman, "Coleridge and the 'Review Business,'" *The Wordsworth Circle* 6: 1 (1975): 3–50 (18).

But the passage in the *Biographia* renders questionable the extent to which Jeffrey himself is guilty of "personality." Circling back to Chapter 3's long footnote on Jeffrey and its concern with the gap between public and private behavior, this anecdote foregrounds irresponsibility rather than malicious feelings. The term "boast" implies that Jeffrey takes pride in his inconsistency, while the image of the book "lying open on his table" suggests that Jeffrey invites his inner circle to notice and thus sanction his self-conscious hypocrisy. The extravagance of the detail of Jeffrey having memorized "nearly" all Wordsworth's lyrical ballads implies that the reviewer takes a mischievous pleasure in deceiving readers of the *Edinburgh* not personally acquainted with him. The anecdote ostensibly functions to disprove the idea that Wordsworth exaggerated in accusing the reviewers of "palsied imaginations" (*BL* 2: 156) in his 1815 "Essay Supplementary to the Preface." But instead it intensifies the *Biographia*'s ambiguity over whether "aggressions" can be avoided, since they are apparently not only built into the system of reviewing but also both less and more "malignant" than they seem at first sight.

Coleridge's Complaints about Hazlitt

Despite the recognition that the defamatory language of the reviewers is a "*game*" and that "their vocation" makes them "rogues" against their private judgment, in the final chapter of the *Biographia* Coleridge returns to the idea that hostile reviews reflect the reviewers' own hostile feelings, yet once again, the issue branches off in various directions. In this chapter Coleridge tells two stories, one of the reception of *Christabel* and one of his *Statesman's Manual* (1816), both of which center on attacks in the *Edinburgh* that Coleridge presumed to be by Hazlitt. In places, complaining about Hazlitt seems to be a way of continuing to attack Jeffrey, as well as the other way around. Coleridge's general reflections on reviewing only return in passing at this point, but they unsettle his individualized grievances.

Contradicting his earlier insistence that he has long been the target of journalistic insults, Coleridge interrupts his concluding remarks with the assertion, "Strange as the delusion may appear, yet it is most true that three years ago I did not know or believe that I had an enemy in the world: and now even my strongest sensations of gratitude are mingled with fear, and I reproach myself for being too often disposed to ask,—Have I one friend?" (*BL* 2: 238). This extravagant, if internally modified, claim turns out to concern the gulf between private reactions to *Christabel* when Coleridge recited or circulated it in manuscript, and the "abuse" (*BL* 2: 238) that followed the poem's publication. "In the Edinburgh Review," Coleridge continues, "it was assailed with a malignity and a spirit of personal hatred that ought to have injured only the work in which such a Tirade was suffered to appear" (*BL* 2: 239). Yet even in this statement, "personal hatred" is not a straightforward explanation for what could be seen as rhetorical "malignity."[24] Alluding to Hazlitt (whom like

---

[24] Lapp, in *Contest for Cultural Authority*, claims that "By invoking the shibboleth 'personal,' Coleridge attempts to preclude the possibility of any other—especially political—motivation for this review" (27).

Jeffrey, he never actually names), Coleridge claims that the supposed author of the review was "a man, who both in my presence and in my absence, has repeatedly pronounced it the finest poem of its kind in the language" (*BL* 2: 239). The charge replicates the image of Jeffrey admiring the *Lyrical Ballads* at home and attacking them in the *Edinburgh*, except that Coleridge goes on to suggest that in this case the private admiration may have been insincere. Authors, warns Coleridge, can attribute negative reviews to "private enmity, of the very existence of which they had perhaps entertained no suspicion— ... personal enmity behind the mask of anonymous criticism" (*BL* 2: 239). Although he is generalizing again, he implies that the "malignity" of the *Christabel* review can be explained by Hazlitt's "private" ill will.

The notion of a "*game*" seems to have disappeared, but Coleridge modifies his point about "personal enmity" by adding that authors should also remain aware of "the necessity of a certain proportion of abuse and ridicule in a Review, in order to make it saleable" (*BL* 2: 239). Having circled back to private feelings as the primary explanation of the reviewers' nastiness, he here returns to the issue of profit, raising the question of how to distinguish between "private" and calculated hostility. He adds that face-to-face admiration in response to "recitation" may be caused by a merely "temporary sympathy of feeling" (*BL* 2: 239). One problem with this explanation is that Coleridge has just mentioned that Hazlitt had praised *Christabel* "both in my presence and in my absence." Coleridge seems to be offering at once too many and too few reasons for why *Christabel* was attacked— by Hazlitt in particular (though his review may have been revised by Jeffrey) and by reviewers in general.[25] He continues to vacillate over the extent to which the reviewers' hostility (or just Hazlitt's, or just Jeffrey's) is "personal" in the sense of expressing private feelings, which, the example of *Christabel* implies, are not necessarily the same as sincere feelings.

Coleridge's final complaint about Hazlitt, concerning the scathing reception of his first lay sermon, *The Statesman's Manual*, slides into a jibe directed at Jeffrey. Hazlitt's first attack on *The Statesman's Manual*, which had appeared in the *Examiner* on September 8, 1816, is an exemplary instance of the lack of connection between a work's content and a reviewer's response, because Hazlitt's

---

[25] Authorship of the *Edinburgh*'s review of *Christabel* review has been disputed. Coleridge later thought that Thomas Moore had written the review (*CL* 4: 736). Elisabeth Schneider tried to confirm this suggestion in "The Unknown Reviewer of *Christabel*," *PMLA* 20 (1955): 417–32. By contrast, Reiman, in *The Romantics Reviewed*, claims that though Hazlitt may have contributed, Jeffrey heavily revised the article (*RR, A* 482), and Jonathan Wordsworth, in *Francis Jeffrey. On the Lake Poets* (Poole: Woodstock Books, 1998), assumes that Jeffrey wrote it. See also John Beer, "Coleridge, Hazlitt, and *Christabel*," *RES* n.s. 37 (1986): 40–54. Duncan Wu, in "Rancour and Rabies: Hazlitt, Coleridge and Jeffrey in Dialogue" in Duncan Wu and Massimiliano Demata, eds, *British Romanticism and the* Edinburgh Review (New York: Palgrave Macmillan, 2002), 168–94, convincingly argues that Hazlitt was indeed the author, but notes that it was "standard practice" for Jeffrey to "recast" contributions to the *Edinburgh* (176).

article appeared before *The Statesman's Manual* had been published. According to Coleridge, "it was reviewed ... by anticipation with a malignity, so avowedly and exclusively personal, as is, I believe, unprecedented even in the present contempt of all common humanity that disgraces and endangers the liberty of the press" (*BL* 2: 241–2). In what sense is Hazlitt's "malignity ... avowedly ... personal"? The article in question, arguing that the meaning of Coleridge's "compositions" is equally unintelligible whether "published" or "unpublished" (*CCH*, 249), certainly insults Coleridge in calling him "the Dog in the Manger of literature, an intellectual Mar-plot" (*CCH*, 249), "the Man in the Moon" and "the Wandering Jew" (*CCH*, 251). It even mentions that Coleridge's "face ... cut[s] no figure" (*CCH*, 253). Despite this name-calling and the allusion to Coleridge's physical appearance (or "person"), Hazlitt leaves it to be inferred that he personally hates Coleridge the individual.

After his reference to this article's "unprecedented[ly]" personal malignity, however, Coleridge does not pause to explain whether the malignity lies behind as well as within it. Coleridge continues, "After its appearance, the author of this lampoon was chosen to review it in the Edinburgh Review: and under the single condition that he should have written what he himself really thought, and have criticized the work as he would have done had its author been indifferent to him, I should have chosen that man myself, ... before all others" (*BL* 2: 242). Hazlitt's review of *The Statesman's Manual* in the *Edinburgh*, Coleridge alleges, was neither sincere nor objective; Coleridge leaves open the possibility that Hazlitt, in writing what he did not "really" think, took a tone that was less rather than more severe. The tribute to Hazlitt's "mind" may suggest that even the best and brightest are corrupted by the institution of reviewing, while the phrase "I should have chosen that man myself" underlines Coleridge's own entanglement in the world he is depreciating.

After a pointed quotation from Catullus about a friend turning into one's worst enemy, Coleridge distinguishes between his own emotional reactions: "I can truly say, that the grief with which I read this rhapsody of predetermined insult, had the Rhapsodist himself for its whole and sole object: and that the indignant contempt which it excited in me, was as exclusively confined to his employer and suborner" (*BL* 2: 242). By calling Hazlitt's review a "rhapsody of predetermined insult," Coleridge insists that it cannot be sincere; Hazlitt deliberately set out to wound his erstwhile friend—hence Coleridge's "grief." Hazlitt's "malignity" is then both deeply felt and willful—but Coleridge no sooner ascribes agency to the younger man than he takes it away by blaming his "employer and suborner," Jeffrey. With his "indignant contempt" Coleridge claims the moral high ground, but such a reaction cannot necessarily be differentiated from a presumably blinder and less controlled rage.[26] As so often in the *Biographia*, the dividing line between

---

[26] On the distinction between righteous indignation and mad rage, see Andrew M. Stauffer, *Anger, Revolution, and Romanticism* (Cambridge: Cambridge University Press, 2005), 59.

Coleridge's "personal" and his "LITERARY LIFE" (*BL* 2: 247) is difficult to pin down. Malevolent intentions and defamatory subject matter ultimately seem less important than the spirit with which the victim approaches a hostile review. Readers of the *Biographia*, however, may respond with emotions other than sadness or contempt because unlike Coleridge, they may or may not have the good or ill fortune of being personally acquainted with this particular reviewer and the *Edinburgh*'s notoriously slippery editor.

"Personality" in Coleridge's Letters

The final chapter of the *Biographia* invites the question of why Coleridge blames Jeffrey more than Hazlitt, or chooses to say that he does. After complaining earlier in the *Biographia* about being spattered by the "water-fall of criticism" aimed at his friends, Coleridge himself seems to be indulging in the same transfer of enmity from one person to the next. Coleridge's letters from 1816 and 1817 concerning the reception of *The Statesman's Manual* and *Christabel* suggest that behind the scenes he harbored far more ill feeling against Hazlitt than he did against Jeffrey, partly because of his complicated private relationship with Hazlitt, dating back to 1798, the year of their first meeting, the occasion commemorated in the younger man's at once damning and elegiac essay, "My First Acquaintance with Poets." In his letters Coleridge uses strong language about Hazlitt, calling his anticipatory review of *The Statesman's Manual* "brutal" (*CL* 4: 669) and Hazlitt himself a "monster" (*CL* 4: 693), a man with "a wicked heart of embruted Appetites" (*CL* 4: 686).

In letters to at least three different correspondents, Coleridge alludes to the incident that made him break off friendly relations with Hazlitt: Hazlitt's so-called Keswick escapade of 1803, which forced him to leave the Lake District in a hurry. Coleridge does not specify the nature of Hazlitt's "unmanly vices" (*CL* 4: 735)— calling them "too disgusting to be named" (*CL* 4: 693). The incident is thought to have involved sexual violence directed against a lower-class woman.[27] Coleridge's letters however return obsessively to the subjects of how this misdemeanor constituted a betrayal on Hazlitt's part of Coleridge's and Southey's hospitality, and to their role in helping Hazlitt to flee from retribution, legal or otherwise. Coleridge tells several correspondents that because of this incident, Hazlitt, owing him a debt of gratitude, now resents him and therefore, when reviewing his former friend's work, wrote the opposite of what he believed (*CL* 4: 735, 4: 831, 4: 972). Coleridge quotes his former friend's "own words": "Damn him! *I hate him*: for I am under obligations to him" (*CL* 4: 693).

Despite this focus on Hazlitt in his letters, Coleridge entangles him with Jeffrey by suggesting, implausibly, that Jeffrey deliberately chose Hazlitt to review his work because he knew how much the younger man loathed Coleridge: "This man

---

[27] Sonia Hofkosh, in *Sexual Politics and the Romantic Author* (Cambridge: Cambridge University Press, 1998), 104–13, discusses the gendered literary historical implications of the incident, as well as "the problematic process of historical reconstruction itself" (107).

Mr Jeffrey has sought out, knowing all this, because the wretch is notorious for his avowed Hatred to *me*" (*CL* 4: 735). As in the *Biographia*, Coleridge may be momentarily displacing his hostile attitude to Hazlitt onto Jeffrey. Although his letters therefore express animosity towards both these individuals, Coleridge several times drifts into the same kind of general language that he uses in the *Biographia*, referring, for example, to "the utmost malignity of personal Enmity" (*CL* 4: 716) with which *Christabel* was reviewed, and "a number of enemies whose very faces I have never seen" (*CL* 4: 699). Unlike in the *Biographia*, and despite the concurrent *Wat Tyler* controversy, there is no awareness of persecutory reviewing as a "*game*": Hazlitt's attacks are deemed personal, that is to say, in the sense of being motivated by private malignity. Coleridge wrote in the postscript of a letter to John Murray: "Now what can I think of Mr Jeffries [sic], who knows nothing personally of me but my hospitable attentions to him, and from whom I heard nothing but very high-seasoned Compliments, and who yet can avail himself of *such* an instrument of his most unprovoked Malignity toward an inoffensive man in distress and sickness" (*CL* 4: 706–7). Coleridge claims to understand the reason for Hazlitt's "malignity" (*CL* 4: 716), while Jeffrey's "proved pre-determined Malice" (*CL* 4: 707) remains baffling.

Instead of considering how the rhetoric of reviewing turns honest men into rogues, Coleridge is much more preoccupied in his letters with the notion that negative reviews impoverish him. He proclaims, "I cannot be indifferent to Starvation" (*CL* 4: 736) and "Thank God! these things pass from me like Drops from a Duck's Back, except as far as they take the Bread out of my mouth" (*CL* 4: 717). Both before and after the publication of the *Biographia*, he tends not to imagine the possibility that any publicity, good or bad, may improve sales, although this assumption may underlie his complaint that the "studied silence" of the *Quarterly* is "far more mischievous" than the "Mohawk truculence of the Edinborough [sic]" (*CL* 4: 949). Coleridge's letters confirm that his self-consciousness in the *Biographia* about the existence of a "*game*" does not allow escape to a higher vantage-point. Because he knows, or thinks he knows, the identities of his anonymous persecutors, Coleridge implies that reviews are transparent indicators of personal malignity, rather than texts that have to be interpreted. Finding malicious feelings behind the texts of reviews—a reader-based approach to personal attacks—can have a hall of mirrors effect in that once Coleridge sees "Malice" behind a review, he tends to find it everywhere. The immediate public reception of the *Biographia* however, invites a more nuanced conception of personal attacks, one that acknowledges the continuities between "personalities," psychological exploration, and the creation of fictional characters.

The *Edinburgh*'s Review of the *Biographia*

Coleridge's complaints against Hazlitt and Jeffrey in the *Biographia* did not deter the latter from choosing Hazlitt to review the *Biographia* in the *Edinburgh*. On the contrary, Jeffrey may have considered that the *Biographia* dictated his choice.

Jeffrey did however, as mentioned earlier, affix to the review a long footnote of self-vindication, signed "F. J." Even before the *Edinburgh* review appeared in mid-September 1817, an article in the *Literary Gazette* anticipated a reply from Jeffrey. The *Literary Gazette* devoted almost a quarter of its review of the *Biographia* to the dispute, quoting in full Coleridge's footnote on Jeffrey from Chapter 3 with the comment, "The next story is one we would gladly suppress for the honour of our tribe: but fiat justitia, even though a Reviewer should be wounded. Authors have a fair right to a fling in return for the buffets they endure" (*RR, A* 592). Despite this expression of sympathy for Coleridge, the writer refuses to elaborate, adding, "Leaving Mr. Jeffrey to answer, as we doubt not he will, this charge of having violated the sacred rights of hospitality and amicable correspondence, we pursue the tenour of our way along with the aggrieved Mr. Coleridge" (*RR, A* 593). Unlike some other reviewers, the *Literary Gazette* writer thus names the editor of the *Edinburgh*, arguably making Coleridge's attack more "personal"; his "as we doubt not he will" takes for granted that Coleridge's accusation will provoke a rebuttal, while the sardonic tinge of his adjectives "sacred" and "amicable" hint that after all, Jeffrey has justice on his side.

Hazlitt's substantial article, which grudgingly begins, "There are some things readable in these volumes" (*ER* 28: 488), does not focus exclusively on what it calls Coleridge's "attacks on the Edinburgh Review" (*ER* 28: 489), but instead broadens to address the failure of Coleridge's literary career.[28] Robert Lapp, in *Contest for Cultural Authority*, offers an astute and detailed analysis of the review, seeing Hazlitt's interpretation of the *Biographia* as a "'prototype' of the various materialist and historicist rereadings of this seminal text in our own day" (132–3). Yet even Lapp's materialist reading of Hazlitt's attack acknowledges the "'music' of Hazlitt's own phrasing" (147) and finds "the painful narratives of apology and apostasy ... seemingly transcended by an aestheticization of history and memory" (152). I will go further in seeing the article as not just a demystification of Coleridge's idealizing impulses but a reworking of them. At first sight, Hazlitt's stringent assaults on Coleridge's philosophical and political opinions would seem to demolish the assumption that poets "live in an ideal world of their own" (*ER* 28: 514). But at the same time, Hazlitt's account of Coleridge's poetic career appears drawn to—even as it sets aside—themes characteristic of the Romantic lyric: the loss and recuperation of inspiration and the "flights" of "imagination" (*ER* 28: 514).

Hazlitt certainly demystifies brilliantly. Foreshadowing his later breathtaking account of Coleridge's fluctuating interests in his *Spirit of the Age* essay "Mr. Coleridge" (1825), he describes the poet as "going up in an air-balloon filled with

---

[28] Although for convenience I will refer to the author of the review as Hazlitt and to the author of its long footnote as Jeffrey, it is of course likely that Jeffrey, as the editor of the *Edinburgh*, contributed to the body of the review. In his footnote he admits to having made "some retrenchments and verbal alterations" to Hazlitt's review of *The Statesman's Manual*. Lapp notes that Jeffrey's footnote "emerges from a point in the text where the plural 'we' covers a complex interchange of critical voices" (*Contest for Cultural Authority*, 143).

fetid gas from the writings of Jacob Behmen and the mystics, and coming down in a parachute made of the soiled and fashionable leaves of the Morning Post" (*ER* 28: 491). The image literalizes the bringing down to earth of Coleridge's transcendentalism. Hazlitt also mires the writer in the world of gossip that Coleridge scorns. Allegedly "Out of regard to Mr C. as well as to our readers," he quotes at some length from the more autobiographical passages of the *Biographia*, on the grounds that their "easy, gossiping, garrulous" style makes them "more likely to be popular" (*ER* 28: 498).[29] As Lapp points out, "The same market demand that makes 'some things readable' in Coleridge's *Biographia* encourages Hazlitt to ensure, through generous quotation, that 'there are some things readable' in his own review as well" (149). Lapp adds that "by remaining anonymous, [Hazlitt] himself is not free to indulge in anecdote; his commitment to the plural 'we' constrains him to rely on Coleridge to bring personal presence to his text" (149). Hazlitt himself thus embraces gossip at one remove.

Elsewhere in the review, Hazlitt generates more gossip while denying an interest in it. Besides Jeffrey's long footnote, the review contains discussions of Southey and Wordsworth, the first of which dwells on the irrelevance of "personal" information (*ER* 28: 492). Hazlitt makes much of Coleridge's footnote concerning the attack on Coleridge, Lamb and Southey in the *Anti-Jacobin*, calling the passage "not a little remarkable" (*ER* 28: 492). He introduces his extensive quotation from the footnote with a sardonic jibe at Coleridge's defense of Southey's private life:

> Mr Coleridge proceeds (by what connexion we know not) to a full, true and particular account of the personal, domestic, and literary habits of his friend Mr Southey,—to all which we have but one objection, namely, that it seems quite unnecessary, as we never heard them impugned,—except indeed by the Antijacobin writers, here quoted by Mr Coleridge, who is no less impartial as a friend, than candid as an enemy. (*ER* 28: 492)

With friends like Coleridge, is the familiar implication, who needs enemies?[30] Hazlitt will have more to say about Coleridge's account of Southey's "personal ... habits," but first he reiterates the accusation of political apostasy that has resounded throughout the *Wat Tyler* controversy: "The charge is, that [Southey] wrote democratical nonsense in his youth: and that he has not only taken to write against democracy in his maturer age, but has abused and reviled those who adhere to his former opinions" (*ER* 28: 493). Southey, rather than being the victim of abuse, is instead the producer of it. "Now," continues Hazlitt, "What has Mr Coleridge to oppose to this? Mr Southey's private character!" (*ER* 28: 493). Hazlitt then proceeds to caricature Coleridge's defense of his friend: "Some people say, that Mr Southey has deserted the cause of liberty: Mr Coleridge tells us, that he has not separated

---

[29] Hazlitt refers familiarly to "Mr C." (*ER* 28: 491) even while writing in the conventionally formal first person plural.

[30] For a thorough explication of Hazlitt's treatment of the *Anti-Jacobin* note, see Lapp, *Contest for Cultural Authority*, 139–40.

from his wife. ... It is also objected, that the worthy laureate was as extravagant in his early writings, as he is virulent in his present ones: Mr Coleridge answers, that he is an early riser, and not a late sitter up. ... With all this we have nothing to do" (*ER* 28: 493–4). Hazlitt presents a set of amusingly sharp distinctions between public and private, but his remarks on Southey in the very next paragraph show the difficulty of separating the two: he describes the Laureate as a "mere book-worm" who writes "with little thought or judgment" (*ER* 28: 494). Treating an author as an "impersonation" of his "work"—to return to Coleridge's phrase—can still sound like a personal attack.

Despite his situating of Coleridge within the trenches of print warfare, Hazlitt reveals Romantic leanings. His review lingers over Coleridge's description of his youthful imaginative awakening and his ideas concerning "the essence of poetry" (*ER* 28: 513), including the notion that poetry has "a logic of its own" (*ER* 28: 489). His initial lengthy quotations from the *Biographia* offer the story of Coleridge's "long and blessed interval" of "love of nature, and the sense of beauty" (*ER* 28: 491), his early engulfment by the "mental disease" (*ER* 28: 490) of metaphysics and his later return to "abstruse researches" (*ER* 28: 491) as an escape from "mismanaged sensibility" (*ER* 28: 491). Hazlitt's selections from the first chapter of the *Biographia* (*BL* 1: 17) thus rehearse the plot of Coleridge's "Dejection: An Ode" (1802), especially since the reviewer then comments, in a rewording of Coleridge's "we receive but what we give" (l. 47), "but the disease, we fear, was in the mind itself" (*ER* 28: 491).[31] Further, Hazlitt mocks the philosophical section of Coleridge's book in language that at once registers the precariousness and the allure of Romantic figurings of transcendence, referring to "the formidable ascent of that mountainous and barren ridge of clouds piled on precipices and precipices on clouds, from the top of which the author deludes us with a view of the Promised Land that divides the regions of Fancy from those of the Imagination" (*ER* 28: 495). The imagery in this only partly sardonic sentence perhaps recalls the sublime cloudscape in Book 2 of Wordsworth's *Excursion*, in which the speaker finds "forms uncouth of mightiest power, / For admiration and mysterious awe" (ll. 903–4).

Moreover, later in the review, Hazlitt seems more accepting of Wordsworth than he at first admits. He plays at setting aside Coleridge's account of Wordsworth's poetry: "as a very great part of it is occupied with specific inculpations of our former remarks on that ingenious author, it would savour too much of mere controversy and recrimination, if we were to indulge ourselves with any observations on the subject" (*ER* 28: 507). Despite this disclaimer, he defends "*poetic diction*" (*ER* 28: 512)—thus disagreeing with a key point in Wordsworth's Preface to *Lyrical Ballads* (1800)—but characterizes it in ambivalent language as "a paste of rich and honeyed words" and "a glittering tissue of quaint conceits and sparkling metaphors" (*ER* 28: 512). In partial acquiescence with a central

---

[31] This quotation and the one from Wordsworth that follows are from Duncan Wu, *Romanticism: An Anthology*, second edition (Oxford: Blackwell, 1998).

contention of Wordsworth's Preface, he also defends "the real language of nature and passion" and poetry's access to "the musical in thought and feeling" (*ER* 28: 513). Explicitly Augustan definitions of literature coexist in the article with more Wordsworthian assumptions.

Jeffrey's Footnote

Meanwhile, competing for the reader's attention, Jeffrey's signed footnote takes up more than four pages of the review, certainly "indulg[ing]" at least to some extent in "controversy and recrimination." Jeffrey's rationale for "com[ing] forward in his own person," as a later writer put it (*CCH*, 367), is that personal attacks must be responded to before they damage one's reputation. The first paragraph of his footnote emphasizes this point:

> If Mr C. had confined himself to matter of argument, or to statements contained in the Review, we should have added no note to this passage, but left him in quiet possession of the last word on the critical question he has thought fit to resume. But as he has been pleased to make several averments in point of fact, touching the personal conduct and motives of his Reviewer, we must be indulged with a few words to correct the errors into which he has fallen: For, though we have no ambition to maintain public disputations with every one who may chuse to question the justice of our opinions, it might appear as if we acquiesced in averments of a personal and injurious nature, if we were to review a work in which they occur, without taking any notice of their inaccuracy. (*ER* 28: 507–8)

The assumption underlying this claim was perfectly standard in the period, and one that Coleridge definitely shared. However, given the *Edinburgh*'s convention of anonymity and its longstanding reputation for "controversy," the fact that Jeffrey on this particular occasion chooses to sign his own name (or at least his initials) remains mysterious. What is it about Coleridge's "averments" that makes them unacceptably "personal"? Apparently Coleridge's description of his private, face-to-face meeting with Jeffrey in the Lake District triggered this response, because, according to Jeffrey's biographer, it was "founded upon most inaccurate statements of what had passed at [the] visit."[32] Responding to a supposedly personal attack with a self-vindication creates the illusion that a "personal" conflict can be cleared up—when in practice a self-defense often leaves something unexplained and contains something else to provoke more "recrimination." As we have already seen in Chapter 1, rather than counterattacks fitting attacks and closing down debate, they tend to escalate it. Moreover, Jeffrey's gestures of shedding his anonymity and providing autobiographical detail to challenge Coleridge's account of their meeting are misleading, partly because he refrains from responding to certain other passages in the *Biographia* and partly because he continues to evade the question of his private views.

---

[32] Cockburn, *Life of Lord Jeffrey*, 2: 199.

The rest of Jeffrey's footnote summarizes the charges against him in the "long note" to Chapter 3 of the *Biographia*, but it adds Coleridge's complaint about the *Edinburgh*'s "malignant" review of *Christabel* from Chapter 24, as if that had also been directed at Jeffrey rather than Hazlitt. Jeffrey then proceeds to give what seems to be a point-by-point refutation, in the middle of which he responds to the accusation about *Christabel* again as if he was its target, even though he later refers to an unnamed "gentleman" (Hazlitt of course) who reviewed *The Statesman's Manual* (*ER* 28: 512). Jeffrey thus takes advantage of the custom of anonymity while claiming to have temporarily discarded it.

The two glaring omissions from his self-vindication concern Coleridge's comparison between Jeffrey's taste and that of the two vulgar Frenchmen in Italy, and the passage in which Coleridge claims that he "heard" the *Edinburgh* editor admit to having the *Lyrical Ballads* "open on his table." One might think that these two allegations demand more rather than less attention than some of the others, given that they appear in the text rather than in a footnote of the *Biographia*. Perhaps Jeffrey considered these two allegations unanswerable, or not worth answering—or not "personal and injurious" like the other "averments." Yet as mentioned earlier, the *Lyrical Ballads* passage gives a glimpse of Jeffrey's (hypocritical) "private admiration of Wordsworth's genius." Jeffrey may have considered the information "personal" but not "injurious"—a circumstance, on the contrary, to "boast" of (Coleridge's term). Nevertheless, in his signed footnote he comes across as extremely anxious to clear his name, proclaiming, "These are Mr C.'s charges against the principal conductor of the Edinburgh Review; to which, in order to avoid all equivocation, that individual begs leave to answer distinctly, and in the first person, as follows" (*ER* 28: 508). Jeffrey, however, does not "avoid all equivocation."

The central and most autobiographical section of his note, his account of his meeting with Coleridge in 1810, begins on the offensive: "as Mr C.'s statement is so given, as to convey an imputation of great ingratitude or violation of the laws of hospitality on my part, I shall mention, in a few words, as nearly as I can now recollect them, the circumstances of this famous visit" (*ER* 28: 509). Jeffrey himself seems to want to immortalize the "famous visit" (the sardonic choice of adjective raises the question of which of the two protagonists is the one recording his brush with fame), as he supplies far more detail than in Coleridge's account:

> It was in 1810, I think, that I went with some of my near relations to Cumberland. I had previously been in some correspondence of a literary nature with Mr C., though I had never seen him personally. ... When I came to Keswick, I had not the least idea that Mr C. lived in Mr Southey's house; and sent a note from the inn, saying, I should be glad to wait on him. He returned for answer, that he *and Mr Southey*, would be glad to see me. I thought it would be pitiful to decline this invitation; and went immediately. Mr Southey received me with cold civility—and, being engaged with other visiters [sic], I had very little conversation with him. With Mr. Coleridge I had a great deal; and was very much amused and interested. I believe coffee was offered me—and I came away in an hour or two. I did not see Mr Southey afterwards. Next day, Mr C. and I spent all the morning

together in the fields,—he did me the honour to dine with me at the inn,—and next morning I left Keswick, and have not seen him since. (*ER* 28: 509)

Did Jeffrey actually drink the cup of coffee he was offered, and does it matter? Jeffrey attempts to puncture the illusion that Coleridge tries to create in the *Biographia*, that he is one hapless individual pitted against the entire institution of reviewing, implying instead that the question concerns one man's word against another's as in a court of law. But the "I" of "F.J." the innocent traveler to the Lake District cannot be separated that easily from the juridical "we" of the *Edinburgh*. Part of the overload of information here is because Jeffrey apparently feels he has to explain the social awkwardness involved in visiting a writer (Southey) whose works he had attacked. The line, "I had not the least idea that Mr C. lived in Mr Southey's house," indirectly suggests that despite all Coleridge's complaints about being lumped with his friends, Jeffrey had thought of them as individuals. He sounds slightly dismayed at finding the Lake Poets living in closer contact than he could possibly have imagined.

The next part of the narrative resembles a witness-statement, with precise lines drawn between different levels of "recollect[ion]" about what Jeffrey did and did not say to Coleridge during their conversation.[33] But it also contains a questionable assertion. Jeffrey says, "I remember perfectly that he complained a good deal of my coupling his name with [Southey's and Wordsworth's] in the Review" (*ER* 28: 510). He then adds, "I promised that I would take his name out of the firm for the future; and I kept my promise" (*ER* 28: 510). The assertion gives the impression that by so doing Jeffrey had ceased to attack Coleridge, and yet the *Edinburgh*'s later attacks on him as an individual writer, in the reviews of *Christabel* and *The Statesman's Manual*, had been far more virulent and sustained than the brief slurs linking him with his fellow Lakers. As if to draw attention to this inconsistency, Jeffrey then segues to Coleridge's allegation that the *Edinburgh* reviewer of *Christabel* had been guilty of hypocrisy. Emphatically continuing in the first person, Jeffrey refutes this particular charge on his own behalf as if no such person as Hazlitt had ever existed: he adds, "We spoke too of *Christabel,* and I advised him to publish it; but I did not say it was either the finest poem of the kind, or a fine poem at all; and I am sure of this, for the best of all reasons, that at this time, and indeed till after it was published, I never saw or heard more than four or five lines of it. ... I did not review it" (*ER* 28: 510). The brevity of this final sentence implies that the case is therefore closed, yet Jeffrey has side-stepped the question of whether the *Edinburgh*'s review was as "malignant" and hypocritical as Coleridge claims.

Returning to his past tendency to link the names of Southey, Wordsworth and Coleridge (and Joanna Baillie), Jeffrey denies that he treated them with "personal pique or hostility" when discussing their "antiquated forms of expression" (*ER* 28: 511). Coleridge had implied that for him to be attacked merely because his friends were attacked made him the victim of a personal vendetta. "But," Jeffrey reminds him pointedly, "the author of the Antient Mariner could not well complain

---

[33] Lapp points out that "Jeffrey's self-defense here is ironically akin in genre to both Southey's *Letter* and the *Biographia* itself" (*Contest for Cultural Authority*, 134).

of being thus classed with the other writers of the Lyrical Ballads" (*ER* 28: 511). Coleridge himself has written anonymously and collaboratively—and Jeffrey himself, he insists, wrote with "sincerity" (*ER* 28: 511). "F.J." at this point assumes Coleridge's own role as the authentic individual confronting a factitious collective entity. "As to the review of the Lay Sermon," he continues, "I have only to say, in one word, that I never employed or suborned any body to abuse or extol it or any other publication" (*ER* 28: 511–2). Jeffrey's denial is difficult to credit, given the extent of his power over the contents of the *Edinburgh* with its trademark lively "abuse." Jeffrey next denies all knowledge of "a malignant lampoon or review by anticipation" (*ER* 28: 512) and adds with reference to the "gentleman" who reviewed *The Statesman's Manual* for the *Edinburgh*, that he "certainly never suspected [him] of having any personal or partial feelings of any kind towards its author" (*ER* 28: 512). It is hard to believe that Jeffrey had never heard of or seen Hazlitt's attacks on *The Statesman's Manual* in the *Examiner*. It is equally hard to believe that the *Edinburgh* editor was oblivious of Hazlitt's troubled relationship with Coleridge, although difficult to imagine that Jeffrey was aware of the lurid story involving Hazlitt alluded to in Coleridge's letters.[34]

Jeffrey concludes with a conventional disclaimer about the embarrassment inherent in autobiography: "It is painful, and perhaps ridiculous, to write so much about oneself" (*ER* 28: 512). As Lapp comments, for Jeffrey, "the convention of anonymity, far from being a mask for the 'personal or partial,' is instead the sign of a decorous subordination of 'one's self' to more important public tasks" (145). However, just as Hazlitt, in Lapp's reading, gives life to his review by quoting Coleridge's more autobiographical passages, Jeffrey has energized his self-justification with his reminiscences about his private encounter with Coleridge in a Lakeland setting. It is certainly the vignette describing Jeffrey's visit to the Lake District that proves most compelling to later reviewers and commentators. Like the *Biographia* itself, Jeffrey's soon-to-be "famous" footnote is self-concealing and self-revealing at the same time.

Other Early Responses to the *Biographia*

Continuing the controversy, several other reviewers of the *Biographia* commented on Coleridge's attack on Jeffrey and Jeffrey's reply. Other writers did so in private, among them Jeffrey's fellow *Edinburgh* reviewer Sydney Smith, who commented in a letter to J.A. Murray in October 1817: "Jeffrey has thrashed Coleridge ... but is it not time to lay up his cudgel? Heads that are plastered and trepanned all over are no longer fit for breaking."[35] Smith unconsciously echoes Coleridge's image

---

[34] Wu, in "Rancour and Rabies," argues that only Hazlitt "fully ... understood" the "unique three-handed dialogue" between himself, Jeffrey and Coleridge (190).

[35] Nowell C. Smith, ed., *Letters of Sydney Smith*, 2 vols (Oxford: Clarendon Press, 1953), 1: 281. J.A. Murray is not to be confused with John Murray the publisher. Compare Griggs: "Coleridge was no match for his opponents in this warfare of invective and insult" (*CL* 4: 668).

of Jeffrey (in a conversation mentioned earlier) as a "thrashed ... fag," but with the roles reversed. By implication, Smith detects excessive violence beneath the surface of Jeffrey's ostensibly decorous footnote. In his diary for October 6, 1817, Coleridge's friend Henry Crabb Robinson formulated a more nuanced reading of the conflict:

> I was interested by the review of Coleridge's Life written by Hazlitt, for which it is said he has received fifty guineas. Jeffrey had added a note with the initials of his name replying to the personalities in Coleridge's book. Jeffrey, of course, being a discreet and artful man, has the advantage over Coleridge in a personal dispute, who has so many infirmities of mind which lay him open to the attack of an adversary; but Jeffrey confesses enough to fix on himself the imputation of gross flattery and insincerity towards Coleridge. He says that he saw Coleridge liked compliments, and therefore gave them. He advised the publication of Christabel on the report of others, and then suffered Hazlitt to heap every species of obloquy on it in his review. He certainly shows the hospitality of Southey not to have been of a kind to demand any vehement gratitude.[36]

The final sentence of this paragraph reads like a tribute to Jeffrey's "artful[ness]" if his footnote "certainly" succeeds in disproving one of Coleridge's allegations. Jeffrey, of course, is not as "discreet" as he looks if he can reveal himself to be guilty of "gross flattery and insincerity," but not every reader saw the "personal dispute" in this light.

The two most elaborate published commentaries, in two Tory monthlies, the *British Critic* and the new *Blackwood's Edinburgh Magazine*, took opposite directions, the first siding mainly with the author of the *Biographia*, and the second launching its own stinging personal attack on Coleridge. Both of these have a creative element, though they branch off into different genres, showing how "personality" can be complicated not just by way of theme but form. The long unsigned article in the *British Critic* gives much space to Coleridge's strictures on the *Edinburgh*. Writing with a veneer of objectivity, this reviewer criticizes Coleridge as well as his opponent, but, presumably motivated by political partisanship, extends rather than merely reproducing Coleridge's attack on Jeffrey. In taking the exchange between Coleridge and Jeffrey as an opportunity to condemn the *Edinburgh*'s vituperative style, however, the *British Critic* reviewer eventually seems to leave politics behind, as he uses the incident to meditate on the limitations of "civility" (*CCH*, 369) and indulge in that favorite occupation of Romantic-era periodical writers, self-referential reflections on the dynamics of periodical discourse.

In the course of his mostly sympathetic account of Coleridge's book, the *British Critic* writer makes a feint of hesitating to address Coleridge's denunciation of "us, 'synodical individuals,' who call ourselves reviewers" (*CCH*, 361). The gesture is

---

[36] *Henry Crabb Robinson on Books and Their Writers*, ed. Edith J. Morley, 3 vols (London: J.M. Dent & Sons, 1938), 1: 209–10.

purely routine, as the reviewer goes on to devote pages to the subject of personal attacks and Coleridge's quarrel with Jeffrey. He argues that Coleridge has "no ... right to complain" about "injury done to his private interests, by anonymous criticism," because authors are "public characters" (*CCH*, 362). At this point the reviewer sounds Jeffrey-esque, remarking flippantly, "misrepresentation and misconception, unreasonable censure and blind admiration—these are matters of course—the penalty paid in all cases for publicity" (*CCH*, 362).

The *British Critic* does not name Coleridge's "anonymous, though well known reviewer" (*CCH*, 364), taking for granted that any reader of the *Biographia* or periodical reviews would be aware that Jeffrey had written the *Edinburgh*'s attacks on the Lake School. He contends that "all that authors or the public, can reasonably expect, is, that critics should *really* speak as they think, and not give decisions which they know to be partial, merely for the purpose of gratifying feelings of a personal nature" (*CCH*, 365). At this point the reviewer seems to sympathize with Coleridge's claims that Jeffrey's dismissive attitude towards him was due to "personal" animosity.

Rather than quoting the "passages ... in which our author gives vent to ... feelings" of persecution, this reviewer sets out to "state the facts" (*CCH*, 366). He presents the evidence of Jeffrey's "private conversation" about having the *Lyrical Ballads* "open on his table" as if it were something of a revelation, but does not immediately offer further commentary (*CCH*, 366). For his next, more elaborate piece of evidence the reviewer backtracks to Coleridge's footnote about Jeffrey in Chapter 3 of the *Biographia*. Before quoting the note he provides his own somewhat slanted and inaccurate commentary:

> In another part of the work Mr Coleridge informs us that some years ago, upon occasion of the reviewer in question paying a visit to Cumberland, he was at his own request introduced to Mr. Southey, drank tea at his house, and was in all respects hospitably treated; but so far was he from permitting the recollection of the courtesies which he had received, to soften the asperity of his criticism, that his very first employment upon returning to Edinburgh, was to write a lampoon upon his host, in language still more offensive than upon any former occasion; designating him and the friends whom he met at his house, as "whining and hypochondriacal poets", and saying many other things, which a critic perhaps had a right to say, but which it was just as easy to have said in civil as in disrespectful language. (*CCH*, 367)

Besides creating confusion about whether Jeffrey was offered tea or coffee at Southey's house, the *British Critic* reviewer exaggerates the hospitality that Jeffrey received and the haste with which he wrote his "lampoon" (not Coleridge's term); he also extrapolates from Coleridge's note in calling Jeffrey's "language" after their meeting "still more offensive than upon any former occasion." The reviewer then quotes Coleridge's footnote in its entirety, on the grounds that "the contents of it have been thought so weighty, as to induce the reviewer to come forward in his own person and under his own name" (*CCH*, 367). The tone here is slight puzzlement, as if the reviewer does not consider Coleridge's allegations "weighty" enough to warrant breaking through the pretence of anonymity. Yet he himself considers them "weighty" enough to provide a detailed analysis, not of Coleridge's note, but of Jeffrey's reply.

The *British Critic* writer finds Jeffrey guilty of hypocrisy: "As to the high-flown compliments with which he gratified Mr. Coleridge's vanity, we are told, that the reviewer paid them, because he thought he could perceive that they were as agreeable to our author, as they are to most people; by which we are left to infer, that what our honest reviewer *says*, is no better criterion of his real sentiments, than what he *writes*" (*CCH*, 368). The term "high-flown" refers back to Coleridge's description, "high-coloured," rather than to Jeffrey's account of their conversation, with the *British Critic* reviewer putting his own twist on Jeffrey's assertion that "it rather appeared to me that Mr C. liked to receive compliments" (*ER* 28: 510).

As this attack progresses, the *British Critic* reviewer portrays Jeffrey as increasingly devious, calculatingly weighing face-to-face flattery against behind-the-back insults. This writer next turns to more subtle evidence of Jeffrey's hypocrisy afforded by his straddling the line between public and private. He continues,

> With respect to the other charge, which he pleads guilty to, it is to be sure rather of a ridiculous nature; he admits that he was received at Mr. Southey's house, and "believes that coffee was handed to him"; but as he was not given to understand that this was offered to him, under any implied condition of praising on all future occasions, the poetry of his host, and that of his friends, he contends that he had a right to speak of them and their writings on his return to Edinburgh, in the same discourteous and abusive language as before. (*CCH*, 368–9)

Conjuring up a scenario in which a cup of coffee could serve as a bribe, the reviewer facetiously distorts Jeffrey's detailed explanation by truncating its narrative, exposing allegedly twisted logic, and substituting the unvarnished phrase "discourteous and abusive language" for Jeffrey's euphemistic reference to his "recurring to the errors and imperfections" of the Lake Poets.

In a less frivolous vein, the *British Critic* reviewer then offers a contorted analysis of the situation, worthy of a novel of manners:

> This is not to be disputed; the circumstance of having been received into his house, and treated with respect and civility, by a person to whom we were personally strangers, would weigh with some minds, to a certain extent at least; it might not, and perhaps ought not, to disarm justice, but it would, at all events, be an additional argument against passing sentence in the language of contempt and insult; it might not call forth any strong expressions of civility, nor make us express a degree of admiration, which we did not feel; but still one should suppose, that it would not produce an opposite effect; it would not excite an unfavourable prejudice, nor induce us to keep down our real feelings, and give utterance to none except such as were harsh and disrespectful. A man is not called upon to flatter another, merely because he has been in his house and received no unfriendly treatment; yet it would surely be still more strange to give this as a reason for abusing him. (*CCH*, 369)

The *British Critic* reviewer makes the most of this relatively rare opportunity to puncture the *Edinburgh*'s mystique, willfully misrepresenting Jeffrey's side of the story.

Jeffrey had not of course actually given his reception in Southey's house as his "reason for abusing" Coleridge, referring instead to the Lake Poets' affectedly archaic "style and diction" (*ER* 28: 511). The mention of Jeffrey's "real feelings" gives renewed credit to the story about Jeffrey admiring Wordsworth in private, without considering whether that "boast" (Coleridge's term) may itself have been insincere. This critique shows the danger of "com[ing] forward in [one's] own person," as the writer ignores the possibility raised in the *Biographia* itself, that "harsh and disrespectful" language is built into the system of reviewing, instead lingering over Jeffrey's apparent perversity. This passage itself could be seen as a personal attack in taking a "disrespectful" attitude to Jeffrey as a human being—except that it is cast in general terms as a hypothetical scenario, an etiquette problem created by the unusual circumstance of being offered a hot beverage in the home of "a person to whom we were personally strangers" (the reviewer ignores Jeffrey's admission that he had met Southey on a previous occasion). Gaining its own momentum, the passage's proliferating clauses temporarily seem to set both real people and politics aside as its hesitancies—"some minds," "to a certain extent at least," "might not, and perhaps ought not"—verge on the novelistic in their attempt to express shades of psychological possibility. As he slides in and out of first person, the writer offers less a quasi-legalistic exposure of Jeffrey than the bemused contemplation of a thorny question of polite manners. Much of the appeal of the dispute seems to lie in the temptation it offers to engage in creative writing of one's own. This is even more the case with the *Blackwood's* review.

Blackwood's on the *Biographia*

The *Blackwood's* attack on the *Biographia* appeared prominently in the first number of the revamped *Blackwood's Magazine*, and provides an excellent example of the blurred line between personal attack and literary biography—between the explicit indulgence in hostile "personality" and the implicit investment in "personality" in the psychological sense. Like Hazlitt's attack, it thus shares Coleridge's own interest in the workings of the human mind. William Blackwood had begun to publish his magazine in April 1817, but he re-launched the publication in October of that year with a talented new editorial team, John Wilson and John Gibson Lockhart.[37] Wilson and Lockhart collaborated on two immediately notorious items in the October number, the scurrilous "Chaldee Manuscript" and "Z"'s initial violent attack on Leigh Hunt and the Cockney School. The equally hostile review of the *Biographia*, while confirming the *Biographia*'s account of personal attacks as multi-causal, introduces the *Blackwood's* policy of inconsistency for its

---

[37] On the success of *Blackwood's*, see, for example, Philip Flynn, "Beginning *Blackwood's*: The Right Mix of *Dulce* and *Utile*," *Victorian Periodicals Review* 39 (Summer 2006): 136–57.

own sake. Although the vitriolic language of the review can easily be explained in terms of its entertainment (and thus commercial) value, the ideological motives behind the attack seem less clear, since the Tory *Blackwood's* might have been expected to approve of Coleridge's politics.[38]

The attack on the *Biographia* also exemplifies the *Blackwood's* practice of unpredictability in that its author, Wilson, was personally acquainted with Coleridge and would go on to defend Coleridge in later contributions to *Blackwood's*, just as he would go back and forth in attacking and defending Wordsworth in the pages of *Maga*.[39] Coleridge himself saw the review as "contain[ing]" an "atrocious Calumny" (referring to its revival of the allegation from the *Anti-Jacobin*), yet acknowledged that the "Slander" in *Blackwood's* was "systematic" (*CL* 4: 786). This review of the *Biographia* does not give as much space to the Coleridge–Jeffrey controversy as the *British Critic*, but, in putting its own spin on the incident, it fanned the fire. Wilson's article, like Hazlitt's review of the *Biographia*, forcefully demystifies Coleridge's precious transcendental notion of selfhood, while indulging in a little mysticism of its own. At the same time, in giving Coleridge himself (though not, at this stage, Jeffrey) a tinge of fictionality, this article also helps to lay the ground for the later more comical and indulgent treatment of the feud in *Blackwood's*.

As mentioned in the introduction, *Blackwood's* changed early nineteenth-century reviewing, intensifying the virulence inherited from the *Edinburgh* and the *Quarterly*, and going a step further than the quarterlies in embracing the practice of character assassination. *Blackwood's* also initiated a different kind of personal attack, supplementing outright slander with more playful (and arguably more benign) "personalities." Peter Murphy has analyzed *Maga*'s "obsessive interest in the interaction, attachment and slippage between authors (published names) and persons (bodies indicated by names)."[40] In its reviews, squibs and parodies, the

---

[38] John Strachan, in *Blackwood's Magazine, 1817–25*, points out that "the *Edinburgh Review* is a principal target of the relaunch issue"; according to him, *Blackwood's* set out to "savage the Laker Coleridge in a way which would have made even Francis Jeffrey blush" (6: xxi).

[39] Erdman, in "Coleridge and the 'Review Business,'" claims that Wilson's "temporarily unfriendly manner" was "induced chiefly by expediency but partly by annoyance" at Coleridge's footnote on Jeffrey (30). On Wilson's contribution to the *Blackwood's* ethos of controversy, see Robert Morrison, "*Blackwood's* Berserker: John Wilson and the Language of Extremity," *Romanticism on the Net*, 20 (November 2000), http://www.erudit.org/revue/ron/2000/v/n20/005951ar.html [accessed July 30, 2012]. See also Andrew Noble, "John Wilson (Christopher North) and the Tory Hegemony," in Douglas Gifford, ed., *The History of Scottish Literature*, Volume 3: *The Nineteenth Century* (Aberdeen: Aberdeen University Press, 1987): 125–52. Noble sees Wilson as a "Scottish Salieri to these English Mozarts" (134). On the inconsistent treatment of Wordsworth in *Blackwood's*, see David Higgins, *Romantic Genius and the Literary Magazine* (London: Routledge, 2005), Chapter 4.

[40] Peter T. Murphy, "Impersonation and Authorship in Romantic Britain," *ELH* 59 (1992): 625–49 (626). See also Margaret Russett, *De Quincey's Romanticism: Canonical Minority and the Forms of Transmission* (Cambridge: Cambridge University Press, 1997), 99–100.

Tory monthly soon developed a reputation for blurring fact and fiction, with its pseudonymous contributors and the objects of its attack alike taking on a quasi-novelistic status that would seem to extend the *Biographia*'s notion of reviewing as a *"game."*⁴¹ Both the attack on the *Biographia* and the first attack on the Cockney School enact this transition in periodical writing. Margaret Russett comments, "The first edition of the new *Blackwood's* was calculated to shock and awe, but more especially to claim the magazine as *literature*, not mere journalism."⁴²

As with the *Edinburgh* review of the *Biographia*, the substantial length of the *Blackwood's* review belies its claim that Coleridge's book lacks value. Wilson asserts that from "a literary point of view," the *Biographia* is "most execrable" (*BM* 2: 5), yet like Hazlitt, Wilson uses anecdotes from the text to enliven his article, though less kindly, he uses Coleridge's own stories against him. In claiming that Coleridge obtrudes his own ego in his account of his literary career, Wilson's conflation of man and author (as in the *Blackwood's* attacks on Leigh Hunt, Keats, and Hazlitt) itself constitutes an aggressive form of life-writing. For example, he objects that "there seems to [Coleridge] something more than human in his very shadow" (*BM* 2: 5). Yet in one sense the attack is not personal as defined by the *Biographia* even though Wilson insinuates that the charges in the *Anti-Jacobin* might be true, because ironically the *Blackwood's* review does not have to bring in information "elsewhere obtained" in order to make a calumnious allegation; the information from the *Anti-Jacobin* is already there in the text of the *Biographia*. Coleridge considered taking out a libel prosecution against *Blackwood's*, but instead, confirming Wilson's insistence on Coleridge's entanglement within periodical culture, two years later he himself began contributing to *Blackwood's*.⁴³

The *Blackwood's* reviewer takes pains to debunk Coleridge's attempt to raise himself above routine journalistic warfare, comparing his writings to "a lying lottery puff or a quack advertisement" (*BM* 2: 6), and mocking his preoccupation with the hostile reception of his works:

> Above all, he weeps and wails over the malignity of Reviewers, who have persecuted him almost from his very cradle, and seem resolved to bark him into

---

⁴¹ Higgins, in *Romantic Genius and the Literary Magazine*, comments on *Maga*'s "confusing world of fictitious and semi-fictitious characters" (58), and Peter T. Murphy, in *Poetry as an Occupation and an Art in Britain, 1760–1830* (Cambridge: Cambridge University Press, 1993), claims that in *Blackwood's*, "the fictional characters poach reality from the real ones" (120).

⁴² Margaret Russett, *Fictions and Fakes: Forging Romantic Authenticity, 1760–1845* (Cambridge: Cambridge University Press, 2006), 178.

⁴³ For a detailed account of Coleridge's negotiations with *Blackwood's*, see Erdman, "Coleridge and the 'Review Business,'" 29–41. Analyzing the poet's contributions to *Blackwood's*, Julian Knox, in "Coleridge's 'Cousin-German': *Blackwood's*, Alter-Egos, and the Making of a Man of Letters," *European Romantic Review* 21.4 (August 2010): 425–46, argues that Coleridge played "the magazine's game of dramatizing and exploiting the inherent performativity of the journalistic 'I' or writerly 'self'" (438), and that his *Blackwood's* publications pull together his worldly and "idealist" personae (444).

the grave. He is haunted by the Image of a Reviewer wherever he goes. They ... may abuse whomsoever they think fit, save himself and Mr Wordsworth. All others are fair game—and he chuckles to see them brought down. But his sacred person must be inviolate; and rudely to touch it is not high treason, it is impiety. Yet his "ever-honoured friend, the laurel-honouring Laureate," is a Reviewer—his friend Mr Thomas Moore is a Reviewer ... —almost every friend he ever had is a Reviewer;—and to crown all, he himself is a Reviewer. Every person who laughs at his silly Poems, and his incomprehensible metaphysics, is malignant—in which case, there can be little benevolence in this world; and while Mr Francis Jeffrey is alive and merry, there can be no happiness here below for Mr Samuel Coleridge. (*BM* 2: 14)

Wilson here exposes the rich seam of paranoia running through the *Biographia*, reducing Coleridge's analysis of the failings of the *Edinburgh* to nothing more than a private obsession.

However, Wilson's demystification of Coleridge's literary life is unsettled elsewhere in the article. In his lengthy opening assault on the Romantic autobiographical impulse—the contemporary turn to self-exploration and introspection—the reviewer's eloquent wording betrays his fascination with this central Wordsworthian and Coleridgean concern even as he scorns it. (His ostensible initial target is Jean-Jacques Rousseau.) He sees efforts at recollection as yielding "a glimmering land of dreams, peopled with phantasms and realities undistinguishably confused and intermingled—here illuminated with dazzling splendour, there dim with melancholy mists,—or it may be shrouded in impenetrable darkness" (*BM* 2: 3). Wilson's word choices here register the appeal of the Romantic preoccupation with the intertwining of memory and identity, even as he sets out to expose its dangers. So even though he overtly objects to "the ransacking of [one's] inmost spirit for all its hidden emotions and passions," he reveals the attraction of themes such as "the melancholy that breathes from vanished delight" (*BM* 2: 3).

The article also contains eloquent tributes to the poetry of Walter Scott, Thomas Campbell, Byron, and Thomas Moore, to make the point that their lack of "self-elevation" (*BM* 2: 6) contrasts with Coleridge's "inveterate and diseased egotism" (*BM* 2: 5). Yet this passage on the "great living poets" values Scott's "romantic" evocation of the past (*BM* 2: 6) and Byron's ability to "[sound] the depths of our nature" (*BM* 2: 7), unsettling the article's contemptuous dismissal of Coleridge's "dreaming Imagination" (*BM* 2: 18). Moreover, emphasizing the way in which Coleridge "fluctuates from theory to theory" (*BM* 2: 18), Wilson would seem to appreciate a unity of mind not unlike the Coleridgean ideal, even as his complaint draws attention to the *Biographia*'s competing multiplicitous presentation of the self.

The more playful and creative element of Wilson's attack on the *Biographia* involves the way in which he invests Coleridge himself with what he calls a "phantasmagorial splendour" (*BM* 2: 5), although his treatment of Coleridge's dispute with Jeffrey leaves behind the fantastical realm of romance. According to

Wilson, Coleridge's writing in the *Biographia* transforms daily life into a land of ghosts: "while he darkens what was dark before into tenfold obscurity, he so treats the most ordinary common-places as to give them the air of mysteries, till we no longer know the faces of our old acquaintances beneath their cowl and hood, but witness plain flesh and blood matters of fact miraculously converted into a troop of phantoms" (*BM* 2: 5). Wilson at once develops and defuses this touch of uncanniness in hinting that *Christabel* contains something scandalous: "[The poet] then walked in broad day-light into the shop of Mr Murray, Albemarle Street, London, with two ladies hanging on each arm, Geraldine and Christabel,—a bold step for a person at all desirous of a good reputation, and most of the trade have looked shy at him since that exhibition" (*BM* 2: 9). Consigning Coleridge's revisionary romance to the hustle and bustle of the literary marketplace, this scenario anthropomorphizes Coleridge's imaginary characters and in doing so threatens to contaminate Coleridge himself with fictionality as well as sexual misbehavior.

A later sentence in the *Blackwood's* review also treats the poet's heroine as having some sort of extra-textual existence: "But alas! no sooner had the Lady Christabel 'come out,' than all the rules of good-breeding and politeness were broken through, and the loud laugh of scorn and ridicule from every quarter assailed the ears of the fantastic Hoyden" (*BM* 2: 15). These allusions to Coleridge's poem confirm Karen Swann's argument that the hostile reviewers of *Christabel* displace dismay over the impropriety of its (Gothic) genre onto notions of sexual impropriety,[44] although Wilson seems to deny the poem's homoeroticism and moral ambiguity in casting its heroine as promiscuous and Coleridge himself as potentially adulterous.

The humorous blurring of the line between real life and literary romance may give some credit to Coleridge's "genius" (*BM* 2: 5), but Wilson's tone changes when he turns to a "matter" that he treats in detail despite or perhaps because of its "personal and private nature" (*BM* 2: 14). In heightened language, Wilson announces that Coleridge "has, in this Work, accused Mr Jeffrey of meanness—hypocrisy—falsehood—and breach of hospitality. That gentleman is able to defend himself—and his defence is no business of ours" (*BM* 2: 14). The latter claim is a little misleading, given that Wilson proceeds to reproduce details, not just from Coleridge's footnote about Jeffrey, but from Jeffrey's footnote about Coleridge. Wilson insists that "instead of humbling his Adversary, [Coleridge] has heaped upon his own head the ashes of disgrace—and with his own blundering hands, so stained his character as a man of honour and high principles, that the mark can never be effaced" (*BM* 2: 14). The matter is not of course so cut and dried, since as Henry Crabb Robinson's comments on Jeffrey suggest, the "stain" may not be restricted to a single "character": no one comes out of this looking good.

Wilson continues in forceful language:

---

[44] Karen Swann, "Literary Gentlemen and Lovely Ladies: The Debate on the Character of *Christabel*," *ELH* 52 (1985): 394–418.

> All the most offensive attacks on the writings of Wordsworth and Southey had been made by Mr Jeffrey before his visit to Keswick. Yet does Coleridge receive him with open arms, according to his own account—listen, well-pleased, to all his compliments—talk to him for hours on his Literary Projects—dine with him as his guest at an Inn—tell him that he knew Mr Wordsworth would be most happy to see him—and in all respects behave to him with a politeness bordering on servility. And after all this, merely because his own vile verses were crumpled up like so much waste paper, by the grasp of a powerful hand in the Edinburgh Review, he accuses Mr Jeffrey of abusing hospitality which he never received, and forgets, that instead of being the Host, he himself was the smiling and obsequious Guest of the man he pretends to have despised. (*BM* 2: 14)

The details about dining at the inn and spending "hours" in conversation are clearly taken from Jeffrey's version of the encounter, not Coleridge's; the reference to Wordsworth being "happy" to meet Jeffrey seems to be pure embellishment, unless Wilson, as a former resident of the Lake District, has access to private information. Yet in casting scorn on Coleridge's "open arms" and "smiling" demeanor, Wilson gives the impression that he is relying on the poet's "own account," even as he extrapolates from Jeffrey's version of events in the *Edinburgh*.

With no irony or self-consciousness about the triviality of the incident, Wilson in his one-sided narrative assembles every possible detail that can add to Coleridge's discredit. The reviewer goes on to claim that Coleridge's conduct rebounds upon himself: "With all this miserable forgetfulness of dignity and self-respect, he mounts the high horse, from which he instantly is tumbled into the dirt; and in his angry ravings collects together all the foul trash of literary gossip to fling at his adversary, but which is blown stifling back upon himself with odium and infamy" (*BM* 2: 14). Wilson here attempts to occlude Jeffrey's role in perpetuating the quarrel, not to mention his own participation in the dissemination of the "foul trash of literary gossip." In contrast with the transcendentalizing and Gothicizing touches in this review, "literary gossip" here is perfectly material and earthly. Yet within the pages of *Blackwood's*, the Coleridge–Jeffrey feud would soon afterwards acquire a more imaginative and tolerant slant.

True to the dialogistic ethos of *Blackwood's*, a humorless letter signed "J.S." appeared in the December 1817 number of the *Magazine*, objecting to its review of the *Biographia* and offering a disapproving reference to its treatment of the Coleridge–Jeffrey feud. Claiming to be motivated by "a hate to every thing which appears personal," the otherwise anonymous author accuses the reviewer of "neglect[ing] the work for the purpose of vilifying the man" (*BM* 2: 287). Momentarily losing the moral high ground, "J.S." himself indulges in a little vilification: "That Coleridge has, in gone by days, vilified Mr. Southey, is no excuse for Mr. Jeffrey's conduct to Mr. C.; and till a better defence has been made for him than you have volunteered, I must think him, what his writings prove him to be, an ungenerous and not one of the best hearted men" (*BM* 2: 287). This statement assumes that readers would be inclined to take Jeffrey's "conduct" seriously (although if, as Alan Lang Strout suggested at one point,[45] the writer was Wilson himself, the whole letter would possess an ironic edge). It thus stands in stark contrast to the final, more extensive treatment of the controversy in *Blackwood's*.

Timothy Tickler's Letter to Jeffrey

In the *Blackwood's* review of the *Biographia*, the *Magazine's* antagonistic attitude to Jeffrey and the *Edinburgh Review* is overpowered by its hostility to Coleridge.[46] The attitude to Jeffrey in the letter from "J.S." is more typical of *Blackwood's*. When *Blackwood's* revived the controversy between Coleridge and Jeffrey in its April 1818 number, however, it treated Jeffrey more indulgently while also attacking him for his treatment of Coleridge. *Blackwood's* addressed at some length the storm in a coffee cup that is the Coleridge–Jeffrey feud in a letter to "Francis Jeffrey, Esq.," the third in an ongoing series of "Letters of Timothy Tickler to Various Literary Characters." The subheading "literary character" captures Jeffrey's dual role as a man of letters and a personage in someone else's work of fiction. Timothy Tickler was one of the many pseudonyms employed (and often shared) by the contributors to *Blackwood's*; Wilson may have written or collaborated upon this letter.

David Higgins has discussed the effect of the way in which *Blackwood's* brought the objects of its attack into "the world of semi-fictional characters that supposedly wrote the magazine," arguing that "although this is an act of coercion, it is also an elaborate joke that seemed to sunder *Blackwood's* victims from their real physical existence, and turn them into (sometimes affectionate) caricatures." Higgins points out that despite the severity of the Cockney School attacks, "by the early 1820s Hunt was treated with a familiar raillery which was similar to the way in which the magazine dealt with 'friends' such as Hogg and De Quincey in the *Noctes Ambrosianae*."[47] The Timothy Tickler letter to Jeffrey takes a similar stance of "familiar raillery," making Jeffrey himself into a semi-fictional character who strangely and amusingly seems to inhabit the Cockney world of aesthetic and social pretentiousness that "Z" was in the process of partly exposing and partly inventing in his ongoing attacks on Hunt and his circle. In this jeu d'esprit, Coleridge's attack on Jeffrey in the *Biographia* is almost entirely left behind as the focus shifts to a humorous rewriting of Jeffrey's self-defense in the *Edinburgh* that threatens to cancel out Tickler's criticisms of Jeffrey.

---

[45] Alan Lang Strout, "Samuel Taylor Coleridge and John Wilson of *Blackwood's Magazine*," *PMLA* 48 (1933): 100–128 (106). However, Strout subsequently conjectured that "J.S." was John Smyth. See Alan Lang Strout, *A Bibliography of Articles in* Blackwood's Magazine *1817–1825* (Lubbock, Texas: Texas Technological College, 1959), 33.

[46] On the ambivalence of *Blackwood's* to the *Edinburgh* and Jeffrey in particular, see Christie, *The Edinburgh Review*, 163.

[47] Higgins, *Romantic Genius and the Literary Magazine*, 57–8.

Familiarly addressed to "My dear Jeffrey," the Timothy Tickler letter fluctuates in tone, beginning with homophobic innuendo with a reference to "that slavish herd of boy-admirers that dog your heels" (*BM* 3: 75) and ending with the pretence that "Tickler" and Jeffrey were more intimate friends in the past (this was actually true of Jeffrey and Wilson). The first paragraph contains relatively harsh criticism of Jeffrey, whom it bluntly describes as "not a great man" (*BM* 3: 76). Part of the purpose of this assessment, however, seems to be to emphasize by contrast the "very trifling and ludicrous" incident to which most of the letter is devoted (*BM* 3: 76). Tickler admits that, given the length of time that has elapsed since it appeared, it "may not be quite fair" to revert to the "note" in which Jeffrey made himself "ridiculous" ("which," he claims implausibly, "by some accident, I saw yesterday for the first time" [*BM* 3: 76])—but of course he does so anyway.

Like the *British Critic* reviewer, this writer leaps on the opportunity to bring down to earth the supposedly oracular editor of the *Edinburgh*, but besides having a keener sense of the "ridiculous," he is more skillful in seizing on demystifying details. Tickler leads into the topic with the rhetorical question, "Who ever thought they would live to see the day, when the Editor of the Edinburgh Review would publish in that work a bulletin of his tea-drinking at Keswick?" (*BM* 3: 76). The mention of "tea-drinking" immediately associates Jeffrey with members of the Cockney School of Poetry, who were repeatedly mocked by *Blackwood's* for effeminate tea-time socializing.[48] Tickler warms to his theme:

> I forget—it was not tea, but coffee. What an image! The stern destroyer of systems, political, poetical, metaphysical—having "coffee handed to him" by Robert Southey's servant-lass! He sips it—while the destined Laureate stands aloof "with cold civility," and the "Ancient Mariner" "holds him with his glittering eye," so that he can with the utmost difficulty snatch a moment's intermission for a mouthful of buttered toast! In this sublimated state of happiness, "an hour or two" passes away,—and then Mr Francis Jeffrey returns to "the Inn," the name of which, my dear friend, you ought to have given, that in future times pilgrims might repair to the spot, and worship the chair on which you took your evening nap, haply beneath the wings of the "Spread Eagle," or the mane of the "Red Lion," or the bushy locks of the "Queen's Head." What is the use of a bulletin at all, unless it be comprehensive and complete? The importance of the subject would have justified the most lengthened detail, for what was the meeting of Kings and Emperors on "that famous Raft," "to the celestial colloquy sublime," of Reviewer and Bard, in the back parlour of an Inn at Keswick? (*BM* 3: 76)

With a misleading use of quotation marks, Wilson uses and in some cases alters the word choices of Jeffrey's note, here rewriting Jeffrey's "I believe coffee was offered me" (which does not specify whether or not the great man deigned to drink it) and inventing "Robert Southey's servant-lass" to give the impression

---

[48] The first attack on the Cockney School by "Z" (John Gibson Lockhart and perhaps Wilson) had compared Leigh Hunt with a "tea-sipping milliner-girl" (*BM* 2: 40).

that Jeffrey has, besides lowering his dignity in recording the incident, stumbled into a social scene that is beneath him. The "image" recalls the vignette in the first Cockney School attack in which a "man of fashion" is "invited to enter … the gilded drawing room of a little mincing boarding-school mistress" (*BM* 2: 39), except that the phrase "servant-lass" suggests old-fashioned rusticity instead of suburban affectation. Southey by implication cannot afford a manservant. The "mouthful of buttered toast" also evokes the attacks on the Cockneys, who will more than once be described in *Blackwood's* as consumers of toasted muffins, a food that figures their inferior social status.[49]

Coleridge himself, as in the *Blackwood's* attack on the *Biographia*, is conflated with his own poetry, resulting in a blend of the preternatural (his "glittering eye") and the proto-realist (the "buttered toast"). Mock-criticizing Jeffrey for not providing enough details, Wilson himself supplies more, inventing Jeffrey's "evening nap" and the "back parlour" (less expensive than the front, one assumes) to further demystify the *Edinburgh* editor. Wilson scales Jeffrey's allegedly inflated ego down to size with his mock-heroic references to "that famous Raft"—an allusion to a meeting between Napoleon, Tsar Alexander I of Russia, and King Friedrich Wilhelm II of Prussia on a raft on the river Niemen that resulted in the Treaty of Tilsit of 1807—and the "celestial colloquy sublime" between God and Adam in *Paradise Lost* (8: 455). But as in mock-epic, the juxtapositions work two ways, adding weight and dignity to Jeffrey's narrative even in belittling it.

The playfully indulgent attitude to Jeffrey continues in the next paragraph:

> How you passed the night—how many blankets you slept under—and whether the hair mattrass was beneath or above the feather-bed, you have, with that forgetfulness so characteristic of genius, omitted to inform the world. But next day "you walked into the fields with Mr Coleridge," he clad, I presume, in "russet weeds," and you in a natty surtout and Hessians. "His whole conversation was poetry;" and when that light fare was digested, "he did you the honour to dine with you at the Inn." Next morning, you parted to meet no more—or, in your own simple words, "I left Keswick, and have not seen him since." (*BM* 3: 76)

This passage offers more than a shred of sympathy for Jeffrey by insinuating that if Leigh Hunt had been in his place, he would have cheerfully informed his readers of his sleeping arrangements. But the writer continues to associate Jeffrey with the world of the Cockneys by mentioning clothing, another motif in the attacks on the Cockney School. In the first of these, Hunt had been imagined as wanting to wear "yellow breeches and flesh-coloured silk stockings" (*BM* 2: 39). Again, Jeffrey in his "natty surtout and Hessians" is the fashionable visitor from the city, while Coleridge wanders in from the realm of romance (the phrase "russet weeds" alludes to Scott's *Lady of the Lake*).

---

[49] See, for example, [John Gibson Lockhart], "On the Cockney School of Poetry, No. VI," *BM* 6: 70–76. This article includes the line, "The affable arch-angel, supping with Adam and Eve in Paradise, is nothing to the Father of Gods and Men eating muffins with the Editor of a Sunday newspaper" (72).

Tickler then expresses bafflement about why Jeffrey "publish[ed] this bulletin" (*BM* 3: 76), suggesting that Jeffrey over-reacted:

> Mr Coleridge, it appears, had brought forward some vague and indefinite charges against you, the head and front of which was, that you had handled severely the poems of a certain bard, after you had eaten his beef and drunk his wine; whereas, the truth is, you had only sipp'd his coffee, and perhaps munch'd his muffins. Even if it had been as the "Ancient Mariner" asserted, the world, who seldom take a deep interest in affairs of that kind, would not have thought a whit the worse of you. But you began to think that the fifteen million inhabitants of these kingdoms had their eyes all fixed upon you—and in the silence of the night you heard voices calling on you to vindicate yourself against the Feast of the Poets. The public, who you imagined were thinking only upon you, were then trifling away their time about the more general, though less interesting affairs of Europe, and could not guess what was the meaning of all this talk of coffee, and all the dark and mysterious charges of wickedness and crime connected with the drinking of it. (*BM* 3: 76–7)

This passage realizes Jeffrey's conventionally expressed fears of being thought egotistical for indulging in a little autobiography. Yet, distinguishing between levels of sociality, it also defends Jeffrey from charges of violating hospitality even as it humorously Gothicizes "all this talk of coffee."

The next paragraph, however, switches gears and seriously accuses Jeffrey of being neither "candid" not "manly." Wilson goes to the heart of Jeffrey's equivocation in his note, telling him bluntly, "It is a poor and unworthy get off, to say that CHRISTABEL was reviewed by another person" (*BM* 3: 77). Ignoring the collaborativeness of periodical discourse practiced so effectively by *Blackwood's* itself, this accusation implies that Jeffrey alone is ultimately responsible for the contents of the *Edinburgh*. Wilson uses the occasion to continue *Blackwood's'* ongoing attack on Hazlitt,[50] berating Jeffrey for

> committ[ing] the task [of reviewing *Christabel*] to a savage and truculent jacobin, the very twitching of whose countenance is enough to frighten the boldest muse into hysterics .... [T]his restless demagogue you let loose upon the friend with whom "you walked in the fields about Keswick," "whose whole conversation was poetry," who stood smilingly by, while "coffee was handed to you," and whom, "as he liked to receive compliments," "you were led to gratify with that kind of fare." There seems some little inconsistency of behaviour in first buttering a man all over with flattery, and then getting a raw-boned prize-fighter to belabour him with a hedge-stake. (*BM* 3: 77).

The forceful metaphors of this final sentence decisively cast blame on Jeffrey, certainly no real "friend" of Coleridge's, but at the end of the letter Tickler switches

---

[50] Lockhart had attacked Hazlitt in passing in his "Letter from Z to Mr Leigh Hunt" in *Blackwood's* 2 (January 1818), and would attack him more fully in "Hazlitt Cross-Questioned by Z" in *Blackwood's* 3 (August 1818).

back to a lighter tone, addressing Jeffrey as "My dear fellow" and signing himself "your affectionate friend" (*BM* 3: 77). As in the Cockney School attacks, the milder ridicule has a more complex effect than the outright vituperation because the lively details of social interactions, with their novelistic tinge, give the antagonists of *Blackwood's* a more human and endearing face.

The Timothy Tickler piece represents the last extended contemporary treatment of the quarrel between Coleridge and Jeffrey. The *Blackwood's* writers would continue to be fascinated by both men, but as separate individuals, not combatants. Where the reception of the *Biographia* is concerned, *Blackwood's* trumped the *Edinburgh* in that the topic of the newer journal's hostility—and inconsistency—to Coleridge overpowered public interest in the Coleridge–Jeffrey feud.[51] John Gibson Lockhart in his satirical three-volume book, *Peter's Letters to His Kinsfolk* (1819), recurred to the *Blackwood's* review of the *Biographia* by describing it as inexplicable and by addressing a postscript to Coleridge in the "third" (really the second) edition.[52] John Scott, editor of the *London Magazine*, subsequently lambasted the "Mohock Magazine" for publishing a letter from Coleridge to "Dr. Morris," the pseudonymous author of Lockhart's book that he mistakenly thought Coleridge had not intended for publication.[53] Coleridge's letter refers to "my unfriends, the Edinburgh Reviewers" (*CL* 4: 968) and to his desire to correct reviewers' misleading accounts of "the events of [his] life," smuggling in "PRINCIPLE" as the "humble companion of PERSONALITY" (*CL* 4: 970). On several levels, Coleridge, as we have seen, in the course of the reception of the *Biographia*, as formerly, is thoroughly absorbed into the "age of personality," despite his aspiration to rise above it. His "real character"—to repeat a phrase from *The Friend* (2: 286)—does indeed disappear behind the "silliest" anecdotes, "worthless" details and "insignificant stories" that constitute commodified gossip.

But on another level, as his feud with Jeffrey develops its own momentum, his "character" comes to life in a way that he could not have predicted. When Coleridge described reviewing as a "*game*" that "*makes* being rogues," he could not have foreseen the arrival on the scene of *Blackwood's Magazine* with its more elaborate and inventive "personalities." Nor when Jeffrey and Coleridge proclaimed the importance of responding to personal attacks, could they have foreseen that their feud would be taken so entirely out of their hands and their

---

[51] Nevertheless, as far as Coleridge was concerned, the feud continued. In July 1825 he wrote to Daniel Stuart: "Jeffray [sic], by the most unprovoked and to me wholly unaccountable antipathy to me, not content with abusing what I have published, has openly avowed his determination to '*cut up*' (I use his own phrase) whatever I shall publish" (*CL* 5. 475).

[52] On the placatory function of the book, see Philip Flynn, "Blackwood's *Maga*, Lockhart's *Peter's Letters*, and the Politics of Publishing," *Studies in Romanticism* 45 (2006): 117–31.

[53] According to Erdman, this article precipitated the duel in which John Scott was killed by Lockhart's friend, Jonathan Christie. Erdman, recounting Coleridge's relationship with *Blackwood's*, describes him as a "hired clown" ("Coleridge and the 'Review Business,'" 37).

identities transmuted into fictitious creations. The *Blackwood's* treatment of both these "literary characters" is particularly intriguing because of the way in which it slides at moments between the genres of comedy of manners and supernatural romance. *Blackwood's*, unlike the *British Critic*, does not merely analyze Jeffrey's legalistic deposition in the *Edinburgh* in terms of its etiquette and psychology. Rather, Timothy Tickler makes the *Edinburgh* editor sound like a member of the Cockney School writing an egotistical travelogue about his stay in the Lake District and his visit to a famous poet, an encounter that is given a supernatural tinge with its allusions to Coleridge's and Scott's poetry. Coleridge meanwhile is on one occasion figured as a rakish adventurer taking the heroine and "Other Woman" from *Christabel* into John Murray's bookshop, and on another occasion imagined transfixing his adversary with a ghostly stare at a tea party in the role of his own Ancient Mariner. These fanciful caricatures constitute a different kind of personal attack relying on little or no external information, "elsewhere obtained," and defused of aggression. If they exploit and reduce Jeffrey and Coleridge, they also make them larger than life. They are intensely readerly, involving as they do humorous rewritings of situations arising from the publication of the *Biographia* and its aftermath, but they also temporarily absorb Coleridge and his adversary into the self-contained and self-referential world of *Blackwood's*. The *Blackwood's* treatment of the Coleridge–Jeffrey feud has a touch of what David Erdman calls, describing the *Biographia* itself, "the incandescence produced when 'the esemplastic power' encounters the resistance of personal anecdote."[54] For a moment at least, even as it feeds off the "age of personality," a collective act of the imagination transcends mere gossip.

---

[54] Erdman, "Coleridge and the 'Review Business,'" 42.

Chapter 3
Hunt, Hazlitt, Lady Morgan, and the *Quarterly*: Creative Reprisals

Addressing the editor of the *Quarterly Review* in his vituperative *Letter to William Gifford, Esq.* of 1819, Hazlitt memorably defined him as "the *Government Critic*, a character nicely differing from that of a government spy—the invisible link, that connects literature with the police" (Wu 5: 343). This often-quoted line from the *Letter* nicely encapsulates the perception, if not the reality, of the *Quarterly*'s hegemonic power. In the same brilliant harangue, Hazlitt called Gifford the "head of the literary police" (Wu 5: 361). Echoing this terminology, Peter Manning, in his essay on Charles Lamb's pseudonymous contributions to the *London Magazine*, contends that Lamb's persona Elia "escapes the critical police," in the sense that he breaks free of the "historical circumstances of magazine writing."[1] In this chapter, I will argue that Hazlitt, together with his fellow reformist writers Leigh Hunt and Lady Morgan, can each be seen as granting the *Quarterly* the power to police more effectively, while displaying unique capacities to "escape" the antagonisms of literary warfare and the culture of "personality."

Beginning with its first issue in 1809, the *Quarterly*, the self-appointed bastion of conservative values, had begun to pursue vendettas against various reform-minded poets, essayists, and novelists. Many of its attacks test the blurred boundaries between "personalities," satire, and textual dissection, or what the *Quarterly* called "verbal criticism" (*QR* 18: 331).[2] Keats and Anna Laetitia Barbauld, for example, were both victims of stinging critiques by the *Quarterly*, but these writers did not publicly respond (although Percy Bysshe Shelley—himself the target of fierce attacks by the Tory periodical—replied on Keats's behalf in *Adonais*). Hunt, Hazlitt, and Morgan are three of the best-known writers who tried to fight back. Each of the three retaliated against the *Quarterly* in various venues with limited rhetorical success, their most effective reprisals appearing in their characteristic genres of poetry, prose satire, and prose fiction respectively. This chapter tells the story of how these three writers embrace what Coleridge called the "critical machine" (*BL* 2: 111), and how they can be seen to step outside it. It also shows how in these highly partisan feuds—like the feuds of

---

[1] Peter Manning, "Detaching Lamb's Thoughts," in *Romantic Periodicals and Print Culture*, ed. Kim Wheatley (London: Frank Cass, 2003), 137–46 (145).

[2] Hazlitt, in his 1821 essay "On Criticism," dismisses "*verbal critics*" as insects that "creep, buzz, and fly-blow," found "crawling over the pages of the Quarterly Review!" (Howe 8: 226).

1817 involving the two great quarterlies and those radicals-turned-conservatives Southey and Coleridge—entertainment eventually trumps politics, as reformist and conservative writers work together to surprise, amuse, and intrigue readers of varying political persuasions.

Hunt, Hazlitt, and Morgan tend to allow the terms of their counterattacks to be dictated by the *Quarterly*, at times resorting to mere point-by-point refutations of the Tories' objections to their alleged offences. An analysis of these three feuds will therefore often give the impression that the *Quarterly* was capable of effortlessly containing its political opponents with its anonymous virulent prose. Like other episodes of print persecution in the era, these feuds reveal the difficulties faced by individuals trying to respond to the voice of an impersonal institution. Nevertheless, the three reformist writers all made efforts to circumvent the convention of anonymity, by blaming Gifford in the case of Hunt and Hazlitt, and the *Quarterly* reviewer John Wilson Croker in the case of Morgan, even though these particular reviewers may not have been directly responsible for most of the attacks in question. Hunt, Hazlitt, and Morgan themselves adopted the mask of anonymity on occasion, with mixed results. The *Quarterly* meanwhile, in its repeated verbal assaults on the three writers, displays plenty of energy but relatively few traces of the literariness that we saw in the attacks by other periodicals on Southey, Coleridge, and Jeffrey. Transcendence of the "age of personality" in these feuds is mainly enacted in three lively post-1817 works that they sparked: Hunt's poem satirizing Gifford, *Ultra-Crepidarius*; Hazlitt's masterly *Letter to Gifford*; and Morgan's pro-Irish and partly satirical novel *Florence Macarthy*. However, as in the controversies involving Southey, Coleridge, and Jeffrey, the proliferation of contributions—whether non-literary, semi-literary, or literary—itself takes on a quasi-literary power to branch off in unexpected directions.

Hunt's and Hazlitt's feuds with the *Quarterly* are intertwined, in that the Tory journal frequently lumped them together and they both published retorts to Gifford in Hunt's *Examiner*. The two journalists also quoted and defended each other, and co-authored a book of essays, *The Round Table*, which the *Quarterly* reviewed with predictable hostility. The *Quarterly* conducted its feud with Morgan separately, beginning in its very first number in 1809, but tarred her with the same brush as Hazlitt in classing their writings with the "ravings" of other politically radical "maniacs" (*QR* 26: 107). Hunt and Hazlitt both made sympathetic references to Morgan in their responses to Gifford. Hazlitt, for example, sardonically attributed to its "Editor" the *Quarterly*'s "chivalrous spirit and [its] attacks on Lady Morgan" (Wu 7: 189). In this chapter I will first trace Hunt's extended "war"[3] with Gifford and the *Quarterly* during the former's editorship of the *Examiner*, a feud that has been neglected by critics in comparison with Hunt's vexed relationship with *Blackwood's*. I will then turn to Hazlitt's overlapping feud with the "Government Critic," before discussing Morgan's concurrent and equally fraught battles with Croker and his fellow Tory reviewers.

---

[3] In a letter to the *Morning Chronicle* of October 3, 1818, John Scott mentioned a fact that "must be known to every one in the least acquainted with the literary gossip of the day": Hunt and "the Editor of The Quarterly Review have long been at war" (4).

Hunt and Gifford

Some commentators on the *Blackwood's* attacks on the Cockney School have pointed to their origins in partisanship and class prejudice, seeing the Cockneys (including Hazlitt and Keats) as a political or social threat to the Tory reviewers.[4] Hunt himself claimed in his *Autobiography* (1850) that the "wrath of the Tory critics" that he suffered was motivated purely by political partisanship.[5] Yet as we have already seen, what Coleridge called the *"game"* of reviewing could have multiple causes and outcomes. The extravagant treatment of Hunt—and his Cockney associates such as "pimpled Hazlitt" (*BM* 2: n.p.)—in the early issues of *Blackwood's* may create a misleading impression of these writers' cultural power. The less often discussed exchanges between Hunt, Hazlitt and the *Quarterly* at first sight constitute a more routine instance of Romantic-era literary warfare, a case of business—or politics—as usual.

Gifford and his fellow *Quarterly* reviewers, like the *Blackwood's* writers, repudiate the leader of the Cockney School on political, moral, social *and* aesthetic grounds, deploring his unorthodox treatment of the classics and his equally unorthodox poetic style. Their objections to Hazlitt are also focused on his radical political views and his alleged abuses of the English language. But whereas the *Blackwood's* reviewers betray an investment in Cockneyism that amounts to an act of collaboration,[6] the attacks on Hunt and Hazlitt in the *Quarterly* seem less inventive, relying mainly on the semi-jocular and semi-aggressive sarcasm that was practically the *Quarterly*'s trademark. Many of Hunt's and Hazlitt's contributions to this war of words, which typically accuse the *Quarterly* reviewers and Gifford in particular of narrow-minded partisanship and intellectual mediocrity, tend to

---

[4] See, for example, Marjorie Levinson, *Keats's Life of Allegory: The Origins of a Style* (Oxford: Basil Blackwell, 1988), and Jeffrey Cox, *Poetry and Politics in the Cockney School* (Cambridge: Cambridge University Press, 1998). My article, "The *Blackwood's* Attacks on Leigh Hunt," *Nineteenth-Century Literature* 47 (June 1992): 1–31, emphasized instead the novelistic aspects of the reviewers' rhetoric. Cox stresses that the "new school" led by Hunt predated the attacks on the Cockneys, but an argument can be made that Hunt was locked from the start into opposition with hostile reviewers: Hunt's self-definition as a Cockney poet—as socially and even sexually marginal—cast himself in terms set by the establishment, while the reviewers tended to approach Hunt by way of his own distinctive self-characterizations. See also Elizabeth Jones, "Keats in the Suburbs," *Keats-Shelley Journal* 45 (1996): 23–43, and "Suburb Sinners: Sex and Disease in the Cockney School" in Nicholas Roe, ed., *Leigh Hunt: Life, Poetics, Politics* (London: Routledge, 2003): 78–94. Roe, in *Fiery Heart: The First Life of Leigh Hunt* (London: Pimlico, 2005), sees racial hostility behind the *Blackwood's* attacks on Hunt (251).

[5] *The Autobiography of Leigh Hunt, with Reminiscences of Friends and Contemporaries*, 2 vols (New York: Harper and Brothers, 1850), 2: 17. Further references in parentheses.

[6] *Blackwood's* also conducted a vendetta against Morgan, describing her, for example, as "the least woman in the world" (*BM* 7: 613), "in *person* a spindle-shank'd old body ... and in *mind*, a haggard demoniac" (*BM* 12: 50).

replicate the Tory periodical's acerbic language, as if their writing becomes infected by the *Quarterly*'s own discourse. An examination of the protracted exchanges between Hunt, Hazlitt and Gifford will therefore initially give a sense less of the liveliness of the Cockneys' public presence than of the constraints on their voices. By contrast, Morgan's responses to the *Quarterly*—in which she attempts to combat their misogyny and anti-Irish prejudice—on the surface seem distinctive, in that they offer a rare example of a woman speaking out against gender-based and nationalistic criticism, but I suggest that they are thoroughly generic when compared with Hunt's and Hazlitt's reprisals. Meanwhile, the writers' more self-consciously literary contributions take us into the broader realm of Romanticism that new historicist critics have helped to excavate—one that accommodates Cockney aesthetics, neo-Juvenalian satire, metaphysical disquisition, and regional prose fiction by a female author.

In the chapter entitled "Literary Warfare" in his *Autobiography*, Hunt accused Gifford of "inhumanity" (1: 257), declaring that Gifford was "the only man I ever attacked, respecting whom I have felt no regret" (1: 254). Apparently the antipathy was mutual: Hunt records a face-to-face encounter with Gifford, who stared at him with loathing (1: 257).[7] The vignette raises the question of the role played by private prejudice in the clashes between the *Examiner*, the *Quarterly*, and their editors. Hunt himself brings up this point when he writes, "Readers in these kindlier days of criticism have no conception of the extent to which personal hostility allowed itself to be transported, in the periodicals of those times" (1: 262). This statement suggests the idea of emotions out of control in an era back when print opponents were more likely to meet in person, while also drawing attention to a cultural shift, contrasting the relative decorousness of Victorian reviewing with the brutality of Regency "personalities." But if, as Hunt remarked retrospectively, "Calumny has been out of fashion for some time" (1: 261), the question arises, why did he still hate Gifford long after his enemy's death? Hunt reveals that he had "conceived some disgust against [Gifford] as a man" (1: 254)—strong words from the proponent of a cheery Cockney tolerance.[8] The fact that his feud with Gifford began and ended outside the pages of the *Examiner* and the *Quarterly* dramatizes the possibility of a distance between individuals and the institutions with which

---

[7] Of course, Gifford may have looked at everyone he met with the same nasty facial expression. Martin Aske, in "Critical Disfiguring: The 'Jealous Leer Malign' in Romantic Criticism" in *Questioning Romanticism*, ed. John Beer (Baltimore and London: The Johns Hopkins University Press, 1995): 49–70, argues convincingly that the mutual hatred of Hunt and Gifford is emblematic of a Romantic-era discourse of envy and *ressentiment*, but he does not address the question of why Gifford is the "only man" whom Hunt continues to hate.

[8] Timothy Webb, in "Correcting the Irritability of His Temper: The Evolution of Leigh Hunt's *Autobiography*" in *Romantic Revisions*, ed. Robert Brinkley and Keith Hanley (Cambridge: Cambridge University Press, 1992): 268–90, discusses the discrepancy between Hunt's ethos of "universal tolerance" and the "adversarial asperities of *The Examiner*" (279). Arguing that Hunt's "philosophy of good cheer" degenerates into "quietism" (287–8), Webb shows that Hunt's judgments of others soften in the *Autobiography*, except for his opinion of Gifford.

they tend to be conflated. Yet Hunt's description of his glimpse of his adversary suggests that he only set eyes on him once. His dealings with Gifford suggest the thin dividing line between public and private. The bitter hatred of these foes was multilayered.

Hunt had two particular fixations that surfaced almost every time he addressed the related subjects of Gifford and the *Quarterly*. The first is the fact that he himself was asked in 1809 by John Murray, the publisher, to contribute to the *Quarterly*, when it was just starting up.[9] Hunt refused because his political stance was so remote from that of the Tory periodical, a circumstance that he publicizes presumably to emphasize his own integrity, although his exploitation of the incident may call his independence into doubt. Hunt's other fixation was with what he claims to be the source of his "disgust" with the *Quarterly*'s editor: an attack by Gifford in *The Baviad* (1791) on the poet Mary Robinson, the former mistress of the Prince of Wales.[10] Hunt's defense of Robinson makes an important political point in contrasting his own feminist sympathies with Gifford's verbal mistreatment of women. But, as with his tendency to dwell on Murray's invitation to write for the *Quarterly*, his repeated references to Gifford's insult are problematic.

Hunt's preoccupation with Robinson also raises the familiar question of the effectiveness of reprisals. Hunt prided himself on having "never retaliated" (1: 262) to personal attacks, but he retaliated on other people's behalf (notably P.B. Shelley's) as well as his own, perpetuating the dynamic of attack and counterattack that threatens to degenerate into a monotonous spinning of wheels. Neither the recycling of material nor the act of speaking back in defense are necessarily rhetorical weaknesses per se. In this case, however, one wonders at what point personal revulsion and the desire for revenge become a matter of policy or expediency. As we will see, Hunt's longstanding hatred of Gifford comes to seem less a deep-seated obsession than a set of ritualistic maneuvers to which he habitually returns. His reliance on these maneuvers, like his adoption of the *Quarterly*'s vitriolic language, confirms that he is mostly content to let his skirmishes with Gifford proceed within certain pre-scripted parameters.

Despite his claim about never retaliating, Hunt wrote several poems attacking Gifford, and responded at some length in the *Examiner* to the *Quarterly*'s hostile reviews—but the size of his share of the dialogue did not necessarily enable him

---

[9] Murray's letter to Hunt, apparently a second request, can be found online in the *Quarterly Review* Archive at http://www.rc.umd.edu/reference/qr/correspondence/murray/Murray_to_Leigh_Hunt_3-13-1809.html [accessed July 31, 2012]. A reply by John Hunt is quoted by Samuel Smiles, *A Publisher and his Friends*, 2 vols (London: John Murray, 1891), 1: 154.

[10] Gifford's attack on Mary Robinson was something of a fixation with Hazlitt too; Hazlitt brought it up both in his *Letter to William Gifford* (Wu 5: 355) and in his account of Gifford in *The Spirit of the Age* (Wu 7: 182–3). Like Hunt and other contributors to periodicals, Hazlitt did not hesitate to re-use material. Morgan also referred to the attack in her *Letter to the Reviewers of "Italy"* (Paris: A. and W. Galignani, 1821), 29, n.1. Further references to the *Letter* in parentheses.

to dominate it. As he himself pointed out in his *Autobiography*, Hunt had quoted approvingly from Gifford's 1795 satire *The Maeviad* in his *Critical Essays* of 1807, but he afterwards attacked Gifford, first in verse and then in prose, in his own satirical work *The Feast of the Poets* (1811–15). It is strange that Hunt would turn to satire, given that his new school of poetry would initially define itself against the work of Alexander Pope, and his relative discomfort with the genre may reflect its changing status as much as its alien sensibility. In crossing swords with Gifford, Hunt was attempting to satirize a writer who was one of the foremost satirists of the preceding generation. While, as editor of the *Quarterly*, even Gifford could no longer dispose of his opponents as decisively as he had done in the late 1790s as editor of the government-sponsored *Anti-Jacobin*, he still had plenty of "power," as Steven Jones puts it, "to abuse"[11]—the power of Juvenalian outrage. While Hunt later claimed that "the new satirist had ceased to regard the old one as a 'critical authority'" (1: 254), Gifford's institutional role carried critical authority with it.

Hunt struck back at the *Quarterly* more often than he did at the elusive "Z" of *Blackwood's*, presumably since in this case he had a particular individual to pinpoint, even though that individual had not necessarily written the reviews in question. Hunt assumed that Gifford was to blame—or at least responsible for—not only the *Quarterly*'s attack on Hunt's own *Story of Rimini* (1816) and *Foliage* (1818), but also the *Quarterly*'s attacks on Shelley and Keats, as well as its attacks on Hazlitt. In most of his counterattacks, Hunt appears to let the *Quarterly* reviewers set the terms of debate, perhaps because he saves his time and energy for other battles—a choice which is itself an implicit recognition of the *Quarterly*'s near-impregnable authority and influence.[12] The climax of the feud is represented by *Ultra-Crepidarius*, subtitled "A Satire on William Gifford," a minor masterpiece of Cockney classicism that succeeds in shifting the power dynamic between Hunt and his Tory adversary.

---

[11] Steven E. Jones, *Satire and Romanticism* (New York: St. Martin's Press, 2000), 133. While, as Gary Dyer brings out in *British Satire and the Politics of Style 1789–1832* (Cambridge: Cambridge University Press, 1997), satire was alive and well in the Romantic period, Jones sees the decline of the genre's status in terms of canon formation. See also Jones, ed., *The Satiric Eye: Forms of Satire in the Romantic Period* (New York: Palgrave Macmillan, 2003). Dyer stresses the ingenuity behind reformist writers' mixed—as opposed to neo-Juvenalian—satiric styles, but concedes that "Radical satire is fundamentally reactive" (87).

[12] As with *Blackwood's*, the dialogue between the *Quarterly* reviewers and the leader of the Cockney School was uneven, with the elite reviewers strictly adhering to their convention of anonymous authorship; unlike Jeffrey, who as we have seen on one occasion initialed a reply to an attack on him by Coleridge, Gifford never publicly identified himself as the author of any review in the *Quarterly*. Nor did he respond except in the *Quarterly* to Hunt's attacks on him. Hunt, by contrast, not only published *The Feast of the Poets* and *Ultra-Crepidarius* under his own name but wrote only semi-anonymously when attacking the *Quarterly* in the *Examiner*. This imbalance does not work to Hunt's advantage because it gives the impression that he is more fascinated by Gifford and his periodical than Gifford is by him.

The short earliest version of *The Feast of the Poets*, with its relatively mild attack on Gifford, hints that Hunt and his Tory opponents can speak the same language.[13] *The Feast* brings out some of the continuities between satirical portraiture and the reviewers' "recourse," as a writer in the *Examiner* in 1822 put it, to "the basest personalities" (*E* 733: 33). Its theme of Apollo's selection of genuine poets places the poem's author in the position of critic even while Hunt attempts to set up an opposition between himself as a poet and Gifford as a reviewer, an opposition complicated by Gifford's past career as a writer of satire. Gifford is introduced as a "sour little gentleman" (l. 135) who presents himself as a would-be guest at Apollo's banquet. After a few querulous remarks about "Scotch reviews" (l. 141) and "reformers, and stuff" (l. 142), he has to remind "the God" (l. 5) of his identity: "William Gifford's a name, I think, pretty well known!" (l. 147).

An amused Apollo insists that Gifford is, first and foremost, a reviewer rather than a scholar, translator or poet:

> Ah! now I remember, said Phoebus, ah true
> My thanks to that name are undoubtedly due;
> The rod, that got rid of the Cruscas and Lauras—
> That plague of the butterflies—sav'd me the horrors;
> The Juvenal, too, stops a gap in one's shelf,
> At least in what Dryden has not done himself;
> And there's something, which even distaste must respect
> In the self-taught example, that conquer'd neglect:
> But not to insist on the recommendations
> Of modesty, wit, and a small stock of patience,
> My visit just now is to poets alone,
> And not to small critics, however well known. (ll. 148–59)

Hunt makes the point that "however well known" Gifford may have been as an anti-Jacobin satirist, he is professionally (as well as physically) "small" now that he has dwindled into a mere reviewer. The dismissiveness of the passage is softened by its obtrusive Cockney rhymes ("Lauras"/"horrors") and modified by the references to the success of Gifford's satire on the Della Cruscan poets and to the competence of his translation of Juvenal. Hunt expresses unambiguous "respect" for Gifford's struggle to achieve an education. Yet, at the same time, in holding up the *Quarterly* editor as its only example of that despised race, reviewers, the poem initiates Hunt's career-long tendency to single him out for negative comment and, in doing so, to adopt his opponent's own tone. Although some of the passage offers grudging praise, the line about Gifford lacking wit, modesty and patience has a sarcastic ring not very different from the patronizing style favored by Gifford himself and his fellow *Quarterly* reviewers.

---

[13] The first version, without notes, was published in Hunt's *Reflector* (1811). I quote from an anonymous and probably unauthorized 12-page Boston reprint of 1813, taken from the *Boston Weekly Messenger* of May 21, 1813. Hunt's expanded 1814 edition of the poem included lengthy notes. My prose quotations below are from *The Feast of the Poets* (London: James Cawthorn, 1814), hereafter *FP*.

Hunt's prose discussion of Gifford in the 1814 edition of the *Feast*, for which the verse attack serves as a peg, continues to establish the terms for Hunt's later attacks on Gifford and does so in a style that is not so far from the one Gifford helped to blend for the *Quarterly*: a style described by one reviewer of the *Feast* as a mix of "asperity and personality."[14] Although the note on Gifford is one of the harshest (and longest) in the volume, Hunt's enlarged critique of the Tory editor, while more severe than the passage in verse, is not an *ad hominem* attack in the sense of bringing in biographical information to discredit Gifford (rather the reverse). Nevertheless, Hunt insists that Gifford's intolerance as a writer is inseparable from his nastiness as a person. Hunt begins by expressing "respect" for Gifford's "sense" and "acquired talents," and even contends that Gifford's own account of his "early difficulties" might inspire "regard" (*FP*, 57).[15] "But," continues Hunt (and it is quite a "but"), "a vile, peevish temper ... breaks out in every page of his criticism, and only renders his affected grinning the more obnoxious" (*FP*, 57–8). Worse, in Gifford's "indignation," Hunt finds a class and gender bias: "from a wrathful, personal satirist of vice and folly, he has softened and settled himself into an editor of old dramatists and government reviews, who is only wrathful in speaking of the objectors to princely vices, and only personal upon dead men or respectable ladies" (*FP*, 59). Since Hunt himself was such a well-known objector to princely vices, he clearly sees himself as a target of Gifford's "wrath," even though Gifford has not yet attacked him.

Hunt goes on to denounce Gifford's tendency to ignore what the *Quarterly* calls "the imputed weaknesses of the great" (*FP*, 60) and his disrespectful attitude towards women. Hunt provides a list of examples, extending from Gifford's expressions of slavish admiration for the Prince Regent to his various attacks on female writers. He says sarcastically, "Princes might formerly have kept mistresses; they might also have discarded them; and these discarded mistresses, if they sinned in rhyme, might be denounced accordingly, even to their rheumatism and their crutches;—but no such things are done now" (*FP*, 60). Hunt explains the reference to rheumatism and crutches in a brief footnote: "See a pleasant and manly fling at Mrs. Robinson's 'crutches' in the *Baviad*" (*FP*, 60). The sentence continues with another passing mention of Gifford's attack on Mary Robinson: "there were vices at court formerly—vices in Juvenal's time—vices even in our own time, when bad poets were going and ladies fell lame—but now—talk of no such thing" (*FP*, 60).

The indignant tone of these first references by Hunt to Gifford's "fling" at Robinson would seem to indicate the extent of his private anger on her behalf, but Hunt's allusions to the incident are surprisingly brief considering that it will become central to his critique. It is almost as if on subsequent occasions Hunt retrospectively identifies Gifford's cruelty to Robinson as the main motive behind

---

[14] *British Critic* 1 (May 1814): 550.
[15] In alluding to the Tory writer's early disadvantages, Hunt lessens his attack. But in doing so, Hunt also relies on a premise underlying the reviewers' personal attacks—the assumption that a person's private life is relevant to a judgment of his work.

his treatment of the Tory writer, in order to justify the unusual bitterness of his language. And even this cryptic reference to ladies falling lame carries rhetorical pitfalls. As with Hunt's later defenses of Keats and P.B. Shelley, he can be seen as exploiting the supposed weakness of a victim to gain strength for himself.[16] Hunt uses the Mary Robinson insult to proclaim his own chivalrousness, coming across as the stalwart defender of female dignity, but one could argue that he acquires masculinity not only through contrast with the less than "manly" Gifford but also at the expense of the persecuted woman (who is literally, as well as figuratively, weak—physically incapacitated as well as morally "fallen").

Hunt and the *Quarterly*

The Feast of the Poets provoked a flurry of reviews, but the *Quarterly* did not deign to notice Hunt until he published his major poetic endeavor, *The Story of Rimini*, in 1816. Since Murray, the *Quarterly*'s publisher, had published *The Story of Rimini*, one might have expected the *Quarterly* to treat the poem kindly; the fact that it did not illustrates the less than straightforward relationship in the period between reception, politics, and aesthetic judgment. The review of *Rimini* is attributed to Lady Morgan's arch-enemy Croker, who would go on to "cut up" Keats's *Endymion* (1818). Although in his *Autobiography*, Hunt implied that *The Story of Rimini* was attacked by the *Quarterly* as retribution for the *Feast*, he also asserted that "it would have met with no such hostility, or indeed any hostility at all, if politics had not judged it" (2: 17). Hunt's claim seems overly narrow given the daring experimentation of *Rimini*; in this poem, Hunt goes out of his way to set forth the poetics as well as the values of Cockneyism, deliberately challenging both the Augustan tastes and the conservative ideologies of the reviewers, and in some sense inviting their strictures.

Duly rising to the occasion, Croker anticipates the Cockney School attacks in *Blackwood's*—which would not be launched until the following year—but unlike the *Blackwood's* reviewers, he does not risk getting carried away by his contempt. He expresses blatant class snobbery (Hunt has "the vulgar impatience of a low man" [*QR* 14: 481]), but most of his energy in this carefully written review is devoted to ridiculing the "*principles*" and practice of Hunt's "new theory" (*QR* 14: 484), his "inaccurate, negligent, and harsh versification" and his "ungrammatical, unauthorised, chaotic jargon" (*QR* 14: 477). Although these attacks on Hunt's language can be seen as politically motivated, the reviewer seems to be content to exploit *Rimini* primarily for amusement.[17]

---

[16] Compare Jones, who, in *Satire and Romanticism*, sees the "defenses" of satiric "victims" in "the attackers' terms" as a larger Romantic phenomenon (132). Jones calls Hunt's defense of Robinson in his *Autobiography* "a transparent gesture of sexist chivalry" (133). Hunt also defended Lady Morgan in his later poem *Blue-Stocking Revels; Or, The Feast of the Violets* (1837).

[17] William Keach, in "Cockney Couplets: Keats and the Politics of Style," *Studies in Romanticism* 25 (1986): 182–96, stresses the political dimension of metrical choices but also cautions against the automatic lining up of "politics and form" (191).

Croker's indulgence in game-playing can most clearly be seen in his calculatedly disingenuous opening: as Donald Reiman points out, he "establish[es] the tone by pretending not to know who Hunt is—though he was a national celebrity" (*RR, C* 752). After an initial dismissive reference to Hunt's editorship of the *Examiner* (which the writer loftily refuses to name), one sardonic assertion follows another:

> A considerable part of this poem was written in Newgate, where the author was some time confined, we believe for a libel which appeared in a newspaper, of which he is said to be the conductor. Such an introduction is not calculated to make a very favourable impression. Fortunately, however, we are as little prejudiced as possible on this subject: we have never seen Mr. Hunt's newspaper; we have never heard any particulars of his offence; nor should we have known that he had been imprisoned but for his own confession. We have not, indeed, ever read one line that he has written, and are alike remote from the knowledge of his errors or the influence of his private character. We are to judge him solely from the work now before us. (*QR* 14: 473)

The highly dubious claim that the reviewer has never seen a "line" by Hunt comes across as the prelude to an exercise of self-satisfied wit at the expense of Hunt's "private character."[18] Yet although Hunt described it in 1819 as an expression of "blind fury" (*E* 613: 620), this article is not a personal attack in the sense of exposing details concerning his private life (though the *Quarterly* would soon descend to such a practice in the case of P.B. Shelley). Except for a final jibe about Hunt's "wretched vanity" (*QR* 14: 481), the review mainly mocks Hunt's Cockney style. In this kind of "verbal" criticism, certainly not the sole province of the *Quarterly*, the reviewers parade choice specimens of what they see as Hunt's faulty diction and syntax, italicizing particular infelicities in their quotations for the delectation of their superior readers.

Subsequent issues of the *Quarterly* made passing jabs at "Mr. Examiner Hunt" (*QR* 16: 248) in articles on the evils of the radical press, but the Tory periodical's next sustained attack on Hunt de-emphasized his political role in favor of a display of its typically heavy-handed humor. In its review of *The Round Table*, the collection of essays on which Hunt had collaborated with Hazlitt, the writer—probably John Taylor Coleridge—claims that the book's political messages were what "chiefly excited us to take the trouble of noticing the work" (*QR* 17: 159). Hazlitt's critique of Edmund Burke is dismissed as "loathsome trash" (*QR* 17: 159). Nevertheless, the reviewer, like the *Blackwood's* reviewers soon afterwards, is more interested in belittling Hunt by exploiting his own distinctive self-representations, a strategy that suggests a certain amount of fascination. Mocking the book's depiction of (Cockney) "manners" (*QR* 17: 155) and its "affected, silly, confused, ungrammatical style" (*QR* 17: 159), he refuses to "discriminate between the productions" of Hunt and Hazlitt (*QR* 17: 159), belatedly finding Hunt's share of the collection to be frivolous rather than seditious:

---

[18] For his libel on the Prince Regent, Hunt was not in fact "confined" in Newgate but in Horsemonger Lane Gaol.

> Mr. Hunt sustains the part of the droll or merry fellow in the performance: it is he who entertains us with the account of his getting the night-mare by eating veal-pye, and who invents for that disorder the facetious name of Mnpvtglnau-auww-auww; who takes the trouble to inform us that he dislikes cats; to describe "the skilful spat of the finger nails which he gives his newspaper," and the mode in which he stirs his fire: it is he who devotes ten or twelve pages to the dissertation on "washerwomen," and who repeats, no doubt from faithful memory, the dialogues which pass between Betty and Molly, the maid-servants, when they are first called in the morning, and describes, from actual observation, (or, it may be, experience,) the "conclusive digs in the side" with which Molly is accustomed to dispel the lingering slumbers of her bed-fellow. (*QR* 17: 159)

While the class-based disdain in this passage has a political edge, the reviewer's main concern seems to be his own patronizing distillation of the topics celebrated by Hunt's familiar prose.[19] The reviewer scorns the idea that he and his social equals (the "us" of the passage) could be "entertain[ed]" by the trivialities of day-to-day Cockney living, yet he clearly expects his readers to appreciate the absurdity of these accumulated details, not to mention the sexual innuendo with which he supplements them.

Showing even less distance, the *Quarterly*'s only other full-fledged attack on Hunt during Gifford's lifetime, its review of *Foliage*, reflects the direct influence of the essays on the Cockney School in *Blackwood's* and therefore in some sense represents a road not taken for the *Quarterly*. By mid-1818, when this article appeared, Cockneyism, as something at once self-created by Hunt and elaborated upon by "Z" of *Blackwood's*, had solidified as a cultural phenomenon. In ridiculing the pretensions of Cockney classicism, for example, the author—John Taylor Coleridge—of the *Quarterly*'s attack on *Foliage* seems to take for granted his readers' familiarity with the *Blackwood's* attacks, referring casually to "the Arcadian Hunt" (*QR* 18: 324) and commenting with irony on a translation by Hunt of a passage from the *Iliad* (*QR* 18: 333).[20] J.T. Coleridge's mockery of Hunt's "rural retreat at Hampstead" (*QR* 18: 325) also echoes Z's ridicule of Cockney suburbanism.

Likewise, his gender-inflected slurs on Hunt's class status and sexuality echo Lockhart and Wilson's insults: one of Hunt's poems is "just what might have been expected from a pert, forward boarding-school girl in her seventh or eighth year" (*QR* 18: 332), and Hunt himself "pant[s] with womanish impatience for immediate notoriety" (*QR* 18: 334). Again following the lead of *Blackwood's*, the *Quarterly*

---

[19] Emily Lorraine de Montluzin, in "Killing the Cockneys: *Blackwood's* Weapons of Choice Against Hunt, Hazlitt, and Keats," *Keats-Shelley Journal* 47 (1998): 87–107, points out that "Hunt's own authentic whimsies and ritualized affectations provided enough raw material to satisfy an army of satirists" (89).

[20] *Blackwood's*, in its sixth essay on the Cockney School, a review of *Foliage*, later mocked Hunt's "*love of the fine imagination of the Greeks*" (*BM* 6: 74; reviewer's italics). Nicholas Roe, in *John Keats and the Culture of Dissent* (Oxford: Clarendon Press, 1997), emphasizes the "politically contentious associations of neoclassicism" (69).

reviewer both attempts to diminish Hunt (a man of "a namby-pamby disposition" [*QR* 18: 327]) and aggrandize him as the "author of a dangerous moral tenet" (*QR* 18: 327)—an anti-Christian Epicurean. J.T. Coleridge thus takes Hunt seriously as a moral or political threat, but only momentarily: most of the article implies that the Cockney leader is beneath serious consideration even as it builds up (via a personal attack on P.B. Shelley) to a climax of condemnation: "[Hunt] will live and die unhonoured in his own generation, and, for his own sake it is to be hoped, moulder unknown in those which are to follow" (*QR* 18: 335).

Counterattacks

Hunt, like Hazlitt, blamed Gifford for both the *Round Table* article and the review of *Foliage*. Hazlitt published in the *Examiner* for June 14, 1818 a scathing reply, subsequently expanded into his *Letter to Gifford* (discussed later in this chapter). Two weeks later, as a "specimen of the calumnies" of which he is a victim, Hunt quoted in the *Examiner* a letter from an anonymous "Wellwisher" (Hunt himself?) informing him that the virulence of the *Quarterly* article reflects rumors that Hunt is a predator of women who has fathered "at least one child" by his wife's sister (*E* 548: 411). Hunt ridiculed these charges, commenting that "It might as well be said of him, that he had Mr. GIFFARD's temper [sic], or used his grandmother's shin-bone for a switch" (*E* 548: 411). Regardless of the validity of the accusations, to publish these rumors at all and to stoop to refute them smacks of recklessness.[21]

Although Hunt also responded in the *Examiner* in 1819 to the *Quarterly*'s attack on Shelley, neither Gifford himself nor any other *Quarterly* reviewer responded directly to Hunt. At times, their "war" seemed distinctly one-sided. The *Quarterly* did, however, continue to attack Hunt's fellow reformist writers, reviewing Hazlitt's *Table-Talk* (1821), William Hone's *Apocryphal New Testament* (1821), and Shelley's *Prometheus Unbound* (1820). A series of counterattacks followed in the *Examiner* in January 1822. None of these was by Hunt. But, despite the absence of Hunt's familiar pointing hand signature, they kept alive the feud between the *Examiner*'s former editor and his worst enemy. In the first piece, "The Three Asses.—Wm. Gifford," the writer picks up on a reference in the *Quarterly* to "the sacrifice of Asses," meaning Hone, Hunt, and Hazlitt (*QR* 26: 103). He does not even toy with the idea of ignoring the bait: "As Messrs. Hone, Hunt, and Hazlitt, are fortunately not at all deficient in the means of reply, the writer of this

---

[21] The *Blackwood's* reviewers predictably responded by attacking Hunt for his "tone": "A pleasant subject of merriment, no doubt, it is—though somewhat embittered by the intrusive remembrance of that unsparing castigator of vice, Mr. Gifford, and clouded over by the melancholy breathed from the shin-bone of his own poor old deceased grandmother" (*BM* 3: 455). In the opinion of Lockhart and Wilson, that is to say, Hunt's jibe suggests that the Cockney leader is haunted by the punitive Gifford; whether or not that is the case, the somewhat disconcerting image of a shinbone-wielding Hunt detracts from his retort. On the "triangular relation" between Hunt, his wife, and his sister-in-law, see Roe, *Fiery Heart*, 292.

article has no intention to attempt to do that for them, which they are so much more capable of doing for themselves; yet there are one or two matters he chooses to strike upon, which may chance to throw out a little light upon Mr. Gifford's gloomy endeavour at pleasantry" (*E* 731: 4).

The article makes the first public reference to the fact that Murray had asked Hunt to "bray in the *Quarterly*" (*E* 731: 4), and quotes Hunt's attack on Gifford from the 1814 *Feast*, together with its long accompanying note (complete with reference to Mary Robinson's rheumatism and crutches). Two weeks later, the lead article in the *Examiner* continued the assault at more length, complaining of the "disgraceful perversion of what affects to be a literary Journal into a vehicle of the lowest passion and personal abuse" and mentioning that "it was only [Hunt's] own squeamishness which prevented him from becoming one of the learned band of Thebans at his own price" (*E* 733: 34). Hunt's refusal to sell himself to the *Quarterly* is again proclaimed as if it automatically places him in an unassailable position.

While Hunt continued to defend P.B. Shelley in the *Examiner*, Hunt himself was by this time in Italy preparing to collaborate on the *Liberal* with Shelley and Byron; Shelley, as is well known, drowned before beginning work on the new periodical. The short-lived *Liberal* can be seen as an attempt to forge a reformist counterblast to the *Quarterly* on its own ground, that of the upmarket quarterly periodical—albeit an explicitly literary one—rather than the *Examiner*'s weekly newspaper format.[22] To the extent that the enterprise was a failure, it confirms Hunt's difficulty in challenging Gifford, although the amount of hostile publicity provoked by the first number of the *Liberal* in particular could be seen as an achievement in itself. However, that outcry had more to do with the reception of Byron, who was seen as tainted by his association with the Cockney School; when the reviewers defended Byron at Hunt's expense, their strictures against Hunt tended to run along the lines already laid down by the *Blackwood's* writers.

One of the attacks on Hunt was in *The Illiberal! Verse and Prose from the North!!*, a late 1822 pamphlet. (The Preface to the first volume of the *Liberal* had sneered at "the Illiberals."[23]) This lively satirical prose work has been attributed to Gifford.[24] If it is true, the content of *The Illiberal!* would suggest that Gifford's attitude to Hunt was becoming increasingly influenced by the *Blackwood's*

---

[22] Roe, in *John Keats*, quotes a letter from Charles Ollier to William Blackwood referring to the projected *Liberal* as "the neutralizer of the Quarterly Review" (274). In his *Lord Byron and Some of his Contemporaries* (London: Henry Colburn, 1828), Hunt claims that for Byron the rivalry was more commercial than ideological: Byron had hoped for "Edinburgh and Quarterly returns" (51).

[23] *The Liberal: Verse and Prose from the South* 1 (1822): ix. On *The Liberal*, see Daisy Hay, "Liberals, *Liberales* and *The Liberal*: a reassessment," *European Romantic Review* 19.4 (2008): 307–20.

[24] See, for example, William H. Marshall, *Byron, Shelley, Hunt, and "The Liberal"* (Philadelphia: University of Pennsylvania, 1960), 120. Quotations from the *Illiberal!* are taken from Marshall.

campaign against the Cockney School, torn between the impulse to condemn Hunt and the impulse to milk humor from his dilettantish self-characterizations. The text consists of a brief play set in Pisa and acted out by Mr. H—T, "Versifier" (219) and his collaborator the lofty Lord B—N, who derides him as "that damn'd Sonnetteer" (220). Lord B—N dreams about the ghost of "SHELLY" [sic] and later receives a letter from him in hell advising him to repent for his irreligion.

The *Illiberal!* tells what will become an entrenched story of the doomed collaboration, a story that—in Thomas Medwin's *Conversations of Lord Byron* (1824), for example—will always reflect badly on Hunt and his family. Hunt's children appear in the play as "THE LITTLE AITCHES," who have been "Imported from the Land of Cockney, as Assistant Scribblers to the Liberal" (219). The author plays the reviewers' game of pretending that Hunt's poems were actually written by his children. The *Quarterly*'s review of *Foliage* had already initiated this jest by suggesting that some lines in that volume had been "dictated" by Hunt's son "master Dick" (*QR* 18: 332). In January 1824, *Blackwood's* would follow suit, first by joking that *Ultra-Crepidarius* was written by Dick's older brother John and second by insisting that it was in fact written by Hunt's (non-existent) 96-year-old grandfather. Yet interestingly, the *Illiberal!* does depict "Lord B." as ambivalent towards "Mr. H.": the former declares that "I'll no more be badgered with partnerships" (221), but is later described as "leaning on the Arm of Mr. H." (223) while he confides to him the contents of his vision. Compared with the monster of vulgarity in the *Blackwood's* attacks, "Mr. H—T" comes across as a relatively dignified figure who tries to reassure his troubled aristocratic colleague; where the reception of the *Liberal* was concerned, its detractors had bigger fish to fry than Hunt.

Hunt probably neither saw the *Illiberal!* nor suspected its author to be Gifford. That Gifford was not far from his thoughts during his stay in Italy, however, is confirmed by a satirical poem that he published anonymously in the third volume of the *Liberal*, "To a Spider Running Across a Room" (1823). The heightened animosity of this piece may be accounted for by the generally outraged Tory response to the *Liberal* rather than by any fresh grudge against Gifford. (The *Quarterly* did not review the *Liberal*.) The speaker of the poem hesitates whether or not to kill a disgusting insect, pointing out that "The vagrant never injured me or mine, / Wrote no critiques, stabb'd at no heart divine" (*Liberal* 3: 178)—presumably a reference to the *Quarterly*'s attacks on Shelley or, possibly, Keats. He contrasts the relatively harmless spider with Southey and other venomous reviewers, including "the brisk crowers in Scotch magazines." Since they are lower than the "vermin" and he has "spared" them (*Liberal* 3: 178–9), why should he smash the spider? One passage of the poem applies the same argument to a "dog" that is clearly Gifford:

> Have I, these five years, spared the dog a stick,
> Cut for his special use, and reasonably thick,
> Now, because prose had fell'd him just before;
> Then, to oblige the very heart he tore;

> Then, from conniving to suppose him human,
> Two-legged, and one that had a serving-woman;
> Then, because some one saw him in a shiver,
> Which shewed, if not a heart, he had a liver;
> And then, because they said the dog was dying,
> His very symptoms being given to lying? (*Liberal* 3: 179)

The "stick" withheld for "five years" refers to *Ultra-Crepidarius*, which Hunt would eventually publish later the same year. The "prose" which had "fell'd" Gifford must be Hazlitt's *Letter*, although the idea that its effect on Gifford was decisive may be illusory. The "very heart he tore" belongs of course to Shelley, figured as more forgiving than the speaker, who can only "conniv[e] to suppose [Gifford] human." The "serving-woman" (Ann Davies) is a servant to whom Gifford had addressed several poems, one of which Hunt admired. The speaker appears to be trying to claim credit for his withholding of the "stick," but the move in which he blames Gifford for the misleading state of his health does not exactly strengthen this attacker's ethos. The end-stopped couplets of this poem, so much more obtrusively derivative than the jaunty anapestic meter of *The Feast of the Poets* (and *Ultra-Crepidarius*) are presumably an attempt by Hunt to give himself a Popean weight and authority. *Ultra-Crepidarius* will redouble this effort by explicitly invoking Pope's *Dunciad*. In the case of "To a Spider" the attempt backfires: the poem's emphasis on the alternative, more ethical, response of refusing to be drawn into an exchange of insults weakens the force of its invective.

Ultra-Crepidarius

Ultra-Crepidarius, published towards the end of 1823, on one level merely perpetuates the animus behind the "Spider" poem, but it also marks Hunt's breaking away from what he called, in a letter to Percy and Mary Shelley, "old rusty resentments."[25] This longer poem offers an astonishing mix of violence and fancifulness, Huntian cheer, and *Quarterly*-like asperity. In this text, Hunt confronts Gifford by flaunting the Cockneyism that the Tory reviewers themselves had helped to harden into easy recognizability. The Cockneyism can be seen both in the subject matter of the poem, its ostentatiously suburbanized and eroticized treatment of classical mythology, and in its style: loose rhyming couplets, a chatty fast-moving meter, and the eye-openingly informal vocabulary for which Hunt had made himself notorious. Hunt had drafted *Ultra-Crepidarius* in 1818 in response to the *Quarterly*'s attack on *Foliage* but had refrained from publishing it then, because, he explains in the Preface, he is "deficient" as a "'hater.'"[26] Hunt finally

---

[25] Kenneth Neill Cameron, Donald H. Reiman and Doucet Devin Fischer, eds, *Shelley and His Circle*, 10 vols, ongoing (Cambridge, MA: Harvard University Press, 1961–70 and 1973–2002), 6: 740.

[26] Hunt, *Ultra-Crepidarius: A Satire on William Gifford* (London: John Hunt, 1823), iii. Further references in parentheses.

decided to publish it while working on the *Liberal*, because, stuck in Italy, he hoped it would make money (though the poem did not sell well).[27] Hunt no doubt hoped that the belated appearance of his satire would give the impression that he had finally been stung into reluctant reprisal.[28] However, since by 1823 most readers would probably have forgotten the attack on *Foliage*, *Ultra-Crepidarius* risks coming across as an unprovoked attack, although as we have seen, there were more recent attacks by the *Quarterly* on writers associated with Hunt to which this could be seen as a reply. As if in reaction against his alleged previous unwillingness to trade blows with Gifford, Hunt published with the poem extracts from Hazlitt's *Letter to Gifford*, in an apparent attempt to bolster his verse satire with Hazlitt's vitriolic prose.

Ultra-Crepidarius falls into two distinct halves, a Cockneyfied elaboration of Greek myth followed by an outburst of Juvenalian railing. The title of the poem (not explained by Hunt) plays on the fact that Gifford had been in his youth an apprentice to a shoemaker. The label "ultra-crepidarius" ridicules the Tory editor for constituting the essence of a shoemaker—the poem's premise is that Gifford is as lowly as the "soul of a shoe" (l. 188)—while mocking him for presuming to look higher than a shoe.[29]

Anticipating the relatively uncompelling second half of the poem, Hunt's Preface to *Ultra-Crepidarius*, written in 1823, proceeds across familiar terrain. The Preface attacks Gifford's "ill temper," "malignity" and "mediocre pretensions" (iii)—the same charges that he had originally made in the note on Gifford in the 1814 *Feast of the Poets*. Hunt goes on to give an account of his relationship with his enemy, and this, too, runs along predictable lines:

> It is said I attacked him first. It is not true. He attacked a woman. He struck, in her latter days, at the *crutches* of poor Mary Robinson—a human being, who was twenty times as good as himself, and whose very lameness (that last melancholy contradiction to qualities of heart and person which he might well envy) was owing to a spirit of active kindness which he never possessed. The blow was bound to make every manly cheek tingle; and I held up the little servile phenomenon in the "Feast of the Poets." For this, and *for attacking powerful Princes instead of their discarded Mistresses*, he has never forgiven me. My first notice of him was in his praise; to which, if I mistake not, I owe the importunate requests which Mr. Murray made me to write in the Quarterly Review. (iii–iv)

---

[27] According to Ann Blainey, *Immortal Boy: A Portrait of Leigh Hunt* (New York: St. Martin's Press, 1985), Hunt immediately "regretted" publishing the poem (139).

[28] One anonymous critic, commenting on *Ultra-Crepidarius* over two years later, did view the poem in this light. See "Poetry and Poets. No. VII: Hunt and Gifford," *The Nic-Nac* 4 (January 14, 1826): 12–14.

[29] Hazlitt referred to Gifford twice in his *Letter* as "an Ultra-Crepidarian critic" (Wu 5: 346, 368); he also used the phrase in his "Reply to 'Z'" (Howe 9: 9). Howe hypothesizes that the adjective was invented by Lamb (Howe 9: 251). Dyer explains the term in *British Satire*, 86.

Here we find the standard reference to Mary Robinson's lameness (also mentioned in the poem itself); as before, Hunt tries to masculinize himself at Gifford's expense (Hunt is the one with the "manly cheek"), but this move is also made at the expense of the "poor" long-dead woman herself.

Hunt's mention of Murray similarly rebounds somewhat on the writer. The idea that Hunt's initial praise of Gifford caused Murray to invite Hunt to contribute to the Tory periodical relies on a questionable reading of events. While priding himself on his own political staunchness, Hunt seems to relish the compliment of having been asked to write for the *Quarterly* (Murray may have repeated his invitation, but were his "requests" really "importunate"?), an attitude that detracts somewhat from his disdain for its views. Hunt concludes the Preface by offering a "word" (v) on Gifford's humble beginnings: Hunt asserts that Gifford's lower class background merely intensifies his repugnancy for the Tory editor's sycophantic attitude towards the royalty and the aristocracy. He explicitly denies (at suspiciously defensive length) that he looks down on Gifford because of his former class status. The claim is a little problematic, however, because of the ambiguity in the poem, signaled by the title, over whether Gifford is being attacked for looking too (socially) high as well as being so (morally) low.

In contrast with the outworn protestations of the Preface, the opening lines of the poem spill over with life and energy:

> 'Tis now about fifty or sixty years since,
> (The date of a charming old boy of a Prince)
> Since the feather'd god Mercury happen'd to lose
> A thing no less precious than one of his shoes. (ll. 1–4)

The first half of the poem defiantly embraces the excesses of Cockneyism as established by Hunt and some of his followers, and reified by "Z" and other hostile reviewers, including those in the *Quarterly*. Hunt brazenly presents his readers with an insistently irreverent rewriting and updating of Greek myth, a technique encapsulated by the emphasis on both divine and human footwear. This opening immediately pulls the god Mercury down to earth by locating him firmly in a particular historical context—the beginning of the reign of George III. The story begins with Mercury lounging around in bed with Venus and complaining about having lost one of his winged shoes. It turns out that Venus, sneakily planning to get a pair made for herself, has sent the shoe away to be copied—its earthly destination being Ashburton, a town in Devonshire, the birthplace, as it happens, of William Gifford. Venus accompanies Mercury to Ashburton; the arrival of the celestial lovers makes its inhabitants more affectionate, all except for "one Shoe" (l. 86) that is not Mercury's lost sandal but a grouchy item of footwear "deaf and blind to all beautiful things" (l. 110). Continuing the juxtaposition of the heavenly and the earthly, an elaborate account of the wonders of Mercury's feathered sandals contrasts with a reference to the shoe that is Gifford, described as "screaming weak like a leather-toed bat" (l. 137).

In creating a tale centering on the post-coital quest for a missing shoe, Hunt goes out of his way to accept his assigned role as a spoiler of the classics.

Cockney poetry usually has a self-parodic element, and in this poem the self-parody is positively gleeful. Hunt clearly takes pleasure in magnifying the coy eroticism and disconcertingly domestic treatment of the classics that had called down the ire of conservative reviewers in their responses to *The Story of Rimini* and *Foliage*. Hunt's divine protagonists are almost jarringly humanized:

> "I wonder," said Mercury,—putting his head
> One rosy-fac'd morning from Venus's bed,—
> "I wonder, my dear Cytherea,—don't you?—
> What can have become of that rogue of a shoe." (ll. 15–18)

These lines exemplify Hunt's breezy, self-mocking playfulness. Their cheerful rhythm and cheekily prosaic diction lend this statement of the story's premise an air of gusto that is intensified by their seemingly deliberately clumsy attempt at erotic titillation.[30]

In presenting his prettified and suburbanized Greek gods, Hunt specializes in literalistic details:

> [T]he God put a leg out of bed,
> And summon'd his winged cap on to his head;
> And the widow in question flew smack round his foot,
> And up he was going to end his pursuit,
> When Venus said softly (so softly, that he
> Turn'd about on his elbow)—"What! go without me?" (ll. 37–42)

Quite apart from the emphasis on Mercury's body and the glaring colloquialism of Venus's snippet of speech, the reference to a shoe as a "widow" comes across as humorously bizarre. Setting out for Ashburton (not the most glamorous destination, needless to say), Mercury and Venus "chalk'd out their journey, got up, took their nectar" (l. 66)—a substitute for a morning cup of tea. Hunt's own enjoyment and his command over the narrative come out in a lively section of dialogue between the "amused" god and goddess (l. 116) and the bad-tempered shoe who does not know their identities: "'Here,'" says Venus, "'come kiss my foot, as a proof we agree:' / But the Shoe huff'd,—as who should say, 'Don't talk to me'" (ll. 94–5).

Hunt also takes evident pleasure in exhibiting the vagaries of his self-consciously informal style. Croker's review of *Rimini* had italicized certain rhyme words in his quotations as if to ridicule their feebleness (*"upon it"* and *"bonnet,"* for example [*QR* 14: 475]), and the *Blackwood's* attacks had followed suit. In *Ultra-Crepidarius*, Hunt plays around with rhymes involving proper names in a manner that hints at a continuity between his satire and Byron's: "please a"/"Eloisa" (ll. 43–4), "flurry"/"Murray" (ll. 213–4), and "fifer'd"/"Gifford" (ll. 287–8). Other rhymes proclaim their looseness rather than their cleverness: "qualities"/"small it is" (ll. 90–91); "lady"/"'Hey-day!'" (ll. 124–5); "penchants"/"ancients" (ll. 203–4).

---

[30] Because of the loss of his "fair widow'd feather" (l. 36), Mercury has been in bed with his paramour for "a whole week" (l. 23).

As mentioned previously, Croker had also attacked Hunt for his awkward versification. In *Ultra-Crepidarius*, as in earlier poems, Hunt is far from being a slave to the demands of meter. Both the rhyme and the rhythm of the following couplet, referring to the arrival of Mercury's shoe at Gifford's birthplace, draw attention to themselves: "Till it came to Ashburton, where something so odd / Seem'd to strike it, it could not help saying, 'My God!'" (ll. 57–8). These two lines read like a self-reflexive comment on the oddness of the poem. In addition, certain word choices simply ask to be singled out for rebuke by the reviewers: for example, Mercury is described as traveling "with such fine overlooking of face" (l. 72). The phrase recalls a line from *Rimini* that irked at least one reviewer: "*So lightsomely dropt in his lordly back*" (*RR, C* 57). The Tory *British Critic* predictably disparaged the notion of "a fine overlooking of face," referring to it as "an expression which we leave to the interpretation of our readers, suggesting in the way of conjecture that it may mean that he neglected to wash it."[31] *Ultra-Crepidarius* would appear to invite exactly this kind of patronizing dismissiveness, and to revel in it.

If the first half of the poem offers a blatant Cockneyism that refuses to be squelched by the reviewers' disapproval and indeed seems to welcome it, however, the second half aspires to a Juvenalian outrage at odds with Huntian playfulness. While some satires may be all the more effective for their mix of styles, Hunt's attempt to shift tactics half way through the poem and treat Gifford with his own Juvenalian medicine seems misguided. Except that it has more pretensions to satiric vigor, the harangue that Hunt puts into the mouth of Mercury is too much of a piece with his previous attacks on the editor of the *Quarterly*, reiterating his usual charges. In this part of the poem, the god curses the offensive shoe by announcing its transformation into the obsequious, woman-hating editor of a certain prestigious quarterly reviewing periodical. Mercury tells the "cross-grained" shoe (l. 118) that after its metamorphosis it will be "human" but not "a man" (l. 155); it will be petty, sycophantic, abusive and lacking in wit; and it will have a "great horror of lowness, because it is low" (l. 192). The final fling of Mercury's speech is, all too predictably, an allusion to Gifford's attack on Mary Robinson: "But meet with a Prince's old mistress discarded, / And then let the world see how vice is rewarded" (ll. 275–6).

The invective has some energy, and the attempt to imitate the great eighteenth-century satirist is not wholly unsuccessful. In contrast with his usual verbosity, Hunt in places tries to mimic the pithiness of Pope's description of Sporus in the "Epistle to Dr. Arbuthnot": Gifford will be "A thing made for dirty ways, hollow at heart" (l. 159). He also attacks the *Quarterly* in some unusually self-contained couplets that—despite the use of anapestic rather than iambic meter—approach the trenchancy of some of Pope's attacks on bad writers in the *Dunciad*:

> Misquote, and misplace, and mislead, and misstate,
> Misapply, misinterpret, misreckon, misdate,
> Misinform, misconjecture, misargue; in short,
> Miss all that is good, that ye miss not the Court. (ll. 231–4)

---

[31] *British Critic*, Second Series 21 (June 1824): 651.

Ultimately, however, Hunt comes across as an improbable follower in Pope's footsteps. His numerous allusions to the *Dunciad* only serve to call attention to the degeneration of Juvenalian satire in the Romantic era. The climax of Mercury's speech is the prophecy that Pope's dunces will be reincarnated in Gifford:

> And finally, thou, my old soul of the tritical,
> Noting, translating, high slavish, hot critical,
> Quarterly-scutcheon'd, great heir to each dunce,
> Be Tibbald, Cook, Arnall, and Dennis at once. (ll. 263–6)

Identifying Pope's targets in a note (p. 24), Hunt gives the impression that Pope has successfully killed off these dunces in the process of immortalizing his own name. That Hunt aspires to dispose of Gifford as efficiently while securing for his poem a fame as lasting as Pope's is suggested by his reference to Mercury's diatribe as "words, that shall die on no shelf" (l. 143), a claim perhaps justifiably ridiculed by hostile reviewers. Leigh Hunt is no Alexander Pope: all he can do is allude to Pope. Hunt cannot have it both ways: delight in self-debasement through taking his Cockney idiosyncrasies to an extreme *and* at the same time lay claim to a satiric authority that would enable him to crush Gifford.

The Reception of *Ultra-Crepidarius*

The tension in the poem between outworn hostilities and a fresher, less constraining aesthetic (both of which might have had more impact if the poem had been published the year it was written) is reflected in the few reviews of *Ultra-Crepidarius*. The ones in the (predictably pro-Hunt) *Literary Examiner* and the (predictably anti-Hunt) *British Critic* both merely feed into the familiar power dynamic, whereas the extremely hostile review in *Blackwood's* registers the unsettling potential of Hunt's Cockneyism. The review in the *Literary Examiner* offers two possible justifications for "an elaborate expenditure of satire on a particular individual": first, "absolute self-defence," and second, the "chastisement" of "a public nuisance."[32] The writer argues that Hunt's attack on Gifford is justified on both grounds, finding in Gifford's treatment of Hunt "malignant insinuation, envenomed slander, and knowingly false and rancorous imputation" (369). He then goes on to accuse the *Quarterly* (with which he conflates the "wretched-tempered" Gifford) of partisanship (a rather hackneyed charge, to say the least) and "brutal performances" (370) for financial gain.[33] This reviewer quotes at length from the Preface (including the references to Hunt's refusal to write for the *Quarterly* and

---

[32] *Literary Examiner* 24 (December 13, 1823): 369. Further page references in parentheses. The *Literary Examiner* was a short-lived supplement to the *Examiner*. James R. Thompson, in *Leigh Hunt* (Boston: Twayne, 1977), suggests that this review was written by Hunt himself (41).

[33] He also predicts the imminent self-destruction of the *Quarterly* (which would in fact last, though admittedly not in the same format, until 1967).

Gifford's attack on Mary Robinson) as well as from the long speech by Mercury that takes up the second half of the poem. This reviewer therefore contributes to the recycling of material that has characterized Hunt's side of his conflict with Gifford from the start. He concludes by asserting that Gifford "cannot reasonably complain" about *Ultra-Crepidarius* (372). "Most likely he will not take any open notice of it. Why should he, when he can spit vipers in return, at least once a quarter; or, more characteristically still,—*anguis in herba*,—await *sweltering* amidst the rank literary vegetation of his review, until his natural venom can be ejected with equal safety and malignity" (372). These final lines of the review merely envisage an endless round of attack and counterattack.

The review of *Ultra-Crepidarius* in the *British Critic*, as unfavorable to Hunt as the *Literary Examiner* is sympathetic, similarly does nothing to break the sequence. The reviewer describes the poem in terms that typify Tory hostility to the Cockney School, but without the effervescence of *Blackwood's*. Allegations of criminality and insanity are standard: "with ... a blank, dark chaos of unmeaning jingle, an Avernus where the creative spirits of wit and imagination have never dared to wave their wings,—[*Ultra-Crepidarius*] combines an atrocity of malignity which we never believe to have been before publicly expressed without an application of the corrective influence of Newgate or Bedlam" (*British Critic* 21: 648). The extravagant expressions here are standard fare. In an equally routine move, the reviewer quotes Mercury's speech to Gifford in its entirety, together with copious extracts from Hazlitt's *Letter to Gifford*, thus helping to perpetuate the anti-Gifford point of view even while suggesting that Hunt should be legally "punished" (*British Critic* 21: 657). But for his attack on Gifford, Hunt can only be chastised by reviewers, not by the law. There would be no decisive ending to this story.

By contrast, the more entertaining unsigned review of *Ultra-Crepidarius* in *Blackwood's* appears to expend almost as much creative energy ridiculing the Cockneyism of the poem as Hunt had put into developing it in the first place. If *Ultra-Crepidarius* involves a shift of tactics in keeping alive the strife between Hunt and Gifford, this strategy presents itself as a gift to *Blackwood's* to be toyed with. The *Blackwood's* reviewers responded with relish, and as usual with their attacks on the Cockney School, the relish itself at times risks undercutting the stance of contempt with which they try to keep the upper hand. As mentioned earlier, the writer of this review, probably John Wilson, begins by pretending that the poem is by Hunt's son John; he next claims that it is actually by Hunt's aged grandfather; and then reveals that Hunt himself is the author. In describing "young Master Hunt" (*BM* 15: 86), the reviewer's wit is as labored as Gifford's own, but he becomes momentarily carried away by his account of "the superannuated Zachariah Hunt": "One thinks of some aged cur, with mangy back, glazed eyeballs dropping rheum, and with most disconsolate mazzard muzzling among the fleas of his abominable loins, by some accident lying upon the bed where Love and Beauty are embracing, and embraced" (*BM* 15: 87). The comparison with a "cur" turns Hunt's image of Gifford as a dog back upon himself. The loaded language typifies the *Blackwood's* habit of embellishment; in what follows, the reviewer responds with what he himself calls "good humoured jocularity" (*BM* 15: 90) to Hunt's treatment of the classics, continuing to expand on Hunt's narrative. He imagines Mercury and Venus's bed to have "dimity curtains" (*BM* 15: 87) and tries to debunk—while actually supplementing—the playful eroticism of the first half of the poem with sexual innuendo of his own, comparing the behavior of Hunt's two deities with "Roger and Dolly coming down a ladder from the top of a haystack" (*BM* 15: 88).

In line with earlier *Blackwood's* reviews of Hunt which had treated him novelistically, this review also takes the logical next step of trying to blur the line between reality and fiction:

> Not to keep the reader any longer in suspense, this shoe is—Mr. Gifford, Editor of the Quarterly Review—Mercury proves to be no less a personage than Mr Leigh Hunt, Editor of the Examiner Newspaper; and Venus, that identical charwoman, who washed, for so many years, the foul linen of the Knights of the Round Table, and who only ceased to do so "when Rowland brave, and Oliver, and every Paladin and Peer," proposed striking off a penny on every pair of dirty drawers, twopence on every dozen of sweaty socks, and would allow not a single stiver for stains on the celebrated yellow breeches. (*BM* 15: 88)

Hunt's "yellow breeches" had frequently been mentioned in previous essays on the Cockney School in order to help characterize Hunt as a dandified upstart. Not content with providing such extraneous detail, this writer goes a step further in seizing the opportunity to conflate Hunt and Mercury. It is tempting to end with the idea of Hunt as a character in his own poem, simultaneously shrunk and elevated into a Cockneyfied Greek god. But Hunt practically disappears from sight as the reviewer elaborates on the conceit: in linking *Ultra-Crepidarius* with the essay on washerwomen formerly derided by the *Quarterly*, this passage slides from attempted sexual titillation of its audience to schoolboyish scatological humor that foregrounds the reviewer's "dirty" imagination.

Unsurprisingly, the overlapping feuds between Hunt and Gifford—and Hunt and the *Quarterly*—did not end with *Ultra-Crepidarius*; right before he died, Gifford was capable of a passing stab at Hunt as a "*maître âne*" in the Preface to his edition of the plays of John Ford (1826),[34] even if he did not take the trouble to retaliate in the *Quarterly*. Another major attack on Hunt in the *Quarterly* was still to come, two years after Gifford's death: John Gibson Lockhart's condemnatory review of Hunt's *Lord Byron and Some of his Contemporaries* (1828): "the miserable book of a miserable man" (*QR* 37: 403). Three years later, in his review of Thomas Moore's *Life of Lord Byron* (1830), Lockhart claimed that Hunt shows "that it is possible to possess, in almost the total absence of every other talent, a potent one for producing deep and permanent impressions of disgust" (*QR* 44: 210). These words sound like

---

[34] Quoted from Roy Benjamin Clark, *William Gifford: Tory Satirist, Critic, and Editor* (New York: Russell and Russell, 1930), 221.

Hunt's final judgment on Gifford as well as the *Quarterly*'s final judgment on Hunt. As we saw at the beginning of this chapter, Hunt would still be attacking Gifford 20 years later in his *Autobiography*, claiming to have "conceived some disgust against him as a man." By way of explanation, after mentioning once more that Murray had begged him to write for the *Quarterly* and that he had refused (as if he is still claiming credit for this 40 years later), Hunt returns to the subject of Gifford's attack on Mary Robinson, even though on this occasion (half a century after her death), he has to remind his readers who she was (1: 253–4).

In addition to *Ultra-Crepidarius* and aspects of its reception imaginatively transcending the conflict that generated them, it therefore looks as if Hunt's lifelong private "disgust" towards Gifford made the feud outlast its historical context. I do not want to dismiss the possibility that this feud was driven by what is now called a personality clash, as well as by the culture of "personality." Hunt's enduring contempt for Gifford may also reflect his powerlessness vis-à-vis the *Quarterly* and by extension its editor. We saw that Hunt failed to challenge the institutional weight of the *Quarterly* in trying to discredit its editor's earlier work as a satirist. As the editor of the elite reviewing periodical, Gifford had become elusive, due to the convention of anonymity. Despite Hunt's readiness to identify Gifford as the author of the *Quarterly*'s attacks on him and other Cockney writers, Gifford can be seen as achieving the stance of dignified silence that Hunt desired for himself. In his verse letter to Thomas Moore, published in the *Examiner* in June 1816, Hunt refers to "GIFFARD" as an insect,[35] but in his various attacks on the *Quarterly* Hunt himself seems more in the position of an insect—a tormentor, but a tiny one.

Hunt's continuing resentment, then, may express his frustration at being unable to shake Gifford's authority—a frustration that is not so much personal (though Hunt himself may have believed otherwise) as structural, a response to the combination of a particular cultural situation and the fact that Gifford's institutional framework conferred superior satirical power. Hunt's "Satire on William Gifford" and the immediate responses to it suggest the emotional hazards of choosing to revive the genre of satire in the Romantic era as well as the potential for new kinds of readerly and writerly fun.

Hazlitt, Gifford, and the *Quarterly*

Hazlitt's related feud with Gifford and the *Quarterly* also displays the limitations of Romantic satire *and* its ability to take off in fresh directions. We have already seen, in his attacks on Southey and Coleridge, continuities between Hazlitt's "personalities" and emerging Romantic notions of transcendental selfhood. In his rancorous *Letter to William Gifford,* he claims to rise above the Tory editor through his "metaphysical discovery" of an "ideal self" (Wu 5: 376–8). The *Letter to Gifford* has often been called a "masterpiece of invective,"[36] but it really falls

---

[35] "Harry Brown to his cousin Thomas Browne, Jun., Letter I" (*E* 444: 410).

[36] See, for example, Duncan Wu, *William Hazlitt: The First Modern Man* (Oxford: Oxford University Press, 2008), 267.

into three distinct parts: an awe-inspiring Juvenalian diatribe against Gifford, a detailed refutation of the three attacks on Hazlitt that had appeared by that point in the *Quarterly*, and a summary of Hazlitt's theory of the disinterested imagination, first expounded in his *Essay on the Principles of Human Action* in 1805. The first two sections seem to exemplify Hazlitt's enmeshment within the culture of vituperative criticism and personal attacks, whereas the final section ostensibly offers what one critic calls a "transcendental argument."[37]

Why did Hazlitt use his *Letter to Gifford* as a vehicle for re-publicizing his philosophical theory—a gesture, in Hunt's words, "amounting to the romantic" (*E* 585: 173)? Recent critics have foregrounded the *Essay on the Principles of Human Action*, considered by Hazlitt to be his claim to fame, in discussions of the extent to which Hazlitt is a materialist or an idealist thinker.[38] I will argue that if Hazlitt breaks free from the "age of personality" in his feud with Gifford, it is not because of the power of his theoretical explanation, but because his representations of Gifford enact the workings of the disinterested imagination. In the following pages, I will look briefly at Hazlitt's dealings with the *Quarterly* (already mentioned in passing during my discussion of Hunt), before examining the terms of the *Letter* and Hazlitt's later *Spirit of the Age* essay "Mr. Gifford" to suggest how this writer evades the "literary police."

Hazlitt's feud with Gifford, like Hunt's, was longstanding and had personal, political, commercial and ideological dimensions. Before Hazlitt published the *Letter*, the *Quarterly* had attacked him in three separate reviews, one (as we have already seen) in 1817 of *The Round Table*, one of his *Characters of Shakespeare's Plays* (1817) and one of his *Lectures on the English Poets* (1818). Writers other than Gifford seem to have been mainly responsible for these, but, ignoring—like Hunt—the *Quarterly* editor's tendency to delegate the actual composition of articles, Hazlitt assumed that Gifford had written all three, even though he himself objected strenuously to being conflated with his collaborator in the *Quarterly*'s attack on *The Round Table* (Wu 5: 355). Hazlitt jibed at Gifford and the *Quarterly* now and again throughout his journalistic writings, but his first main counterattack was his essay entitled "The Editor of the Quarterly Review," published anonymously in June 1818 in the *Examiner* (*E* 546: 378–9), which he expanded the following year into the signed *Letter to Gifford*. Like many of his contemporaries, Hazlitt, when attacked, did not believe in staying silent—quite the reverse. Hazlitt followed these

---

[37] A.C. Grayling, *The Quarrel of the Age: The Life and Times of William Hazlitt* (London: Weidenfeld and Nicolson, 2000), 364.

[38] See, for example, Uttara Natarajan, *Hazlitt and the Reach of Sense* (Oxford: Clarendon Press, 1998), on Hazlitt's "symbiosis of the experiential and the ideal" (4), and Tim Milnes, "Seeing in the Dark: Hazlitt's Immanent Idealism," *Studies in Romanticism* 39.1 (2000): 3–26. Milnes claims, in contrast with Natarajan's less materialist approach, that "Hazlitt remained epistemologically empiricist while appearing to be metaphysically idealist" (7). See also Uttara Natarajan, Tom Paulin, and Duncan Wu, eds, *Metaphysical Hazlitt: Bicentenary Essays* (London: Routledge, 2005), a collection that takes multiple approaches to the *Essay*.

reprisals with his withering essay "Mr. Gifford," by which time the *Quarterly* had attacked him twice more, in reviews of *Political Essays* and *Table-Talk*, the first of which may or may not have been written by Gifford himself, and the second of which almost certainly was not. As David Bromwich points out, Hazlitt's opinion of other Tories had mellowed by the time he published *The Spirit of the Age* in 1825, but not his opinion of Gifford. This is because, according to Bromwich, Gifford's "career had become to Hazlitt a living allegory of the spite, rancor, and servility of prostituted intelligence."[39]

At first sight, the *Quarterly*'s attacks on Hazlitt and his acidic responses seem to rely on similar strategies and speak the same language. As mentioned earlier, *The Round Table* review—initially crediting Hazlitt with the entire volume—refers to his remarks on Burke as "loathsome trash." It also labels him a "creature" that "grovel[s]" in "slime and filth" (*QR* 17: 159). Hazlitt accused the *Quarterly* in turn of "slime and filth" (Wu 5: 360). The attack on the *Characters of Shakespeare's Plays*—which Duncan Wu calls "diabolical"[40]—referred to "the concentrated venom of [Hazlitt's] malignity" (*QR* 18: 464), accused him of "senseless and wicked sophistry" (*QR* 18: 466), and described him as a "poor cankered creature" (*QR* 18: 464). Somewhat less harshly, the churlish review of Hazlitt's *Lectures* dismissed their "vacancy of thought" and "incoherent jumble of gaudy words" (*QR* 19: 434).[41] In his *Letter*, Hazlitt complains of Gifford's "wretched verbal criticism" (Wu 5: 354), but Hazlitt himself, with what seems like equal pettiness, offers defensive refutations of the *Quarterly*'s first three attacks that take up more space than the attacks themselves. He says that the *Quarterly*'s article on his *Lectures* "requires a very short notice" (Wu 5: 369), yet then proceeds to reply to its nitpicking allegations at tedious length.

In "Mr. Gifford," he accuses his enemy of "personal calumny" and "harshness of invective" (Wu 7: 189), both of which allegations could be turned back against himself. For example, despite claiming that Gifford "sneers at people of low birth" (Wu 7: 183), he calls Gifford "ill-bred" (Wu 5: 346), mocks him for being "bred to some handicraft" (Wu 7: 180), and accuses his poetry of a "low, mechanic vein" (Wu 7: 188). More vividly, he figures Gifford as an obsequious servant of uncertain gender: "Again, of an humble origin yourself, you recommend your performances to persons of fashion by always abusing *low people*, with the smartness of a lady's waiting-woman, and the independent spirit of a travelling tutor" (Wu 5: 345). Hazlitt accuses the Tory editor of satirizing "personal" (meaning physical) "defect[s]" (Wu 7: 182), yet he does the same. Although—following Hunt—he violently objects to Gifford's jibe in the *Baviad* about Mary

---

[39] David Bromwich, *Hazlitt: The Mind of a Critic* (New Haven: Yale University Press, 1999), 102.

[40] Wu, *Hazlitt*, 246.

[41] The *Times*, on November 12, 1818, reported that in the spoken version of the lectures, Hazlitt "raised a tumult by abusing Gifford, which a few hissed at and many applauded" (3, quoted in Wu, *Hazlitt*, 494, n.81).

Robinson's lameness and her "crutches" (Wu 5: 355), he complains that Gifford "must have crutches, a go-cart and trammels" (Wu 7: 182), expressions that might seem purely metaphorical except that in a later essay he mentions in passing "lame G—" (Howe 20: 376). More generally, he accuses Gifford of an "utter want of independence" (Wu 7: 182), even though one could object that Hazlitt needs Gifford as much as Gifford needs him.[42]

Hazlittian Transcendence

Hazlitt's apparent reliance on questionable tactics, however, may be a symptom of how his representations of Gifford reflect assumptions underlying his theory of the disinterested imagination. When turning to his account of his theory, Hazlitt notes that "I have written this Letter partly to introduce it through you to the notice of the reader" (Wu 5: 376). Hazlitt recapitulated the argument of his *Essay on the Principles of Human Action* at various points throughout his career. Besides summarizing it in the *Letter* and referring to it in his "Reply to Z" (an attack on *Blackwood's*), drafted in 1818 but not published during his lifetime, he used it as the starting point for two essays in *Table-Talk* ("On the Past and Future" and "On the Fear of Death"), and two dialogues on "Self-Love and Benevolence," published in the *New Monthly Magazine* in 1828. Hazlitt never changed his theory or his high opinion of it.

Hazlitt's basic argument is against the idea that people act self-interestedly. He makes this contention on the grounds that although one is committed through memory and sensation to one's own past and present self, it is as easy to identify with other people's future selves as with one's own, since the future is essentially unknowable. He calls the unified self "this fine illusion of the brain, and forgery of language" (Wu 5: 377), but also claims that because the imagination is "common, discursive, and social," we all collaborate upon this necessary fiction despite taking a "disinterested" attitude to our "own future welfare" (Wu 5: 379). As the Charles Lamb character in the essay on "Self-Love and Benevolence," protests, Hazlitt shatters "this self, this 'precious jewel of the soul,' this rock ... to pieces" with a "sledge-hammer" (Howe 20: 172). Yet he gives us back an imaginary identity grounded upon the ability to sympathize with others. In the words of the Hazlitt figure in the same essay, "fellow-feeling" paradoxically "constitutes" self (Howe 20: 175).

Recent analyses of Hazlitt's *Essay* have drawn attention to its anti-empirical elements. Deborah Elise White sees its theory as a version of the Romantic

---

[42] Hazlitt's use of the opinion of a fellow "Cockney" writer is also rhetorically problematic. He reprints Hunt's modified attack on Gifford from *The Feast of the Poets*, just as Hunt will later quote at length from Hazlitt's *Letter* in *Ultra-Crepidarius*. Hazlitt also relies on a quotation from Hunt for the *Letter*'s only kind words about Gifford. This maneuver marshals a collective voice that sounds weak, because ambivalent, in the face of the unyielding ethos of the *Quarterly*.

ideology, in that although Hazlitt's discontinuous notion of the self seems anti-Wordsworthian, it assumes the possibility of transcendence. As White points out, for Hazlitt, because consciousness "comes from the future," it is also transcendental, "in Wordsworth's phrase, 'something evermore about to be.'"[43] At the same time, Hazlitt recognizes the fictionality of the self, that "bubble of the brain" (Wu 5: 382), but admits the irresistibility of the delusion of a continuous "personal identity" (Wu 5: 377). As he puts it in the *Letter to Gifford*, the imagination "impregnates" the future "with life and motion," and "clothes the whole possible world with a borrowed reality" (Wu 5: 382). Jacques Khalip stresses that "Hazlitt's demystification of the self" has strong temporal and ethical dimensions: it depends on an absolute disjunction between present and future identities and in doing so frees up the ideal, impersonal self to act ethically.[44] By the same token, according to White, "The romanticization of morality ... proves to be its enabling condition" (72).

Transcendence, however, comes with a twist. White observes of Hazlitt's account of imagination in the *Essay*, "It both projects the 'self' out of itself and projects it, so to speak, out of its projections, so that one must think, necessarily and not just by force of habit, that a self really exists whose future is one's own" (88). Hazlitt's summary of his theory in the *Letter* is not so explicit about the imagination's capacity to fool the "brain" into thinking that the self "really exists," yet he asserts that "we ... live in a waking dream" (Wu 5: 382). The obvious reason why Hazlitt yokes together his theory and his disgust for Gifford in the *Letter* is that Gifford represents the triumph of self-interest in contrast with the ostensible selflessness of the Hazlittian imagination. But Gifford himself in places, as a figure for that evil institution the *Quarterly Review*, is something evermore about to be, a necessary transcendental fiction that carries a hint of its own critique.

On one level, Hazlitt brings up his theory in the *Letter* seemingly to show his *personal* moral superiority to Gifford. At the end of the *Letter* he informs Gifford that the discovery of his theory made him a happier person: "From that time I felt a certain weight and tightness about my heart taken off, and cheerful and confident thoughts springing up in the place of anxious fears and sad forebodings" (Wu 5: 383). A freer body and a freer mind go together. Gifford, of course, has neither—or does he? One might object, why should a belief in the unknowability of the future give "confident thoughts"? Hazlitt also claims that because of his metaphysical discovery, he is "little discomposed" by worldly setbacks like attacks in the *Quarterly Review* (Wu 5: 383). The bulk of the *Letter* however implies that he was extremely bothered by the *Quarterly*'s attacks. Although he contrasts his own sublime disinterestedness with Gifford's disgusting self-love, by retaliating at such length he gives the impression that his own self-love is wounded. Such apparent

---

[43] Deborah Elise White, *Romantic Returns: Superstition, Imagination, History* (Stanford: Stanford University Press, 2000), 70. Further references in parentheses.

[44] Jacques Khalip, *Anonymous Life: Romanticism and Dispossession* (Stanford: Stanford University Press, 2009), 29.

contradictions grant the pull of "habit and circumstances" (Wu 5: 380), yet the figurative language that Hazlitt applies to Gifford also ascribes a larger scope to "mere fiction[s] of the mind" (Wu 5: 379).

His attacks on Gifford, especially in the *Letter*, appear to set up a firm distinction between the self-interested self, figured as corporeal and repellent, and the disinterested self, which "exists in an ideal world" (Wu 5: 382). They show the "fierce obtrusion of the bodily into the written" that Peter Murphy finds in the "personalities" of *Blackwood's*.[45] But Hazlitt depicts Gifford not only in terms of a deformed and unhealthy body, but also in terms of a disembodied entity with a greater potential for evil. Hazlitt's short essay on Gifford in the *Examiner* had referred to his "irritable, discontented, vindictive and peevish effusions of bodily pain and mental infirmity" (*E* 546: 379). Hazlitt here unsympathetically alludes to the fact that Gifford was a chronic invalid. The implication is that sickness of body and mind go together. In "Mr. Gifford" he repeats the slur, denouncing the editor's "slow, snail-paced, bed-rid habits of reasoning" (Wu 7: 182). In the *Letter*, Hazlitt addresses his nemesis as "a little person" (Wu 5: 343), which Wu calls "a none too kind reference to Gifford's short stature" (Wu 5: 449, n.1). Gifford is repeatedly imagined in terms of grotesque physicality. "He has the *chalk-stones* [gouty growths] in his understanding" (Wu 7: 181). Hazlitt tells him, "The air you breathe seems to infect; and your friendship to be a canker-worm that blights its objects with unwholesome and premature decay" (Wu 5: 353–4). According to Hazlitt, as a reviewer Gifford "crawl[s] and leave[s] the slimy track of sophistry and lies" over any material opposed to his political viewpoint (Wu 5: 361).

Hazlitt characterizes the *Quarterly* in similar terms as an institution that is physically repellent. In his essay "Mr. Jeffrey" (in *The Spirit of the Age*), he condemns the *Edinburgh*'s rival periodical as "one foul blotch of servility, intolerance, falsehood, spite, and ill manners" (Wu 7: 192), and "a mere mass and tissue of prejudices on all subjects" (Wu 7: 195). In the *Letter to Gifford*, Hazlitt actually invokes the physical appearance of the *Quarterly*, referring to its "paltry blurred sheets" (Wu 5: 353), and declaring that "The dingy cover that wraps the pages of the Quarterly Review does not contain a concentrated essence of taste and knowledge, but is a receptacle for the scum and sediment of all the prejudice, bigotry, ill-will, ignorance, and rancour, afloat in the kingdom" (Wu 5: 344).

But in conflating Gifford with the *Quarterly*, Hazlitt ascribes to him an "essence" that makes him bigger and more elusive than his own short, sick, slimy body, a ghostly personification of the periodical that makes him more threatening than mere "scum and sediment." The *Examiner* attack and the *Letter* both begin with an attempted justification for devoting so many words to Gifford. Hazlitt's repeated associations of the Tory editor with bodily weakness and dirt inevitably raise the question of why he is worth bothering with. Hazlitt calls him "a considerable cat's-paw; and so far worthy of notice" (Wu 5: 343). He continues

---

[45] Peter T. Murphy, "Impersonation and Authorship in Romantic Britain," *ELH* 59 (1992): 625–49 (636).

with the sentence that I quoted earlier from the *Letter*, an image that turns Gifford from a "little person" into something larger than life: "You are the *Government Critic*, a character nicely differing from that of a government spy—the invisible link, that connects literature with the police." In characterizing the deformed Gifford as an "invisible link," Hazlitt makes the "government automaton" (Wu 5: 353) into the faceless face of the *Quarterly*, "the oracle of Church and State" (Wu 5: 345). He thus allows Gifford an impersonal version of what Manning calls "an identity beyond the words on the page."[46] Later in the *Letter*, Hazlitt pauses in his rebuttal of the *Quarterly*'s (of course false) allegation that he "writes eternally about washerwomen," to fend off the idea that he is wasting his time: "There is a littleness in your objections which makes even the answers to them ridiculous, and which would make it impossible to notice them, were you not the Government-Critic" (Wu 5: 350).

The extent of Gifford's political power, that is to say, justifies investing energy in him, although in reading the *Letter*, it is hard to avoid the suspicion that Hazlitt devotes far more energy to Gifford than he deserves. According to Hazlitt, this power is self-perpetuating: "every indulgence of his hired malignity makes him more disposed to repeat the insult and the injury" (Wu 5: 347). Gifford is the mere "tool" and "cat's-paw" of his patrons and employers, but also seems to float free, invested with an almost preternatural ability to maintain the status quo. As Hazlitt puts it, in the "machine" that is the *Quarterly*, the "slime of hypocrisy" is spread by "the iron hand of power" (Wu 7: 189). Hazlitt continues to make grand claims for the ambitions of the *Quarterly*: "The intention is to poison the sources of public opinion and individual fame—to pervert literature, from being the natural ally of freedom and humanity, into an engine of priestcraft and despotism, and to undermine the spirit of the English Constitution and the independence of the English character" (Wu 7: 189). Such language helps make the *Quarterly* into a threat.

Hazlitt thus ascribes to Gifford and the *Quarterly*—to self-interest itself—the capacity to break free from the slime, all the better to do their dirty work, but a few passages in the *Letter* hint that that act of transcendence may be one more "bubble of the brain." At one point it emerges that Gifford is not just bigger than himself in standing for the *Quarterly*, the *Quarterly* itself stands for something larger than itself. Hazlitt tells Gifford with magnificent hyperbole, "You know very well that if a particle of truth or fairness were to find its way into a single number of your publication, another Quarterly Review would be set up tomorrow for the express purpose of depriving every author, in prose or verse, of his reputation and livelihood, who is not a regular hack of the vilest cabal that ever disgraced this or any other country" (Wu 5: 344–5). The idea of a new "Quarterly Review" instantly springing up to replace the current one if it deflected for one moment from its diabolical mission, implies that the *Quarterly* itself transcends the *Quarterly*. Here Hazlitt seems to contradict his theory of the discontinuous self by claiming to be

---

[46] Manning, "Detaching Lamb's Thoughts," 143.

able to see into the future, perceiving Gifford and the *Quarterly* as incapable of ever acting any differently. That very contradiction is evidence of the imagination's dependence on what it already knows. Hazlitt, that is to say, corporealizes Gifford and then transcendentalizes him, but also implicitly recognizes the fictionality of that move outside the "human mind" (Wu 5: 377).

In a similar move, towards the end of the *Letter*, Hazlitt tells Gifford that his "conduct" is part of a "system" reaching back to the *Anti-Jacobin Review* (Wu 5: 375). Again he extrapolates from Gifford himself. The assertion forms part of a seemingly awkward transition in which Hazlitt re-uses material from his attack on the *Biographia* in the *Edinburgh* to bring up the political apostasy of Coleridge and Southey. (He thus punctures the illusion of anonymity in his *Biographia* review.) Hazlitt suggests that his former friends were more liable to change "sides" than Gifford—or Hazlitt himself—because they were true poets (Wu 5: 375). The passage contains a line that sounds as if it belongs in Shelley's *Defence of Poetry*: "Poetry may be described as having the range of the universe; it traverses the empyrean, and looks down on nature from a higher sphere" (Wu 5: 375). Hazlitt thus proclaims his own Romantic credentials, his capacity to hear Wordsworth's "still sad music of humanity" (Wu 5: 365). But, he proceeds to say, poetry is easily soiled, explaining with what Bromwich calls "characteristic generosity,"[47] that he himself did not fall (that is, change his views) because, "I was not a poet, but a metaphysician" (Wu 5: 376). Although the poetic imagination is no match for the "prejudices of absolute power" (Wu 5: 376), a belief in the "natural disinterestedness of the human mind"—by implication a higher (less vulnerable) as well as a lower (less literary) form of transcendence—can prevail. Generous or not, Hazlitt's turn to his own "metaphysical discovery" again shows that the very act of countering Gifford and everything he stands for still has to be done in "personal" terms.

It therefore makes sense that Hazlitt has "cheerful thoughts" even though his *Letter* has exposed the *Quarterly*'s "invisible" and self-renewing capacity for evil. The *Letter* implies two conflicting things simultaneously—that evil is self-perpetuating and that it *can* be resisted. It also makes sense that Hazlitt takes up so much space refuting the *Quarterly*'s misrepresentations of him and reviling Gifford. It is a symptom of how the *Letter* at once repudiates and relies on the fiction of a continuous autonomous self. For the same reason, after his emphasis on the "blank and dreary void" of the future (Wu 5: 382), Hazlitt mentions his desire for (philosophical) "fame" (Wu 5: 383). The same "illusion of the brain" that allows Hazlitt to project himself confidently into the future also indicates that the *Quarterly*'s apparently endless power may be illusory. Hazlitt steps beyond personal concerns and illustrates their hold, offering the possibility of breaking free as a delusion *and* something to believe in. Hence the openness of his theory to both materialist and anti-materialist interpretations. Recognizing this tension, Hunt commented, in his March 1819 review of the *Letter* in the *Examiner*, "The

---

[47] Bromwich, *Hazlitt: The Mind of a Critic*, 102.

trenchant metaphysician, who cuts asunder the disguises of others ... is ... 'fairly caught in the web of his own' simplicity. But how well can he afford to commit himself!" (*E* 585: 173).[48]

As with other print feuds of the era, there is no neat and tidy ending to the Hazlitt–Gifford conflict. As mentioned earlier, the *Quarterly* went on to review Hazlitt's *Political Essays* and then his *Table-Talk*. The first of these scathing attacks, possibly by Gifford, contains an oblique answer to the *Letter*: "We believe that since we last noticed Mr. Hazlitt, he has manifested great wrath against us" (*QR* 22: 159). The article expresses "unqualified detestation" for "the spirit which pervades [Hazlitt's] volumes," condemns "the ludicrous egotism" of "this forlorn drudge of the Examiner," and associates him with "the straw crowns and scepters" of madmen (*QR* 22: 159). Slightly softening these blows, the reviewer sarcastically figures Hazlitt as the "chivalrous squire" to Hunt, possessor of "the Throne of Cockney" (*QR* 22: 159). Alluding again to the *Letter* without naming it, the reviewer attempts to debunk Hazlitt's philosophical aspirations: "We doubt whether a Dutch sign-painter would make his own apotheosis equally ludicrous: even if he were to depict himself recumbent at the table of the Gods, with trunk hose, grasping a tobacco-pipe in one hand, and striving to purple his lips in nectar with the other" (*QR* 22: 162).[49] This image adopts the Cockney strategy of desecrating the classics, yoking Greek mythology to a mundane understanding of Dutch visual art. However, rather than pursuing this line of thought, the article ends by calling "the Hazlitt" a "slanderer of the human race," and a member of a transitory "new species," one of "many new plagues" (*QR* 22: 163). With similar intransigence, the attack on *Table-Talk* labels Hazlitt a "SLANG-WHANGER" (*QR* 26: 103), and sneeringly quotes his own line against him: "What abortions are these Essays!" (*QR* 26: 108). These two articles thus apply Hazlitt's own demystifying impulses against him, but without displaying a simultaneous readiness to re-mystify. Despite the momentary triumph of Hazlitt's disinterested imagination, and as the ongoing Hunt-Gifford saga confirms, "personality" is inevitably alive and well in the third decade of the nineteenth century.

Lady Morgan, Croker, and the *Quarterly*

Lady Morgan, the Irish novelist and travel writer known before her marriage as Sydney Owenson, would not have had it any other way. The victim of violent attacks by the *Quarterly* and other periodicals, she was never afraid to retaliate,

---

[48] Hunt's article was the only review of the *Letter*, but Keats privately celebrated its "force" (*The Letters of John Keats*, ed. H.E. Rollins, 2 vols. [Cambridge: Harvard University Press, 1958], 2: 76).

[49] Hazlitt, in "Mr. Gifford," indignantly (and creatively) paraphrased this image: "It was amusing to see this person, sitting like one of Brouwer's Dutch boors over his gin and tobacco-pipes, and fancying himself a Leibnitz!" (Wu 7: 188). Hazlitt's rewording extends the demystification.

whether or not she knew the identity of her combatants. A Victorian sympathizer claimed that she crushed her hostile reviewers: "with her own fragile female hand she not only parried undauntedly the assaults of a furious and organized host of Critic-Cut-Throats, but absolutely hurled them, one by one, to the ground; and the teeth that had been sharpened to gnaw this brilliant woman's heart, impotently bit the dust beneath her feet. ... The blows aimed at her own fair fame she made recoil upon her assailants."[50] This author concludes that unlike lesser mortals like Aristotle, Racine, and Keats, "That brilliant woman ... grappled with the arm that sought to destroy her fair reputation, and possibly her life, and like the good fairy crushing the Evil Genius in a Pantomime, she smote the arch-Foe to the earth, and placed her tiny foot, clad in white satin, upon his ponderous coat of mail."[51]

In the rest of this chapter, I will offer a less decisive interpretation of Morgan's sporadic but bitter feud with the *Quarterly*. Like Hunt's skirmishes with Gifford, Morgan's battles with the *Quarterly* reviewer who became her nemesis, Croker, preceded the campaign against her in the *Quarterly*. And like both Hunt's and Hazlitt's squabbles with the *Quarterly*, Morgan's feud with the Tory periodical shows the challenges faced by reformist writers in assailing the "ponderous coat of mail" of anonymous conservative reviewers. Morgan's counterattacks, like those of her fellow reformers, rarely find a separate space in which to sidestep her opponents. Her responses to the *Quarterly* embrace what Coleridge called "*the game*," making her often seem less like a winning player and more like a pawn in the reviewers' control. In what follows, I will discuss the *Quarterly*'s three major attacks on Morgan and her print replies, which include a sustained satirical portrait of Croker in her 1818 novel *Florence Macarthy: An Irish Tale*. I will argue that only in this novel does Morgan succeed momentarily in transcending the hostilities of print warfare—not that she ever aspires to do so, since as a thoroughly materialist creature, she gleefully inhabits a politicized literary marketplace.

From Morgan's point of view, she was victorious over her opponents because she made money. Claire Connolly has argued that Morgan's quarrels with her reviewers were "not so much obstacles on the path to fame as constitutive of her writing identity and celebrity."[52] Unlike other writers of the period (such as Coleridge and Hazlitt) who complained that negative reviews damaged sales, Morgan repeatedly boasted in print about attacks aiding the financial success of her publications. She did indeed make thousands of pounds where other novelists such as Jane Austen made hundreds. Her frank references to the commercial basis of authorship and practical concerns such as publishers' deadlines may be an additional reason for the virulence with which she was attacked by the *Quarterly* and other conservative periodicals. The writer of an 1817 *Examiner* article

---

[50] W.J. Fitzpatrick, *The Friends, Foes, and Adventures of Lady Morgan* (Dublin: W.B. Kelly, 1859), 136–7.

[51] Ibid., 138.

[52] Claire Connolly, "'I accuse Miss Owenson': *The Wild Irish Girl* as Media Event," *Colby Quarterly* 36.2 (2000): 98–115.

defending Morgan sarcastically noted that unlike her, "the writers in the *Quarterly Review* are not hired, but act gratuitously" (*E* 514: 698). The same writer mocked Morgan's attackers for implying that "the getters-up of the articles in the *Quarterly Review* are not only not paid, but that they contribute their free-will offerings when they please" (*E* 514: 698).

Morgan assumed that her old enemy Croker was responsible for the attacks on her in the *Quarterly*, even though he collaborated with Gifford. Her exchange with the *Quarterly* builds upon her earlier conflict with Croker, who had anonymously attacked her novel *The Wild Irish Girl* in 1806 in the Dublin newspaper the *Freeman's Journal*, sparking a storm of controversy. Prior to that attack, Owenson had written a pamphlet responding to a book Croker had written anonymously attacking the "Irish Stage," a text that reportedly caused one actor to die of a broken heart.[53] Croker had accused "Miss Owenson" of "having written bad novels, and worse poetry—volumes without number, and verses without end" and more egregiously, of "attempting to vitiate mankind—of attempting to undermine morality by sophistry—and that under the insidious mask of virtue, sensibility and truth."[54] Besides print defenses and counterattacks, the controversy generated advertisements for Owenson's works and various *Wild Irish Girl*-inspired fashion accessories: a brooch named the "Glorvina ornament" after the heroine of the novel, a Glorvina-ish cloak, and an Irish harp. Morgan later said that the novel was "buoyed up into notice by the very means taken to sink it,"[55] one of several places in which she claims that all publicity is good publicity.

The *Quarterly*'s attacks on Morgan began with a review of her latest novel *Woman; or Ida of Athens* (1809). Gifford (not Croker) accused the book's "sentiments" (though not the author herself) of being "mischievous in tendency, and profligate in principle; licentious and irreverent in the highest degree" (*QR* 1: 52). The reviewer condescendingly advises "Miss Owenson" to buy a "spelling book" and "a pocket dictionary" and to study the Bible in order to become "a faithful wife, a tender mother, and a respectable and happy mistress of a family" (*QR* 1: 52).

Morgan's response to this verbal assault was belated, but superficially effective. In the Preface to her travel book *France*, published in 1817, Morgan throws down a challenge to the *Quarterly* by saying that she expects "condemnation" from it for her book's "sentiments and principles." She refers back to the *Quarterly*'s "unprovoked and wanton attack upon [her] personal character," claiming that "The slander thus hurled against a young and unprotected female ... happily fell hurtless." Morgan protests too much. Her exaggerated account of the attack on *Woman*, which is actually a rather slight review by the *Quarterly*'s standards,

---

[53] Fitzpatrick, *Friends, Foes, and Adventures*, 137. Croker's 1803 book was entitled *Familiar Epistles on the Irish Stage*.

[54] Quoted by Jacqueline E. Belanger, *Critical Receptions: Sydney Owenson, Lady Morgan* (Bethesda: Academica Press, 2007), 74.

[55] Quoted by Connolly, "*The Wild Irish Girl* as Media Event," 100, from the 1846 Preface to a revised version of *The Wild Irish Girl*.

finds in it accusations of "licentiousness, profligacy, irreverence, blasphemy, libertinism, disloyalty, and atheism."[56] Instead of pouring scorn on the *Quarterly* for its patronizing attitude to her as a female writer, she sarcastically thanks the reviewers for giving her advice that had enabled her to find a husband, since by then she had married Sir Charles Morgan, yet this mention of her "reward" could be read as a boast about her success in the marriage market.[57]

This reprisal was certainly successful in the sense that it provoked a long, detailed and extremely hostile review in the *Quarterly*, beginning with an appalled one-syllable sentence, "*France!*" (*QR* 17: 260).[58] The authors, Gifford and Croker, refer explicitly back to their previous attack and Morgan's counterattack, accusing her of misrepresenting the "advice" they gave her formerly and of treating "us" with "the most lofty indignation" in her Preface to the book (*QR* 17: 261). The reviewers make a routine, disingenuous and unconvincing disclaimer that their attacks on Morgan are not personal attacks: "Lady Morgan ... seems strangely anxious to persuade the world that we accused her of *personal* licentiousness, profligacy, &c. but she does both us and herself injustice. We spoke then, as we shall do now, only of her works. We disclaim all personal acquaintance with Lady Morgan—we never saw her; and, except as a book manufacturer, know absolutely nothing about her" (*QR* 17: 262). The term "manufacturer" conveys the reviewers' disdain for a writer who makes money. They later accuse her of letting the world "a little too much behind (as she would call it) the typographical scene" by mentioning her contract with her publisher (*QR* 17: 263). According to them, her "language smells vilely of the shop" (*QR* 17: 261). Clearly, the reviewers are threatened by Morgan's habit of puncturing the illusion that relationships between writers and readers exist in a rarefied realm beyond mere moneymaking. They add, "the uninitiated will be shocked to find that the sylphid Miss Owenson, the elegant Lady Morgan, is in fact a mere bookseller's drudge, (we tremble as we write it!)" (*QR* 17: 263).

The main strategy of the review—which appeared in the same issue as the attack on Hunt and Hazlitt's *Round Table*—is to condemn Morgan "out of her own mouth" as they put it (*QR* 17: 263), by supplying lengthy quotations to support their list of charges, presented as a series of sub-headings: "Bad taste—Bombast and Nonsense—Blunders—Ignorance of the French Language and Manners—General Ignorance—Jacobinism—Falsehood—Licentiousness, and Impiety" (*QR* 17: 264). The reviewers back up this mixture of general allegations with detailed attention to word choices, which, rather than discrediting Morgan, illustrates the petty-mindedness of her attackers. The article builds to a climax of vitriol, dismissing the book as "trash," accusing "this mad woman" (*QR* 17: 284) of

---

[56] These quotations are from Belanger, *Critical Receptions*, 140–41.

[57] Compare Jeanne Moskal, "Gender, Nationality and Textual Authority in Lady Morgan's Travel Books," in Paula Feldman and Theresa M. Kelley, eds, *Romantic Women Writers: Voices and Countervoices* (Hanover: University Press of New England, 1995): 171–93, on how Morgan "allows the *Quarterly* to define the terms of her success" (180).

[58] In passing, Croker had also mocked Morgan's *O'Donnel: A National Tale* (1814) in the previous volume of the *Quarterly* (*QR* 16: 338).

"abominations" (*QR* 17: 285), calling her "insane" (*QR* 17: 285), and referring to her as "this audacious worm" (*QR* 17: 284). With such name-calling, the *Quarterly* loses all pretence at trying to offer authoritative literary criticism and draws attention to itself as a vehicle of entertainment and a stirrer-up of controversy for its own sake.[59]

The *Quarterly*'s follow-up attack on Morgan's second travel book, *Italy*, in 1821, was briefer, merely dismissing the book as "a series of offences against good morals, good politics, good sense, and good taste" (*QR* 25: 529). In this review, Croker claims that "this woman is utterly *incorrigible*" (*QR* 25: 529), and he therefore refuses to lend publicity to her writing—a tacit acknowledgement that he had done so in the past. In his words, "any examination would only serve to let the effluvia escape, and in some degree endanger the public health" (*QR* 25: 530). Instead, he offers reflections on the "system of puffing" (*QR* 25: 530),[60] analyzing her publisher's newspaper advertisements, one of which falsely (according to him) claimed that the book "has *put all the race of intolerant critics* into a STATE OF FURY—Lady Morgan has kindled *their indignation*" (*QR* 25: 532, reviewer's emphasis). This review mocks what it sees as the publisher's failed attempt to use the "'malignant fury of the reptiles [Morgan] has crushed'" to sell her book (*QR* 25: 533). Here we see the *Quarterly* trying in vain to stand outside the "system" in which it is implicated. The article ends by mocking another counterattack by Morgan, her *Letter to the Reviewers of Italy* (1821), which Morgan herself boasted had preempted the *Quarterly*'s intended attack on *Italy*, forcing its writers to "get up a new article."[61]

In the *Letter*, a 45-page pamphlet, Morgan embraces the system by openly acknowledging that print warfare involves game-playing: "If I come forth among my nameless assailants … 'tis more in fun than fear—less in spite than sport" (*Letter*, 4). In this reprisal, she does not square off against the *Quarterly*, claiming that its attack on *France* is "too notorious to dwell upon" (*Letter*, 7), but this move gives the impression that she hesitates to engage directly with the voice of the establishment. Instead, she addresses an attack on her in the *Edinburgh Magazine*, not to be confused with *Blackwood's*, which she claims "*smells* of the *Quarterly* creature" (*Letter*, 10, n.3). The *Edinburgh Magazine* had mocked her for pleading what it calls the "*privilege of sex!*" adding, "The age of chivalry, alas! is gone by; and 'a woman's work' … must, no less than a man's—had *any* man ever written

---

[59] A letter to the editor printed in *The Star* (a daily newspaper), for example, considered the "abusive epithets" of the *Quarterly* to be "rendered doubly base and unmanly, by their application to a female" (September 29, 1817: 1). The same writer claimed that "the Reviewer has clearly overshot his mark, and by a barefaced display of the feeling under which he has written, has divested his observations of all their venom" (1).

[60] On "puffing," see Nicholas Mason, "'The Quack has become God': Puffery, Print, and the 'Death' of Literature in Romantic-Era Britain," *Nineteenth-Century Literature* 60 (2005): 1–31.

[61] Lionel Stevenson, *The Wild Irish Girl: The Life of Sydney Owenson, Lady Morgan* (New York: Russell and Russell, 1969; first published 1936), 228.

such a mass of revolting jargon and abomination,—submit it to the dissecting knife of criticism" (*Letter*, 12). The reviewer offers a *Quarterly*-influenced list of Morgan's offences and goes beyond the *Quarterly*'s attack on *France* in describing *Italy* as "this monstrous literary abortion" (*Letter*, 13).

Morgan's rebuttal plays along with the reviewers by quoting copiously from the *Edinburgh Magazine* article and indulging in indignant refutation of its charges. Like Hazlitt's *Letter to Gifford*, this reprisal offers point-by-point self-vindication with a level of detail that takes "wretched verbal criticism" too seriously. With what looks more like "spite than sport," Morgan goes on to jibe at "cowardly," "cold-blooded" reviewers, "secure in anonymous ambuscade," including the editor of the *Quarterly* (*Letter*, 29), and blames them for killing Keats (as Shelley had claimed in the Preface to *Adonais*) and John Scott of the *London Magazine* (who had died in a *Blackwood's*-related duel earlier in 1821). She ends by appealing to the high price of *Italy* as proof of her victory over her attackers (*Letter*, 45), even though that would seem to anticipate the *Quarterly*'s accusation that she "sell[s]" her "wares to the best bidder" (*QR* 25: 530).[62] Morgan also counterattacked in a book-length anonymous poem *The Mohawks* (1822)—mostly written by her husband—in a section in heroic couplets that, like those of Hunt's "To a Spider," unsuccessfully try to imitate Pope's. She refers to "G—d, with an eunuch's fury fir'd" (a gratuitous allusion to Gifford's celibacy), and ascribes his attack on an unnamed woman (herself) to the "black reflections of his own dark soul."[63]

Florence Macarthy

Although Morgan's counterattacks on the reviewers in general and the *Quarterly* in particular thus risk buying in to their hostile characterizations of her, her attempt at revenge in *Florence Macarthy* is more complex and elaborate. The novel not only contains a spirited portrait of Croker in the character Conway Townsend Crawley, an anti-Jacobin writer and aspiring politician, but also—as in Morgan's other novels—an intriguing self-portrait by Morgan in the character of the heroine. The novel, which Morgan herself privately called "good fun,"[64] and which Maria Edgeworth privately described as "a heap of trash,"[65] features an absurdly convoluted plot and a mixture of pro-Irish polemic, antiquarianism, slapstick

---

[62] The *Edinburgh Magazine* reviewer counterattacked by accusing Morgan of "rak[ing] into the stercoraceous and putrescent puddles of Billingsgate" and by calling her "a blustering virago" (*The Scots Magazine and Edinburgh Literary Miscellany* [New Series] 88 [October 1821]: 340 and 344)

[63] Anon., *The Mohawks; a Satirical Poem with Notes* (London: Henry Colburn, 1822), 99.

[64] Quoted in James Newcomer, *Lady Morgan the Novelist* (Lewisburg: Bucknell University Press, 1990), 89, n.1.

[65] Christina Colvin, ed., *Maria Edgeworth: Letters from England 1813–1844* (Oxford: Clarendon Press, 1971), 166.

humor, comedy of manners, sentiment (sometimes satirized and sometimes not), and the Gothic. This "strange tissue of improbability" (*FM*, 95) offers two heroes, one more Napoleonic and one more Byronic, and foregrounds the familiar Gothic theme whereby "The sins of the fathers must be visited on the childer" (*FM*, 72). It also relies on standard Gothic motifs such as fulfilled prophecies, mistaken identities, and the recovery of his birthright by a long lost heir, mistakenly thought drowned. In the remaining pages of this chapter, I will examine how Morgan uses this rollicking work of prose fiction to strike back at the *Quarterly*. I will suggest that the novel's hybrid genre helps Morgan herself, in the guise of her heroine Florence Macarthy, the "Bhan Tierna" (*FM*, 258), also known as Lady Clancare, to evade the terms of—in her phrase—the "hireling umpires" (*FM*, 301).

The initial summary of the villainous Croker character stands out in a lengthy satirical portrayal of the corrupt upstart Crawley family, "land pirates" (*FM*, 94) who rule in place of absentee Irish aristocrats. Morgan puts plenty of energy into characterizing the "OGRISH" Crawleys (*FM*, 275), but she shows particular investment in Conway (or "Counsellor Con"), whom she describes with mounting invective:

> The dark bile, which from childhood sallowed his cheek, dimm'd his eye, and tinged the spirits of youth with the causticity of age, continued, through adolescence and manhood, to communicate its bitterness to all his views; turning his words to sarcasm, his ink to gall, and his pen to a stiletto; and combining with an education, whose object was pretension, and whose principle was arrogance, it made him at once a thing fearful and pitiable, at war with its species and itself, ready to crush on the verge of the tomb, as to sting in the cradle, and leading his overweening ambition to pursue its object by ways, dark and hidden, safe from the penalty of crime, and exposed only to the obloquy which he laughed to scorn; for opinion has no punishment for the base.
>
> If ever there was a man formed alike by nature and education to betray the land that gave him birth and to act openly as the pander of political corruption or secretly as the agent of defamation, who would stoop to seek his fortune by effecting the fall of a frail woman, or would strive to advance it by stabbing the character of an honest one—who would crush aspiring merit behind the ambuscade of anonymous security while he came forward openly in the defence of that vileness which rank sanctified and influence protected—that man was Conway Crawley. He was yet young, but belonging to the day and the country where he first raised his hiss, and shed his venom, success already beckoned him towards her, with a smile of encouragement, and a leer of contempt. (*FM*, 127–8)

In this vigorous but unsubtle personal attack, Morgan does not resist the temptation to link Croker's allegedly unsavory physical appearance (his sallow complexion) with his "paths of darkness" (*FM*, 128). Morgan's overall depiction of Conway is more nuanced, betraying the satirist's fascination with the target of her satire. She implicitly ridicules his opinion that contemporaries are the "best judges" of fame—"for, after all, the *trash* that is talked about posterity, the true reputation is contemporary reputation, tangible fame, fame that one can lay one's finger on, that one can touch" (*FM*, 141), yet she herself would presumably agree with this anti-Romantic view. "Con," with "the sensitive quickness of self-love" (*FM*, 155), is capable of feeling "mortification" as well as "ire" (*FM*, 144), and of being "confused," while "unsubdued" (*FM*, 209), and "sobered" by a rebuke (*FM*, 297). He is also contrasted advantageously with his comically bigoted and under-educated father.

The portrait is unmistakable: Conway refers to "my friend of the Baviad and Maeviad" (*FM*, 139), and at one point actually utters various phrases from the *Quarterly*'s attack on *France*. Explaining that he is repeating "the criticism of a celebrated periodical review" (*FM*, 297–8), he denounces the "*sylphed* [sic] Miss Macarthy, the *elegant* Lady Clancare," as "in fact, a *mere bookseller's drudge*," castigating "her *impudent falsehoods*, and *lies by implication*, the impious jargon of this *mad woman, this* audacious worm" (*FM*, 297; Morgan's italics). Yet the insistence on the parallel betrays the extent to which Morgan allows her reputation to be defined by the *Quarterly*. And in zooming in on Croker as her enemy, Morgan may underestimate the power of the *Quarterly*'s corporate voice. Moreover, the fact that the heroes and heroine of the novel mask their identities for much of the story, preferring to remain mysteriously "*incognito*" (*FM*, 94), seems to unsettle Morgan's complaint about Conway / Croker's reliance on the "ambuscade" of anonymity.[66] Conway is thwarted at various times in the novel but not ultimately defeated, since at the end of the story, like his real-life counterpart, he is elected as a Member of Parliament for a rotten borough. Morgan, that is to say, instead of punishing Conway, uses him to show the power of the status quo, but this gesture indirectly acknowledges the enormity of what she is up against.

The portrait of Croker in *Florence Macarthy*, then, comes across as an energetic contribution to Morgan's feud with the *Quarterly*, but Morgan's self-portrait as the heroine is something more—a dazzlingly contradictory character capable of inhabiting all the different generic layers in the novel. A mistress of disguise, the heroine is first introduced unbeknownst to the reader and our two heroes in the shape of a repellent genderless elderly religious fanatic named Molly Magillicuddy. Molly, with her "very red nose, and a very large pair of dark green spectacles" (*FM*, 24) and her caged pet magpie, is described as "a most repelling ... thing" (*FM*, 60) who haunts the male protagonists like a "frightful phantom" (*FM*, 68). Imagined at one point as "some Ariel 'correspondent to command' of a concealed Prospero," the heroine is also compared with "the foul witch Sycorax" (*FM*, 78), while the novel's epigraph from *The Tempest* lines her up with Prospero himself. At one point, she passes herself off as an aged housekeeper known as Protestant Moll, who turns out to be deceased. When not masking her beauty of person and mind, the impoverished Lady Clancare improbably divides her time between being lionized in London as a professional woman of letters and digging up potatoes with the peasants outside her ruined castle in Southern Ireland. She

---

[66] In keeping with the novel's slippages of identity, even minor characters such as a coach driver and the lost heir's illegitimate half-brother turn out to be in disguise.

is also a self-proclaimed puppeteer and "magician" (*FM*, 316) who orchestrates the narrative and casts a spell over the two heroes, her love interest the long-lost Marquis of Dunore and the dreamy Lord Adelm Fitzadelm.

Morgan uses the career of Lady Clancare to comment on her own feud with the reviewers, making her a mouthpiece for her view that she has been "lashed into note" by malicious attacks (*FM*, 329). Lady Clancare even imagines a future domestic scene by her "Irish turf fire" with her husband as her "critical reviewer" (*FM*, 364), suggesting the extent to which reception defines her identity. In one problematic moment, singled out for quotation by more than one early reviewer, she admits to cashing in on Ireland's woes in her national tales: "With Ireland in my heart, and epitomizing something of her humour and her sufferings in my own life and story, I *do* trade upon the materials she furnishes me; and [turn] my patriotism into pounds, shillings, and pence" (*FM*, 274). This line makes Morgan's exposure of Irish poverty and squalor seem more financially than ethically motivated. Moreover, her disenchantment with celebrity, of being "shewn off like a wild beast," is perfectly rote (*FM*, 275). Confirming the blatant self-portrait, Lady Clancare announces a plan to write her own autobiographical story, entitled "*Florence Macarthy*" (*FM*, 364).[67]

However, unlike the character of Conway Crawley, Morgan's heroine cannot be pinned down to the novel's real-life concerns. Ina Ferris, in a discussion of the "hyper-hybridity" of the Morgan heroine (in this and her other Irish novels), claims that "she blocks both the transcendental move 'beyond' and the interior turn to a 'deep' subjectivity."[68] As Ferris points out, Lady Clancare even overlaps to some extent with Lord Adelm's sensibility-driven mother, the Marchioness of Dunore.[69] Ferris, commenting on Florence's "motiveless disguise[s]," adds that her "mobility" (*FM*, 245) causes her to "lie outside the wholeness of being conventionally linked to femininity in the period."[70] Florence Macarthy is indeed a figure of surfaces, as befits the multiple roles that she plays, exemplifying a self-dispersal that not only casts doubt on the authenticity of her Irishness, but also runs counter to the fantasy of an autonomous self more often identified with male writers of the Romantic era.

Nevertheless, her ability to occupy the multiple generic registers of the novel simultaneously takes her "beyond" them. As an author-figure, she is in charge of

---

[67] Jenny McAuley, in her edition of the novel, sees in this self-reflexive moment "Owenson's sense ... of the textual construction of women, as of Ireland" (*FM*, xvi).

[68] Ina Ferris, *The Romantic National Tale and the Question of Ireland* (Cambridge: Cambridge University Press, 2002), 84. As Ferris notes, the name Florence Macarthy also blurs gender lines, as it is the name of the heroine's father (76). On the elusiveness of Morgan's self-representations, see also Julie Donovan, *Sydney Owenson, Lady Morgan, and the Politics of Style* (Palo Alto: Academica Press, 2009), 54.

[69] Ferris, *The Romantic National Tale*, 83.

[70] Ina Ferris, "The Irish Novel, 1800–1829" in *The Cambridge Guide to Fiction in the Romantic Period*, ed. Richard Maxwell and Katie Trumpener (Cambridge: Cambridge University Press, 2007), 242.

the comic resolution of her own tale (marriage, of course), and thus of its pro-Irish social commentary, but as a Gothic heroine, her agency is partly subsumed by the Gothic convention whereby desire slides between overlapping characters and between the characters and the settings.[71] She meets her shape-shifting match in the charismatic Marquis of Dunore, variously known as the Commodore, "the Spanish Don" (*FM*, 14), and "General Fitzwalter, of South America" (*FM*, 212). Moreover, although she manipulates the second string hero Lord Adelm (also known as De Vere), she is somewhat contaminated by his attraction to "mystery," "romance" (*FM*, 25), and "fairyland" (*FM*, 77), and his interest in "superhuman agency" (*FM*, 37). Embodying the novel's tension between the mundane and the mystical, Lord Adelm is characterized as possessing "a something imaginative and ideal," and described as a "fop or philosopher, dandy or poet" who, "occupied by an *ideal presence*, ... affected to live independent of all human interests" (*FM*, 7).

In line with this passage's set of oppositions, the treatment of transcendence in the novel is only partly skeptical, and the desire to be "transport[ed] beyond the present" (*FM*, 248) leaks off onto the supposedly more practical protagonists, Florence and the Marquis. The Marquis debunks Lord Adelm's flights of fancy with reference to the "human" and the "material" (*FM*, 224), yet his skeptical voice is drowned out at times by the "wild, unregulated, ideal character" of his foster-father O'Leary (*FM*, 92). Even the "circle" of "Crawley dulness" is comically linked with this idealizing strand of the novel when it is compared with the "hieroglyphical circle of eternity" (*FM*, 169). Moreover, the Gothic settings such as ruined castles, sublime scenery, and gloomy towers—besides destabilizing the story's political message by glamorizing its pictures of Irish poverty—serve to lend the protagonists more than a tinge of "romance."

Contemporary reviewers were divided over whether *Florence Macarthy* had succeeded in wreaking vengeance on Morgan's attackers. The *Anti-Jacobin Review*, for example, with predictable hostility, accused the novel of "gross personality,"[72] and the *British Review* complained of its "distorted caricature of individuals."[73] More kindly, the *Edinburgh Magazine*—one of Morgan's later targets in her *Letter*—predicted that "it will *be read* in spite of all that Counsellor Crawley and his coadjutors of the Quarterly Review can do to the contrary."[74] The *New Monthly Magazine*—a product, like *Florence Macarthy*, of Henry Colburn's publishing house—described it as "a book which promises to be in every body's hands."[75] Morgan herself was delighted with the sensation she had created: by the following year, the novel had gone into five editions and had been adapted for the stage. Although the *Quarterly* responded to *Florence Macarthy* only in passing,

---

[71] On this feature of the Gothic, see Eve Sedgwick, "The Character in the Veil: Imagery of the Surface in the Gothic Novel," *PMLA* 96.2 (March 1981), 255–70.

[72] *Anti-Jacobin Review* 55 (February 1819): 513.

[73] Quoted by Belanger, *Critical Receptions*, 207.

[74] *Edinburgh Magazine* 3 (December 1818): 556.

[75] *The New Monthly Magazine* 10 (January 1819): 533.

dismissing it as a "sooterkin of dulness and immorality" (*QR* 21: 143–4), Morgan's own private comment on the novel was unequivocal: "What a triumph after the persecution I have suffered!"[76] As we have already seen, the "persecution" would continue, and Morgan, whose public identity was bound up with print warfare, would continue to revel in it. Nevertheless, *Florence Macarthy* shows that, while locked into the culture of "personality," like Hunt and Hazlitt, she was able on occasion to create a different sort of identity, in this case "something imaginative and ideal."

---

[76] Quoted by Newcomer, *Lady Morgan the Novelist*, 48.

Chapter 4
John Barrow, John Ross, and the Arctic Sublime

In previous chapters, we have seen that feuds originating with the *Quarterly* and the *Edinburgh* rise above the mire of "personality" in collaborating with emerging Romantic models of selfhood—or, in the cases of the feuds involving Hunt, Hazlitt, and Lady Morgan—in inspiring imaginative rejoinders that propose alternative versions of Romantic identity. The present chapter identifies a literary element within the *Quarterly* itself, focusing partly on a feud between the *Quarterly* reviewer John Barrow and the Scottish Arctic explorer John Ross that was conducted mostly in the pages of the periodical, and partly on a larger context for this feud: the *Quarterly*'s promotion of Arctic exploration. Like the other clashes that I have examined, the feud descends to alleged "personalities," while it expands in surprising directions both in terms of content and genre. While encompassing various single-authored books and pamphlets, this feud also further complicates the blurred relationship between individual and collective authorship.

Barrow, in his capacity as the Second Secretary to the British Admiralty,[1] was the man behind the Romantic-era quests to find the Northwest Passage, a navigable waterway across the top of North America, and to reach the North Pole (a lesser "Arctic Grail").[2] Beginning in 1818, successive British naval expeditions resumed the centuries-long search for the as yet hypothetical Passage. Despite their lack of success, expedition leaders such as Ross, William Edward Parry and John Franklin were hailed as national heroes. Each of their attempts to find the elusive waterway was recorded in print, in publications that included Ross's *Voyage of Discovery* (1819), Parry's *Journal of a Voyage for the Discovery of a North-West Passage* (1821), Franklin's *Narrative of a Journey to the Shores of the Polar Sea* (1823)—and, later, Ross's more controversial *Narrative of a Second Voyage in Search of a North-West Passage* (1835).[3]

---

[1] The First Secretary was Lady Morgan's arch-foe, Croker. More on him, or rather his name, below.

[2] I take the phrase from Pierre Berton, *The Arctic Grail: The Quest for the Northwest Passage and the North Pole 1818–1909* (New York: Lyons Press, 2000).

[3] The adventures of Ross, Parry, and others, have been fascinatingly recounted by historians of maritime exploration. See, for example, M.J. Ross, *Polar Pioneers: John Ross and James Clark Ross* (Montreal: McGill-Queen's University Press, 1994); Fergus Fleming, *Barrow's Boys* (New York: Grove Press, 1998); Ann Savours, *The Search for the North West Passage* (New York: St. Martin's Press, 1999); Glyn Williams, *Voyages of Delusion* (New Haven: Yale University Press, 2003); and Anthony Brandt, *The Man Who Ate His Boots: The Tragic History of the Search for the Northwest Passage* (New York: Alfred A. Knopf, 2010). However, these writers pay relatively little attention to Barrow's

Besides initiating these government-financed expeditions, Barrow regularly reviewed in the *Quarterly* the explorers' published accounts of their travels—anonymously of course. Between 1816 and 1840, he wrote for the *Quarterly* 18 highly biased articles that embraced its self-appointed cultural role as the chief promoter of the British push to conquer the Arctic ice. At first sight, these propagandistic articles do not proclaim their literariness. But Barrow's descriptions of human beings contemplating landscapes and seascapes at least potentially relate to the central Romantic themes of the interaction of mind and nature leading to transcendence, and the power of the supernatural. Rather than consciously seeking sublimity or plumbing the depths of the soul, however, Barrow used his Arctic reviews to advance his imperialistic, nationalistic, and private agendas, including conducting his feud with the naval officer who became his nemesis, John Ross. Barrow's treatment of Ross, culminating in the reviewer's own 1846 book, *Voyages of Discovery and Research Within the Arctic Regions*, eventually goaded the explorer to retaliate in print with indignant accusations of "personality" similar to those that we have seen in other feuds. Viewed holistically, Barrow's *Quarterly* articles on the Arctic can be read as a complex dramatic monologue in which the anonymous speaker's certainties are unsettled at every turn by his choice of evidence and his fixation with the looming figure of his antagonist. Its blindness yielding unsought-for insight, the narrative that unfolds, like certain canonical Romantic texts, offers glimmerings of the mysticism of ice.

Although it might seem artificial to bring together a set of essays written by one person over a period of more than 20 years, the *Quarterly*'s Arctic reviews offer an excellent opportunity to recover an individual voice from a collaborative product. Barrow's own voice is admittedly not easily disentangled from that of the periodical. And, though they acquired their own momentum, his Arctic articles were obviously not planned as a series, being contingent on the outcome of various different expeditions.[4] My intention in this chapter is not to recuperate the myth of solitary inspiration that is part of our Romantic inheritance, but partly to show how Barrow takes advantage of the conventional first person plural. Although Gifford often revised contributions to make them better fit the ethos of the periodical, he seems to have given Barrow a relatively free rein in covering the areas of his expertise, which included not only the British navy but geographical, travel-related

---

reviews of the books written by his "boys." Fleming calls Barrow not just "the father of Arctic exploration" but also "the father of global exploration" (*Barrow's Boys*, 11). He promoted African exploration, in particular the search for the source of the Niger and the quest to reach Timbuktu, in other *Quarterly* articles. See also Peter J. Kitson, ed., *Travels, Explorations and Empires: Writings from the Era of Imperial Expansion*, Volume 3: *North and South Poles* (London: Pickering & Chatto, 2001), a collection of extracts from books by early nineteenth-century explorers.

[4] Janice Cavell, in *Tracing the Connected Narrative: Arctic Exploration in British Print Culture, 1818–1860* (Toronto: University of Toronto Press, 2008), points out that "Barrow did not foresee a forty-year epic quest for the passage" (56).

and scientific matters in general.[5] The *Quarterly*'s most prolific contributor (he wrote over 200 articles in 34 years), Barrow said that "In all my critical labours I avoided touching upon politics, almost, I might say, altogether"—an unconvincing claim given the highly politicized discourse of the *Quarterly*.[6] In fact, Barrow's articles on Arctic discovery offer a remarkable instance of the masking of political power with cultural power.

As we have seen, the magisterial "we" of the *Quarterly* usually purported to represent the semi-official voice of the establishment, but in this case the *Quarterly* really did express establishment authority. The same man, that is to say, forged government policy and tried to sell it to the public. Several of the articles claim responsibility for the current search for the Northwest Passage while occluding the influence actually exerted by their author in his position as a high-ranking bureaucrat. At one point, Barrow gives "ourselves the credit" for making the Arctic "one of the fashionable topics of the day" (*QR* 19: 208), implying that the *Quarterly* single-handedly keeps British zeal for Arctic exploration at fever pitch.[7] He later insists that the government's plans are "no business of ours" (*QR* 38: 357). Yet his role as shaper of public opinion all too conveniently coincided with his act of sending the expeditions out in the first place. Needless to say, the articles do not acknowledge that it was Barrow's connection with the *Quarterly*'s publisher, Murray, that enabled the explorers, including John Ross, to publish their journals in expensive, high-profile editions suitable for reviewing in the elite periodical.

But, as Jonathan Cutmore notes, Barrow tended to signal his own authorship in his review articles.[8] Chafing against the convention of anonymity, he carves out his own space within the pages of the *Quarterly* by showing off his access to inside knowledge and repeatedly referring back to his own previous articles on the same topic. He not infrequently mentions his own name, sometimes citing his own book *A Chronological History of Voyages into the Arctic Regions* (1818) and fairly often alluding to geographical features of the Arctic named after him: he refers casually to "Barrow's Bay" (*QR* 19: 241), "Cape Barrow" (*QR* 28: 392), "Barrow's Strait" (*QR* 25: 181), "Point Barrow" (*QR* 45: 91), "Mount Barrow" (*QR* 56: 292) and a river "named after [the explorers'] mutual friend,

---

[5] According to Jonathan Cutmore, Barrow eventually "bypassed Gifford by sending his articles directly to the printer and by editing the proofs himself," thus endangering the "mystique that the *Quarterly*'s editorial cabal spoke Cabinet-like with a single voice" (Cutmore, "Writers and Readers of the Early *Quarterly Review*," unpublished manuscript, 17).

[6] Sir John Barrow, *An Auto-biographical Memoir* (London: John Murray, 1847), 504.

[7] On another occasion, he says, "we may, perhaps, be pardoned if ... we take some little merit to ourselves for having revived the subject of a North-West Passage ... [and] for having kept alive the public attention to it" (*QR* 25: 176).

[8] Jonathan Cutmore, *Contributors to the Quarterly Review 1809–25: A History* (London: Pickering & Chatto, 2008), 221, n.45.

Mr. Barrow" (*QR* 30: 255).⁹ In his penultimate Arctic article for the *Quarterly*, a review of George Back's *Journey to the Arctic Sea* (1836), Barrow summarizes and approvingly quotes from a letter by "Sir John Barrow" (*QR* 56: 296). (He had by then been awarded a baronetcy.) Later, in his 1846 book on Arctic exploration, he quotes and acknowledges ownership of a passage from the *Quarterly*.¹⁰ There are two overlapping collective voices here then—that of the British Admiralty as well as the periodical—in addition to Barrow's individual voice with its own personal prejudices. He seems to be playing a game with his audience, creating a cultural identity for himself as *the* expert on polar exploration while at once hiding and revealing his position as the mastermind behind it.¹¹

What does this game-playing—and the feud with Ross—have to do with the arrival on the scene of what we now know as Romanticism? I have already suggested that Barrow's Arctic reviews can be seen as a complicated form of self-expression—calculating yet at the same time lacking in self-awareness—that hints at nature's hidden depths. While the articles foreground more tangible agendas, their theme of humanity's encounter with the hostilities of the Arctic resonates against central Romantic texts that linger over the dangers of ice: for example, Coleridge's "The Rime of the Ancient Mariner," even though the ice in that poem is southern rather than northern, and Mary Shelley's *Frankenstein* (1818). But the reviews also look outwards in a different sense to the alien cultural practices of native North Americans, sharing some of the ambivalence underlying Romantic colonialism.¹² Jen Hill has recently addressed the (gendered) nationalistic and imperialistic dimensions of nineteenth-century British Arctic exploration literature.¹³ As we will see, Barrow (or his persona), like many other Romantic-

---

⁹ On the naming of places in the context of Romantic colonialism, see Carol Bolton, *Writing the Empire: Robert Southey and Romantic Colonialism* (London: Pickering & Chatto, 2007), 84.

¹⁰ Sir John Barrow, *Voyages of Discovery and Research Within the Arctic Regions, from the year 1818 to the present time* (London: John Murray, 1846), 1–2.

¹¹ Cavell, in *Tracing the Connected Narrative*, calls Barrow "the epitome of the behind-the-scenes manipulator" (55), while pointing out that "Other journalists referred to Barrow's authorship of the *Quarterly* articles as if to a widely-known fact" (255, n.2). *Blackwood's*, for instance, alludes to "The very able articles connected with [the Arctic], which we have already received, from the pen of Mr Barrow, through the medium of the Quarterly Review" (*BM* 4: 187). A later *Blackwood's* piece praises the most recent *Quarterly* article on the Arctic and refers to its author as "Mr Barrow" (*BM* 14: 84).

¹² See, for example, Tim Fulford and Peter Kitson, eds, *Romanticism and Colonialism: Writing and Empire, 1780–1830* (Cambridge: Cambridge University Press, 1998). On the ambivalence of Southey, Barrow's fellow *Quarterly* reviewer, in particular, see David Simpson, *Writing the Empire*, "Romantic Indians: Robert Southey's Distinctions," *The Wordsworth Circle* 38 (2007): 20–25.

¹³ Hill qualifies Linda Colley's work, in *Britons: Forging the Nation, 1707–1837* (New Haven: Yale University Press, 1992), on the formation of British nationalism in relation to foreign cultures, by showing how nineteenth-century British national and imperial identities were also defined against the supposedly blank, "pure" space of the Arctic (Jen Hill, *White*

era travel writers, displays ethnographic fascination alongside ethnocentric moral judgment. The subject matter of his reviews therefore speaks to our new, expanded sense of Romanticism besides providing an unexpected source of the more familiar Romantic entrancement with the sublime.

As we have seen in previous chapters, the question of continuities between periodical writing and Romanticism involves choices of genre as well as content. Jessica Richard has argued that Mary Shelley's novel criticizes the narratives of Arctic exploration—and by extension her fictional explorer Robert Walton—for being caught up in the quest to master the ice, a quest associated with "imaginative self-assertion"—and, one might add, masculine dominance.[14] Richard claims that the narratives belong to the genre of romance, a genre revived in much Romantic poetry and Romantic-era prose fiction.[15] Barrow's writings on the Arctic exemplify what Richard calls in her title "the improbable romance of polar exploration" in that not only did Barrow believe that "a navigable and practical [Northwest] passage does exist" (*QR* 30: 268), for much of his career he insisted on the existence of an unfrozen "Polar Sea" (*QR* 30: 255). These convictions as expressed in his reviews reflect not only personal and institutional priorities but also tensions within romance: its structure, a search that is constantly replayed yet deferred, reflects the elusiveness of both the Passage and the Pole.[16] Barrow himself never expresses any

---

Horizon: The Arctic in the Nineteenth-Century Imagination [Albany: State University of New York Press, 2007], 9). Hill points out that Barrow metonymically associated that purity with the British navy (11). Hence his opposition to mechanized ships: he ridiculed Ross's use of a steamship (*QR* 54: 5). Francis Spufford, who, in *I May Be Some Time: Ice and the English Imagination* (New York: St. Martin's Press, 1997), presents a cultural or "imaginative," rather than factual "history of polar exploration" (7), points out that the (false) "perception of Arctic emptiness" (58) made the region seem like a blank sheet of paper that could be written on by outsiders. See also Adriana Craciun, "The Scramble for the Arctic," *Interventions* 11.1 (2009): 103–14.

[14] Richard, in "'A Paradise of My Own Creation': *Frankenstein* and the Improbable Romance of Polar Exploration," *Nineteenth-Century Contexts* 25.4 (2003): 295–314 (297), quotes this phrase from Mary Poovey, *The Proper Lady and the Woman Writer* (Chicago: University of Chicago Press, 1984), 149. Richard's essay brings out a "sexualized" element (303) in what she calls "the masculine romance of conquest, penetration, and possession" (301). On the gender implications of imperialistic explorations, see Hill, *White Horizon*, and Lisa Bloom, *Gender on Ice: American Ideologies of Polar Expeditions* (Minneapolis: University of Minnesota Press, 1993). On connections between polar imagery, classical myth, and *Paradise Lost*, see Rudolf Beck, "'The Region of Beauty and Delight': Walton's Polar Fantasies in Mary Shelley's *Frankenstein*," *Keats-Shelley Journal* 49 (2000): 24–9. See also Adriana Craciun, "Writing the Disaster: Franklin and *Frankenstein*," *Nineteenth-Century Literature* 65.4 (March 2011): 433–80.

[15] Compare Cavell, *Tracing the Connected Narrative*, on how Barrow "did not begin as a Romantic" (56), but eventually "espoused a romantic vision" (14).

[16] Drawing on Patricia Parker's theory of romance, in *Inescapable Romance* (Princeton: Princeton University Press, 1979), as involving endless deferral, Richard notes that "Barrow's narratives, filled with ever-proliferating opinions, tales, and arguments about attempts to reach the pole, cannot describe the end of the quest, the perennially postponed

doubt about reaching his goal, but his use of romance conventions reinforces the pull between renewal and postponement that is built into periodical form.

However, I see the romance in this material as competing with other literary genres. I will show that Barrow does indeed present himself as the writer of a traditional quest romance involving the successful overcoming of adversity. He has his hero—Parry—and his villain—John Ross. The first will easily defeat the latter, as well as his other enemy, the Arctic ice, with or without the help of the trusty John Franklin, and the story will end with the happy marriage of the Atlantic and the Pacific. The story has epic as well as comic dimensions, fantasizing the spread of empire through the planting of the Union Jack in the Arctic tundra. As the narrative develops, Barrow is forced to darken it, casting the fearless Parry as a heroic wanderer suffering cruel setbacks. Taking a hint from Barrow's repeated quotation from *Measure for Measure*, "thrilling regions of thick-ribbed ice" (*QR* 26: 357; *QR* 30: 262; *QR* 37: 538)—a phrase that identifies the Arctic with death—we can see his polar articles as resembling a problem play with various morally recalcitrant elements (including native peoples as well as the ice). Barrow's persecution of Ross also draws upon the conventions of the Gothic romance with its standard plot of paranoid pursuit and its preoccupation with epistemological confusion. Read in such ways, these reviews tell a bleak rather than uplifting story that degenerates into farce. Nonetheless, Barrow's narrative is punctuated by moments gesturing towards the Romantic lyric with its figurings of transcendence, rather than prose genres with their more earthly resolutions. These are the moments in which Barrow's voice registers—at several removes—the wondrousness of the Arctic. Here we find the inward turn that characterizes Romantic-era romance.[17] At such points, problems of knowing are not mere matters of mistaken identity as in a comic or Gothic plot; they instead shade into the existential questioning typified by that profound meditation on ice, Percy Bysshe Shelley's "Mont Blanc" (1816).

Setting the Scene

Barrow's first four articles on the Arctic can be read as elaborate scene-setting since he does not yet have his cast of stereotyped characters. And they offer few

---

Paradise beyond the pack ice" ("'A Paradise of My Own Creation,'" 303). In illuminating the polar context of *Frankenstein*, Richard stresses Barrow's interest in the open polar sea as expressed in his 1818 book, as opposed to his articles on the search for the Northwest Passage. On mystical Arctic utopianism, see Adriana Craciun, "The Frozen Ocean," *PMLA* 125 (2010): 693–702.

[17] Compare, however, Greg Kucich on "psychodrama" as a longstanding element of the genre ("Romance," in *Romanticism: An Oxford Guide* [Oxford: Oxford University Press, 2005, 463–81], 466). The Arctic essays often appeared alongside reviews of Romantic poetry, one (*QR* 19: 208–14) even sandwiched right between the *Quarterly*'s attack on Keats's *Endymion* and its praise for Lord Byron's *Childe Harold's Pilgrimage*, Canto 4 (1818).

if any hints of the magic of the polar landscape. But these preliminary pieces introduce one of Barrow's major themes—distorted perception—although this theme is not initially exploited for comic effect, as it will be in his attacks on Ross. Barrow himself had taken a months-long voyage in a whaling ship as young man (besides publishing accounts of his travels to China and South Africa as an "imperial servant"[18]), but he prefers to come across in these and later reviews as a faceless armchair traveler with an unparalleled grasp of the past and present state of Arctic exploration. Writing at his desk in London, Barrow implies that he can see more clearly than people who have actually grappled with the ice.[19]

Nevertheless, as Fergus Fleming remarks in an understatement, "Barrow was never quite right."[20] Richard's essay on the polar context of *Frankenstein* emphasizes "the problem of evaluating evidence, witnesses, and testimony that plagued historians of polar exploration."[21] Nothing if not thorough, Barrow risks leaving his audience behind just when he sounds most authoritative. Place names, dates, references to distances and latitudes and other matters of historical and geographical fact proliferate dauntingly in his Arctic articles. Perhaps overestimating the periodical reader's tolerance for repetition, he tends to reiterate his account of the history of Arctic exploration, material duplicated in his 1818 book.

Barrow's air of assurance is strikingly at odds with the contradictory picture that emerges of the Arctic climate and topography. At the same time, his tone of optimism grates against his exhaustive coverage of the setbacks encountered by explorers, whether historical or contemporary. His frequent self-conscious references to the influence that his articles are having on public thinking about the Arctic thus tend to ring hollow. He also often raises the question of why it is important to find "A NORTH-WEST PASSAGE FROM THE ATLANTIC INTO THE PACIFIC" (*QR* 25: 176, his emphasis). While he claims that geographical discovery and national glory are ends in themselves, he can never entirely let go of a possible commercial payoff. Although the search for the fabled Passage thus seems clouded from various directions, Barrow creates the impression of a progressing narrative by referring in most of his articles to new expeditions currently underway or pending. Meanwhile, his discussions at times become mired in issues of spurious authorship and distracted by some of the more lurid aspects of polar exploration.

Barrow's initial *Quarterly* article on polar matters, dated 1816, approaches epistemological questions only obliquely at first by summarizing a one-sided book about the "atrocities" (*QR* 16: 138) committed by the North West Company of

---

[18] J.M.R. Cameron, "John Barrow, the *Quarterly Review*'s Imperial Reviewer," in Jonathan Cutmore, ed., *Conservatism and the* Quarterly Review*: A Critical Analysis* (London: Pickering & Chatto, 2007), 133–49 (135).

[19] Barrow finally referred to his own youthful travels in the Arctic in his 1843 *Edinburgh Review* article, "Beechey's Voyages towards the North Pole" (*ER* 78: 86).

[20] Fleming, *Barrow's Boys*, 11–12.

[21] Richard, "'A Paradise of My Own Creation,'" 299.

Canada and its bloody feud with its rival fur-traders, the Hudson's Bay Company (the two did not merge until 1821).[22] Barrow concurs with the author of the book, Lord Selkirk, that the North West Company is guilty of "outrageous acts of violence" (*QR* 16: 138) and frustratingly beyond the reach of the law. The story provides an ominous lead-in to the topic of "the discovery of a North-west Passage" (*QR* 16: 144). He then turns to the second of the two books under review, a recent French translation of a manuscript by a (real) sixteenth-century Spanish captain claiming to have navigated the Northwest Passage itself. Barrow concedes that the Spaniard, Lorenzo Maldonado, existed, voyaged up the west coast of America towards Bering Strait, and gave the manuscript of his journal to a Spanish bishop. But he denies that the book he is reviewing is based on that manuscript and insists that Maldonado could not have navigated the Northwest Passage.

Barrow's exposure of the spuriousness of the Spanish text evokes a situation familiar to readers of Gothic fiction with its elaborate strategies for giving improbable events a veneer of believability: the translator, a librarian in Milan, having found a hastily copied document in Spanish with an Italian watermark, supposedly written at the turn of the seventeenth century, decided at first that it was "only ... a tale to amuse the curious" but then "on reading it with attention ... found it stamped ... strongly with the character of authenticity and veracity" (*QR* 16: 146).[23] The deluded librarian then translated the document first into Italian, and then into French. The image of an unearthed manuscript from a foreign library—which brings to mind the first (later repudiated) Preface to Horace Walpole's *The Castle of Otranto* (1764)—might alone serve to discredit this suspiciously embellished frame narrative. Nevertheless, Barrow next proceeds to demolish the contents of the purported "memoir" (*QR* 16: 146). He complains of the author's "gross blunders ... in geography" (*QR* 16: 148) and "gross fictions" (*QR* 16: 150–51). Yet at least one of his refutations adds another layer of questionability: "We suspect this pretended voyage of Maldonado to be the clumsy and audacious forgery of some ignorant German" (*QR* 16: 151). Having exposed the credulity of the Milanese librarian, Barrow seemingly expects his own readers to believe an equally improbable scenario. This will not be the last time that readers of the *Quarterly* hear of Maldonado.

Amid the maze of claims and counterclaims, however, Barrow's central assertion stands out: "We firmly believe ... that a navigable passage from the Atlantic to the Pacific round the northern coast of America does exist, and may be of no difficult execution" (*QR* 16: 153). But as he goes on to demonstrate in much detail, he holds this belief despite not because of the vast extent of his knowledge. His preoccupation with uncovering the truth will soon establish him as

---

[22] This article thus offers a rare moment of what Peter J. Kitson calls "colonial guilt" (*Romanticism and Colonialism: Writing and Empire, 1780–1830* [Cambridge: Cambridge University Press, 1998], 15).

[23] On how the "found-manuscript topos" elicits "suspicion rather than belief," see Margaret Russett, *Fictions and Fakes: Forging Romantic Authenticity, 1760–1845* (Cambridge: Cambridge University Press, 2006), 24–5.

the unconscious victim of irony. As we will see, every failure to find the Northwest Passage only strengthens Barrow's belief that it exists.

The remainder of the 1816 article recounts previous attempts to find the Passage from an earlier golden age of British Arctic exploration, beginning with the Elizabethans Martin Frobisher and John Davis.[24] Barrow introduces the subject by expressing "pride and pleasure" at the thought of early explorers' "daring enterprizes [sic]" (*QR* 16: 153). Yet his account relates a succession of disappearances, mutinies, "ships beset by ice" (*QR* 16: 158), death "by cold and hunger," and murder at the hands of the "natives" (*QR* 16: 157). He dismisses one particular failure in a single throwaway sentence: "Knight and Hall, in 1606 and 1607, lost their lives in a scuffle with the natives before they had made any discovery of importance" (*QR* 16: 156). He even seems to foreshadow Franklin's first dire overland expedition with a reference to the mutinous crew of a ship subsisting on "sea-weeds fryed [sic] with candle-ends, and the skins and feathers of the fowl they had eaten" (*QR* 16: 157). So much for the glorious history of the past. Despite all this discouraging information, Barrow concludes that the Northwest Passage surely exists and that "The solution of this important problem is the business of *three months* out and home" (*QR* 16: 168; his italics).

Later events will destabilize such assertions. In 1819, Parry would begin the practice of wintering in the Arctic in order to maximize efforts at locating the Passage. His third voyage, involving two winters in the ice, resulted in the loss of one of his two ships. In 1833, John Ross would return from his second voyage to the Arctic after four winters stuck in the ice, having been forced to abandon his only ship. The early nineteenth-century quest for the Northwest Passage culminated disastrously in the 1845 expedition of Sir John Franklin, from which no one returned. The waterway was not actually navigated until 1906, by the Norwegian Roald Amundsen, who spent three years on his journey. In his 1816 article, Barrow concedes that the discovery of the Passage might have no commercial significance, "from the uncertainty of its being free from ice any one year" (*QR* 16: 169). But he insists that British "national honour" (*QR* 16: 169) is at stake—he is worried that the Russians will get there first—not to mention the heroic search for geographical knowledge. "We have little doubt," Barrow adds inconsistently, "of a free and practicable passage round [the American continent] for seven or eight months in every year" (*QR* 16: 169). He continues to make such statements even after his explorers find themselves at the "very threshold of the door" only to confront "an unbroken sheet of ice" (*QR* 30: 255).

Ten years into the renewed quest, Barrow conjured up the threat of American rivals to highlight the importance of pressing on: "if we should unfortunately remain satisfied with having opened the door, our transatlantic brethren, with all their love for the dollars, will not be slow in availing themselves of so good an opportunity of passing the threshold" (*QR* 34: 388). In his very last Arctic article

---

[24] Spufford points out that the Northwest Passage's "connection" to "Elizabethan voyagers" made it seem magical (*I May Be Some Time*, 54).

for the *Quarterly*, in 1840, Barrow was still using the image of a threshold and writing with the same nationalistic fervor: "We cannot believe—now the doors have been widely thrown open—that the triumph of first actually passing the threshold shall, after all that we have done to clear the way, be left to any foreign flag" (*QR* 66: 445). Despite insisting that he favors "the pursuit of science for the sake of science" (*QR* 18: 457), Barrow almost invariably gives the main thrust of his argument a nationalistic spin: "To ascertain the existence of a north-west passage from the Atlantic to the Pacific," he emphasizes early on, "is peculiarly a British object" (*QR* 18: 212).

Barrow's second and third Arctic articles, both published in 1818, continue to offer a mixture of "facts" and "hypothesis" (*QR* 18: 444), while putting forward an obtrusive show of authority. These two articles expatiate on the significance of the recent moving and thawing of the polar ice pack, arguing for the "insularity of Greenland" (*QR* 18: 213) and against the "heresy" (*QR* 18: 431) that Bering Strait leads into a bay connecting America and Asia (*QR* 18: 215 and *QR* 18: 431–9). In his determination to "prove" claims that have not yet been substantiated (*QR* 18: 445), Barrow makes copious reference to water temperatures, currents, notes in sealed bottles, and, as he puts it, "wounded whales and drift-wood" (*QR* 18: 444). One of the articles includes a chart of recent thermometer readings, but vacillates over whether the thawing of the polar ice will improve or worsen the climate of Britain (*QR* 18: 206–8). Barrow is sometimes forced to revise "facts" as he goes along. His first Arctic article had claimed that the Aurora Borealis gives out heat and makes a "crackling noise" (*QR* 16: 171); a few years later he dismisses the "numerous ... testimonies to this fact" (*QR* 25: 201). By contrast, in his final Arctic article for the *Quarterly* he refuses to decide: "They all are right—they all are wrong" (*QR* 66: 429). Quite often, he simply contradicts himself: for example, his first article states that "the sea and land swarm with animals in these abodes of ice and snow" (*QR* 16: 170), whereas later ones expatiate on the scarcity or absence of "living creature[s]" in the Arctic (*QR* 25: 183).

Barrow's second Arctic article, according to his 1847 autobiography, "very much increased" the circulation of the *Quarterly* in the opinion of Murray; Barrow misleadingly added that the same article "gave rise to the recent Arctic voyages."[25] Barrow typically implies that his words rather than his actions brought

---

[25] Barrow, *An Auto-biographical Memoir*, 505. Over 12,000 copies of the October 1817 *Quarterly* (in which this article appeared) were sold on the day of publication (Cutmore, *Quarterly Review* Archive). The cultural impact of the article may be indicated by the prefatory note to Eleanor Anne Porden's poem *The Arctic Expeditions* (London: John Murray, 1818), which says that "The objects of the expeditions of which these vessels form a part, the dangers they may have to encounter, and their prospects of success, have been made so familiar to every one by the very able and delightful article in the last Quarterly Review, and the disquisitions to which it has give rise, that any details are unnecessary" (5–6). For discussions of this poem, see Tim Fulford et al., *Literature, Science and Exploration* (Cambridge: Cambridge University Press, 2004), 68–9; and Hill, *White Horizon*, 69–87. No doubt inspired by the same piece of news if not by Barrow's article, Lady Morgan ended *Florence Macarthy* with the disappointed Lord Adelm's "departure for the North Pole" (*FM*, 365).

about efforts at exploration. In fact the article gives details of two expeditions—headed by Captains Buchan and Ross—about to leave for the North Pole and the Northwest Passage respectively. At one point Barrow "throw[s] out" a "hint" about opportunities for research (*QR* 18: 204), as if he has nothing to do with organizing the expeditions. Yet in his next article he includes up-to-date news from the ships on their voyage to the Arctic. In both these articles, Barrow quotes a letter from the whaling captain and scientist William Scoresby to Sir Joseph Banks, President of the Royal Society, about the recent melting of the polar ice. Barrow thus gives a small amount of credit to Scoresby, whose findings had inspired the renewed quest for the Passage, while omitting to mention that he personally had refused to let Scoresby command either of the current expeditions.[26] In his very next article, Barrow again parades his access to behind-the-scenes information. He first pretends that the writer under review, Bernard O'Reilly, had "hash[ed] up a fictitious voyage" to make money (*QR* 19: 208). Yet, "Recollecting, however, that the log-book of the ship Thomas, of Hull, in which this voyage is stated to have been made, was within our reach, we turned to it, and found that Bernard O'Reilly, Esq. was not, as we suspected, a phantom conjured up for the occasion, but that there actually was a person of this name, in the capacity of surgeon, on board that ship" (*QR* 19: 208). Having invented the possibility of the book being spurious so that he can prove its authenticity, he then nevertheless dismisses the "pompous and frothy quarto" (*QR* 19: 208) as nearly all "either fiction or downright falsehood" (*QR* 19: 209).

Both Barrow's second and third articles propound at length their writer's belief in an unfrozen sea at the North Pole. Barrow does not go quite as far as Mary Shelley's Robert Walton in seeing the Pole as "the region of beauty and delight,"[27] but states intransigently that sailing there will be "easy": "A sea of more than two thousand miles in diameter, of unfathomable depth ... and in constant motion, is not likely to be frozen over at any time" (*QR* 18: 222). Barrow made the same argument in his 1818 book (citing his third *Quarterly* article on the Arctic), while

---

[26] For a fuller account, see A.G.E. Jones, "Sir John Ross and Sir John Barrow," *Polar Portraits: Collected Papers* (Whitby: Caedmon, 1992), 219–28 (221–2); Constance Martin, "William Scoresby Jr. and the Open Polar Sea—Myth and Reality," *Arctic* 41 (1988): 39–47; and Fleming, *Barrow's Boys*, 30–33. Fleming points out that in these *Quarterly* articles, Barrow published "Scoresby's plans as his (anonymous) own" (*Barrow's Boys*, 35). A letter from Scoresby about the "singular openness of the Greenland seas" had been published in *Blackwood's* in October 1817 (*BM* 2: 21). Eighteen years later, Barrow took the trouble to challenge Ross's claim that Scoresby had "revived" the quest for the Northwest Passage, instead giving credit to his own earlier *Quarterly* articles (*QR* 54: 1). An *Edinburgh* article dated 1818 by John Leslie deplored the governmental "jealousies or official punctilios" (*ER* 30: 3) that refused to give Scoresby command of a ship. In contrast with Barrow, the *Edinburgh* reviewer expresses skepticism about the break-up of the polar ice, consigning fantasies of an improved climate to the "dreams of romance" (*ER* 30: 5). The *Edinburgh* was markedly less optimistic than the *Quarterly* about the existence of a Northwest Passage.

[27] Mary Shelley, *Frankenstein*, ed. Marilyn Butler (Oxford: Oxford World's Classics, 1994), 5.

sounding a little less optimistic about the navigability of the Northwest Passage. A footnote in the second of this pair of articles ridicules Scoresby's idea (which he admits Scoresby himself has repudiated) of traveling over the ice: "even supposing the polar sea to be frozen, it would present a surface so rugged and mountainous, as to make it an easier task to drive a broad-wheeled waggon over the summit of Mont-Blanc, than a rein-deer sledge to the north pole" (*QR* 18: 451). The whimsicality of this image may intensify rather than diminish the fancifulness of Barrow's "open sea" theory.

Barrow did not entirely relinquish this cherished theory even when reviewing Parry's *Narrative of an Attempt to Reach the North Pole*—an attempt, involving boats and hand-drawn sledges, which failed miserably. In this 1828 article Barrow asserts that "a good stout sailing vessel would have been preferable ... we wish to see our brave fellows in their proper station—on board a ship" (*QR* 37: 535). Despite the insuperable difficulties encountered by Parry, in another article published later that same year Barrow continued to maintain with exaggerated emphasis that "there is every reason to believe that at all times a very large portion of the Polar Sea is entirely free from ice" (*QR* 38: 356). In his final *Quarterly* article on the Arctic, dated 1840, he suggests that it would be even more efficient to travel to Bering Strait via the North Pole than via the (still undiscovered) Northwest Passage. Meanwhile, back in 1818, Barrow optimistically predicts the explorers' enlargement of "the sphere of human knowledge" (*QR* 18: 457). Unfortunately all this eager anticipation will only intensify the reviewer's—and the reader's—sense of dissatisfaction at the perpetual prolonging of the quest.

Barrow versus Ross

Barrow's reviews of the accounts of the initial Arctic expeditions that he himself sent out set up the major conflict within his story—the rivalry between his arch-enemy John Ross and his "golden boy" Parry.[28] In the *Quarterly* for January 1819, Barrow attacked the unfortunate Ross for failing to find the Northwest Passage, in a scathing 49-page review that, as Kitson notes, seriously damaged Ross's reputation. Behind the scenes, Barrow put an end to Ross's career in the British navy. The leaders of the two separate expeditions, David Buchan and Ross, had both made the decision to turn back, Buchan because one of his ships was damaged, and Ross because he thought he saw the passage west blocked by a range of mountains. Ross had chronicled his journey to Greenland and the waterways off the north-east coast of Canada in his 1819 book published by Murray, *A Voyage of Discovery: made under the Orders of the Admiralty, in His Majesty's ships Isabella and Alexander, for the Purpose of Exploring Baffin's Bay, and Inquiring into the Probability of a North-West passage.*

---

[28] Fleming uses the phrase in *Barrow's Boys*, 234.

Barrow begins his article by expressing "disappointment ... in common with the rest of the world, at the total failure of the two Expeditions" of the previous year (*QR* 21: 213). He dispenses with Buchan's North Pole expedition in a single sentence, seeing its "failure" as beyond human control. "Of that of the other," he adds ominously, "we hardly know in what terms to speak" (*QR* 21: 213). Calling Ross's abandonment of his voyage "wholly unaccountable" (*QR* 21: 214), the reviewer claims that "our conviction of the existence" of a waterway to the "Polar Sea" and a navigable Northwest Passage "so far from being in the smallest degree shaken by any thing that Captain Ross has done, is considerably strengthened by what he has omitted to do" (*QR* 21: 214). He continues, "In support of this opinion we shall not, on the present occasion, have recourse to either argument or hypothesis," instead "confining ourselves strictly to the actual facts and circumstances of the voyage, as detailed in the narrative before us" (*QR* 21: 214).

Despite this promise to restrict himself to internal evidence, Barrow marshals various different authorities in support of his attack on Ross, including an essay by Edward Sabine, the expedition's scientist; an article from "one of the monthly journals"—*Blackwood's Magazine* for December 1818—(*QR* 21: 238); the private journal of Parry, Ross's second-in-command; and Barrow's own 1818 book. Although claiming not to feel "a single particle of personal hostility" (*QR* 21: 214), Barrow, as Pierre Berton remarks, finds Ross guilty of cowardice, besides calling him "[i]mpenetrably dull or intentionally perverse" (*QR* 21: 248).[29] He accuses Ross of ignoring "plain facts" (*QR* 21: 234) and neglecting to do "actual researches while on the spot" (*QR* 21: 235), instead relying on "mere assertions" (*QR* 21: 235). He also contrasts Ross's lack of "perseverance" with that of previous "navigators" (*QR* 21: 251). Barrow takes one passage in Ross's book about people "unwilling to concede their opinions while there is yet a single yarn of their hypothesis holding" to be "aimed at us" (*QR* 21: 235), but he is clearly hoping to turn it back against Ross.

The idea of clashing facts and hypotheses foregrounds Barrow's theme of clouded vision. Barrow had already exploited this theme's comic potential in his attack on O'Reilly's *Greenland* (1818). Opposing O'Reilly's claim to authority, Barrow flaunts not only his access to inside information but also his own superior powers of interpretation. Prefiguring his attack on Ross, Barrow mocks O'Reilly's invention of the "Linnean islands" (*QR* 19: 210): "By the 'power of vision' he sees behind them 'very distinctly, an open sea,' and beyond that an 'interminable icy continent.' But on reading a little farther, we find that the sea and the continent have changed places!" (*QR* 19: 210). With the labored humor so often found in reviews of the era, Barrow flogs the joke to death: "The ship Thomas, it is true, was never within sight of any land on this part of the coast; but that is nothing— Bernard O'Reilly's 'power of vision' enables him, like the witches in Macbeth,

---

[29] Berton, *The Arctic Grail*, 33. Berton calls this review "savage" (33). Cavell, in *Tracing the Connected Narrative*, calling it "exceptionally vituperative" (54), discusses the cultural and political reasons for Barrow's "extreme hostility" to Ross (68).

to see 'beyond the ignorant present'" (*QR* 19: 211). Of course one could make the same complaint about Barrow's seemingly preternatural command of the unknown.

Problems of perception return with a vengeance in Barrow's first attack on Ross. The obstacle to Ross's success and therefore to Barrow's approval was a range of mountains across Lancaster Sound that Ross supposedly glimpsed during a 10-minute gap in the fog, causing him to abandon his search for the Northwest Passage and return to England. When Ross saw these non-existent mountains, he was in fact looking at the entrance to the Passage that Parry would discover a year later.[30] Responding to Ross, Barrow does not yet have proof that the mountains are imaginary, but takes the line that they cannot exist because the Northwest Passage must exist. He quotes Ross's account at length: "I distinctly saw the land, round the bottom of the bay, forming a connected chain of mountains. ... At this moment I also saw a continuity of ice. ... The mountains ... were named Croker's Mountains, after the Secretary to the Admiralty. The south-west corner, which formed a spacious bay completely occupied by ice, was named Barrow's Bay" (*QR* 19: 241). Ross's book was even published with an illustration of Croker's Mountains. Barrow lingers over Ross's description, accusing him of "inconsistencies" and "impossibilities" (*QR* 19: 241), mocking his "extraordinary powers of vision" (*QR* 21: 243) and berating him for "blocking up Lancaster Sound with Croker's Mountains, and Cape Rosamond—mountains in nubibus, and Cape fly-away" (*QR* 21: 243). (He sounds equally doubtful about the existence of "Barrow's Bay" but mentions it again twice.) He adds disingenuously, "We have too great a respect for Captain Ross to doubt his word, though we may be permitted to doubt his strength of sight" (*QR* 21: 244).

Barrow's skepticism as to the accuracy of Ross's visual perceptions extends to the appearance of ice. He quotes a passage from Ross's book rhapsodizing over the "exquisite" rainbow-colored "tints" of the icebergs, and comments curtly, "We do not well see how this can be; icebergs display no colour by night, and those exhibited by day are confined to blue and green" (*QR* 21: 215). This emphatic statement is at odds with later moments in which he acknowledges the wonders of Arctic seascapes. Accusing Ross of "habitual inaccuracy and a looseness of description" (*QR* 21: 216), the reviewer dismisses one of the explorer's observations as "utterly unintelligible on any principle of optics and natural philosophy that we are acquainted with" (*QR* 21: 233). He also ridicules Ross's account of a previously unknown native people whom he named "Arctic Highlanders" (*QR* 21: 225). Barrow's condescending pity for these "poor people" (*QR* 21: 226) does not prevent him from pronouncing these "northern Esquimaux" to be "more ugly than their southern neighbours" (*QR* 21: 228). While going on to devote several pages to Ross's descriptions of "this insulated tribe," he insists that studying them further would have been a waste of time (*QR* 21: 225). For Barrow, the expedition was

---

[30] Fleming, in *Barrow's Boys*, confirming that Ross was "utterly mistaken" (48), suggests that the mountain-range that Ross saw may have been a mirage (49).

a total failure. Although, in addition to encountering these natives of Greenland, Ross had mapped new coastline and discovered red snow resembling "raspberry ice-cream" (*QR* 21: 229), Barrow concludes that "he knows no more, in fact, than he might have known by staying at home" (*QR* 21: 251). This breathtakingly unjust comment betrays the reviewer's fanaticism.[31]

The far more favorable review of Ross's book in the March 1819 *Edinburgh* highlights the hostility of Barrow's review by contrast. Much less invested than Barrow in the notion of a Northwest Passage, the unidentified *Edinburgh* reviewer (possibly Sydney Smith), though "rather surprised" to hear of the lack of an exit from Lancaster Sound, comments merely, "It is not for us to reconcile the doubts of those who disbelieve, with the testimony of those who have seen" (*ER* 31: 363). In contrast with Barrow, this reviewer concludes, "That [Ross] has disproved the existence of a North-west Passage, or of any passage, throughout the whole space which he has circumnavigated, appears to us to be ... most clearly demonstrated" (*ER* 31: 363). Questioning the value of the quest for the Passage and referring pessimistically to the "new expedition" (Parry's), the *Edinburgh* claims to have "heard more than enough of the heat which has been excited on this occasion" (*ER* 31: 363). Barrow's ridicule, at which these remarks seem aimed, had taken part in a wider "public lampooning"—as Russell Potter puts it—of Ross: soon before Barrow's attack appeared, an anonymous parody of Ross's book mocked the worthlessness of his quest in a publication entitled *Munchausen at the POLE* (1819).[32]

Barrow on Ross's Successors

Parry's first voyage to find the Northwest Passage, which disproved the existence of Croker's Mountains, confirmed the prescience, even the apparent omniscience of the *Quarterly*. Barrow's review of Parry's account of this voyage takes a triumphant tone despite the fact that Parry was forced to turn back after a long winter in the ice. Barrow's terms of praise for Parry condemn Ross afresh (he begins by quoting part of his own attack on Ross), with special emphasis on truth, lies, and the evidence of the senses. The opening pages strike the note of adulation: "few books, since the commencement of our labours, have afforded us more to blame and less to censure; and ... not one has inspired us with more respect for its author" (*QR* 25: 177). Strong words from the often querulous *Quarterly*. Barrow continues, "In this work we find ... no attempt to deceive, or throw dust in the eyes of the public; no marvellous stories to disgust or confound ... no ... mere fancies of the brain;—but, on the contrary, a plain statement of facts" (*QR* 25: 177).

---

[31] Fleming, in *Barrow's Boys*, calls Barrow a "fanatic" (11). Barrow's contemporary Sir Byam Martin called him "the most obstinate man living ... no public servant has done more harm for so little good" (quoted in M.J. Ross, *Polar Pioneers*, 187).

[32] See Russell A. Potter, *Arctic Spectacles: The Frozen North in Visual Culture, 1818–1875* (Seattle: University of Washington Press, 2007): 49–51 (47). Potter reproduces the book's frontispiece depicting Ross as Munchausen (51).

It is almost as if Parry's expedition was tailor-made to confirm the line taken in Barrow's review of Ross—which in a sense it was. Calling Ross's description of Lancaster Sound "reprehensibly erroneous" (*QR* 25: 176), Barrow claims that "No extraordinary degree of scepticism was necessary to deny the existence of mountains gratuitously asserted, or of continuous ice on the surface of a sea a thousand fathoms deep ... —no great penetration was required to reject alleged facts physically impossible" (*QR* 25: 176). Why physically impossible? Again, simply because Ross's claims directly contradicted Barrow's hypotheses. Barrow clearly takes pleasure in insisting that "the intrepid assertions, descriptions, and *paintings*, the produce of the preceding voyage, were wholly gratuitous" (*QR* 25: 180). He goes on to commend Parry for having "transformed, as with a touch of Harlequin's sword, the magnificent and insuperable range of mountains, which a former expedition had assigned to one Secretary of the Admiralty, into a broad and uninterrupted passage, bearing the name of the other Secretary" (*QR* 25: 180). Barrow here makes a sly reference to the body of water still known as Barrow Strait. "In fact," he continues, "neither mountain nor ice, nor other obstacle, real or imaginary, opposed the progress of Captain Parry" (*QR* 25: 180).

Subsequent articles claim continuing progress towards the goal of finding the Northwest Passage, while reluctantly conceding the enormity of the task. In an article published in 1822, Barrow reports on an "unsuccessful" attempt (*QR* 26: 363) to find the Northeast Passage by a Russian expedition under the command of Otto von Kotzebue (son of August von Kotzebue). Although this voyage was privately financed, Barrow digresses to deplore the imperialistic motives of the Russian government, complaining that "we have actual possession of the six degrees of coast usurped by Russia" (*QR* 26: 346).[33] Looking backwards and forwards, he also takes the opportunity to remind readers of his previous arguments in favor of the Northwest Passage, refers approvingly to "Captain Parry" (*QR* 26: 352), and brings up a detail from Franklin's land expedition, even though Franklin's book had not yet been published.

Changing tack, in an article in the same issue of the *Quarterly* he embarks on a larger digression, revisiting what he calls the "ghosts" of Maldonado and "Bartolomeo de Fonte" (*QR* 26: 514), creator of another "fictitious voyage" (*QR* 26: 520). In this blatantly Francophobic article he expresses resentment at the revival of their "fables" (*QR* 26: 515) in the wake of the "complete exposure" of Maldonado by "Mr. Barrow, and by ourselves" (*QR* 26: 516)—another allusion to his own book on the Arctic. Why then, one might ask, does he help to republicize these "monstrous falsehoods" (*QR* 26: 521)? Discussing the transmission of Maldonado's account, he proclaims, "we have been at the pains to procure, through the means of Don Filipe Bauza, superintendant of the hydrographical department in Madrid, an authenticated copy of the manuscript from the library of

---

[33] In contrast with Barrow's thirst for empire, an *Edinburgh* reviewer commented that an Arctic "territorial acquisition to the empire will not probably be considered by the Colonial Department as ... very interesting" (*ER* 31: 356).

the Duc d'Infantado" (*QR* 26: 518). (Barrow had reprinted the manuscript as an appendix in his 1818 book.) This evidence of his relentless desire for authenticity unfortunately suggests that he himself was not convinced by his own earlier refutation of the "impostor" (*QR* 26: 516).

Ridiculing the book under review, Barrow sarcastically quotes the writer's reference to Ross's 1818 voyage: "'Ross,' he says, 'was stopped by the invincible obstacles which nature threw in his way! Lancaster Sound was *completely closed up with mountains of ice*'" (*QR* 26: 516, his emphasis). Letting his italics speak for themselves, Barrow expresses complete reliance on his readers' memory and their agreement with his point of view. Yet his preoccupation with exposing impostures risks giving the impression that an authentic account of exploration may be nowhere to be found. Barrow dismisses de Fonte's voyage as a "hoax" (*QR* 26: 520), but goes to the trouble of explaining how "the very circumstances under which it was first given to the world were more than sufficient to stamp it as a forgery" (*QR* 26: 519). As elsewhere in Barrow's writings on the Arctic, the quest to find an unknown place becomes sidetracked by his own extensive journeys into the realms of historical research.

Barrow's next five reviews continue to build up the glorious heroic figure of Parry at the expense of Ross, while scaling back the impression of progress. The first of these, his 1823 article on the notorious land expedition of Franklin that I have already mentioned, makes clear the political overtones of the *Quarterly*'s would-be Providential narrative. The review of Franklin recounts a shocking story of starvation, murder, and even cannibalism, but it attempts to foreground the "firm reliance on a merciful Providence" (*QR* 28: 373) of the survivors. Thanks to the "blessings of religion," the British explorers—unlike their native companions—did not succumb to "despondency" (*QR* 28: 399) and thus death, according to Barrow; in an explicitly partisan aside he adds, "Read this, ye Hunts and ye Hones" (*QR* 28: 399). Barrow praises the government for "prosecut[ing]" exploration so assiduously (*QR* 28: 373), quotes "authentic information" from a Russian correspondent that "remove[s] all doubts" (*QR* 28: 406) of a navigable Northwest Passage, and exults in a vision of "steamboats, bearing furs" to Asia via the "polar sea" (*QR* 28: 393). He continues to elevate "the Parrys and Franklins" (*QR* 28: 406) at the expense of Ross and his non-existent mountains, a man lacking "that sort of education which is necessary to form the true character of a British naval officer" (*QR* 28: 405).[34] Barrow also quotes an upbeat letter from Parry "written when on the eve of departure on his present voyage" (*QR* 28: 407) and denies any fear for his "safety" (*QR* 28: 409), despite his two-year absence.

Such complacency is undercut by the dismal account of Franklin's journey in the "most miserable of all countries" (*QR* 28: 382)—Northern Canada. Franklin's story is shadowed from early on by violence. His party and their Native American

---

[34] The routine class snobbery of the *Quarterly* is in this case intensified by its anti-Scots prejudice. Ross had in fact been promoted to the rank of Captain on his return from the Arctic.

guides come across the site of the "inhuman massacre of the Esquimaux ... by the Chipeywan Indians" (*QR* 28: 390), an event that for Romantic-era readers exemplified New World savagery.[35] Barrow had already used this article to present various bizarre pieces of information concerning the northern "Indians" as opposed to the "Esquimaux," several of which perpetuate the racial stereotype of the bloodthirsty Native American. He quotes one man's claim that "tattooing" is more "painful" than amputation of a limb (*QR* 28: 378), and relates an anecdote about a father who succeeded in breast-feeding his child (*QR* 28: 380). More tendentiously, he tells of a certain tribe's recourse to "feed[ing] upon" the bodies of dead family members "to prevent actual starvation" (*QR* 28: 377), and discusses one tribe's custom of "destroy[ing] female children at their birth" (*QR* 38: 342) and another tribe's belief that mothers "guilty of infanticide" haunt the sites of their crimes (*QR* 28: 378). He describes the "*Stone* Indians" as "prepossessing" in appearance but "never fail[ing] to take the scalps of their prisoners as trophies" (*QR* 28: 379).

In relating these anthropological findings with minimal commentary, Barrow covers his moral revulsion with a veneer of objectivity, while making clear his condemnation of customs such as wife-sharing and wife-selling, and the general "degradation" of women among the natives of Canada (*QR* 28: 380). This article thus all too obviously defines British normality against the weirdness of racial and ethnic others. It also tries to conjure up what Jen Hill calls a "heroic British masculinity."[36] Returning to Franklin's adventures, the reviewer quotes a graphic account of the agony inflicted by mosquitoes, "goring us with their envenomed trunks, and steeping our clothes in blood" (*QR* 28: 381), foreshadowing the threat posed by "the murderous hand of an assassin" (*QR* 28: 373). He goes on to report that after unspeakable sufferings, Franklin and his surviving men were reduced to eating "old shoes, scraps of leather, and skins with the hair singed off" (*QR* 28: 398). The Gothic-inflected reference to the explorers' "ghastly countenances, dilated eye-balls, and sepulchral voices" (*QR* 28: 401) gives the veneer of a ghost story to a tale that is too grotesque to be made up. In a transparent attempt to sidestep the tensions within this pivotal article, Barrow ends it incongruously with a tribute to Parry's stupendous powers of leadership. Parry, not the admirable but weakened Franklin, will apparently take readers where they want to be.

Barrow's following four articles, on three different expeditions of Parry's and another one led by Franklin, show the strain of maintaining an optimistic tone. His 1823 review of Parry's second voyage, during which Parry and his men spent two winters in the Arctic and experienced "appalling difficulties" (*QR* 30: 239), claims that Parry's "narrative" has "very considerably strengthened" the *Quarterly*'s belief in the Northwest passage, yet expresses "disappointment" that the expedition has returned from "the north, instead of the south, as was anxiously

---

[35] The event had been described by Samuel Hearne in *A Journey from ... Hudson's Bay to the Northern Ocean* (1795), a source cited by William Wordsworth in his note to "The Complaint of a Forsaken Indian Woman" (1798).

[36] Hill, *White Horizon*, 16.

expected" (*QR* 30: 231). The article offers a quasi-Gothic frisson (even though the context is "amusements" that helped pass the time during the long winter) with its description of "the unexpected appearance, on the 1st February, of a number of strange people coming towards the ships over the ice" (*QR* 30: 243). Barrow takes this opportunity to expand on the brief account of Arctic natives offered in his review of Ross. This article veers between idealizing the "half-civilized" Inuit at the expense of the "Indians" (*QR* 30: 245) and demystifying the stereotypical notion of the noble savage.

It begins with a tone of pitying dismissiveness, referring to "these poor creatures, whom fate has thrown into this dark and dismal corner of the world, amidst eternal ice and snow" (*QR* 30: 244). Yet, following Parry, Barrow sounds intrigued by their "moral character" (*QR* 30: 246), even though he refers in a later article to "the beastly Esquimaux who inhabit these cheerless regions" (*QR* 45: 63). The Inuit, he alleges, are "free from those dark vices of savage life, ferocious cruelty, resentment and revenge" (*QR* 30: 246). A quotation from Parry contrasts the peaceful "Eskimaux" male with "the self-willed and vindictive Indian wantonly plunging his dagger into the bosom of [a] helpless woman" (*QR* 30: 246). Nevertheless, Barrow claims that the Inuit abandon ailing family members and then react hypocritically: "they contrive to shed tears and to howl most clamorously at the death of those whom they wholly neglected when alive, and leave to be devoured by dogs and wolves when dead" (*QR* 30: 246).

Barrow's ethnocentric moral judgment here exaggerates that of Wordsworth's 1798 lyrical ballad, "Complaint of a Forsaken Indian Woman," which implicitly condemns the Native American practice of leaving the sick to die alone. Parry's lengthy anecdote about the "spoil[ing]" of an intelligent Inuit woman (*QR* 30: 251) reads like an unconscious parable of the staining of a pristine landscape through exploration. No such concerns trouble either the explorers or their reviewer, but Barrow, despite his enthusiasm for the Arctic, routinely describes it as hostile to life and enjoyment. He quotes Parry's account of how after the native tribe vanished "we knew not where," the "wretched appearance" of abandoned igloos "excite[d] in the mind a sensation of dreariness and desolation" (*QR* 30: 247). Barrow and his golden boy both use the adjective "dreary" formulaically to describe the Arctic. These "happy and cheerful" natives (*QR* 30: 246) will not be seen again.

The review of Parry's third voyage, which Barrow describes as Parry's "least successful" attempt to find the Northwest Passage (*QR* 34: 378), admits that "it has added little or nothing to our stock of geographical knowledge," leaving the question "precisely where it was at the conclusion of his first voyage, in the course of which he went over the same ground" (QR 34: 379). Yet Barrow insists that Parry himself is not to "blame" (*QR* 34: 379), and he forecasts that "England will yet be the nation to accomplish [the quest] and Parry the happy individual" (*QR* 34: 388). Such language fails to soften Barrow's account of the expedition's monotonous winter in the ice, "there to pine, / Immoveable, infixed, and frozen round" (*QR* 34: 379). (The quotation from Book 2 of *Paradise Lost* refers to imprisonment in hell.) More than once, the exhausting labor involved in struggling with the ice rendered the explorers imbecilic: Parry refers to both "officers and men" being reduced to a state of mental "stupor" (*QR* 34: 383). Parry's abandonment of one of his ships, the *Fury*, after it was "crushed and wrecked" in Prince Regent's Inlet (*QR* 34: 385), is described by Barrow as "disastrous" (*QR* 34: 383). Nevertheless, Barrow ends his review with his usual unconvincing note of reassurance, refusing to imagine "any very great danger" involved in Parry's current journey to the North Pole (*QR* 34: 391), even though he quotes Parry as saying that "on numerous occasions" during the third voyage, he and his men were in "hourly and imminent peril" (*QR* 34: 384–5).

The abortive journey to the North Pole not surprisingly proved to be especially "perilous" (*QR* 37: 525). Barrow's article on Parry's narrative begins with knee-jerk adulation: "It is almost superfluous to say, that the conduct of Captain Parry on the late, as on all former occasions, appears to have been above all praise" (*QR* 37: 524). This review comes close to admitting an irrational aspect to his enthusiasm for Parry: "There is something in the failures of Captain Parry that compensates the want of success, and that reconciles us to the disappointment" (*QR* 37: 524). Parry's account of the expedition trying to travel northward only to find that the "constant southerly drift of the ice" (*QR* 37: 536) counteracted their efforts seems to encapsulate the larger project of Arctic exploration.

Barrow's review of Franklin's *Narrative of a Second Expedition to the Shores of the Polar Sea, in the Years 1825, 1826, and 1827* (1828) gives an equally bleak impression. In this article, Barrow reminds readers of the "intensity" of Franklin's "sufferings" on his previous overland trek (*QR* 38: 336), and admits that exploration involves "the certain endurance of every species of misery" (*QR* 38: 336). He describes Franklin's diet on his former journey as "pieces of bones and scraps of skin, picked out of the ash-heap, and boiled down into a wretched mess of acrid soup" (*QR* 38: 336)—a dish that sounds only slightly less appetizing than the previously mentioned "old shoes." Barrow repeated this description almost verbatim in his later attack on Ross, contrasting Ross's "mince pies and cherry-brandy" with Franklin's "acrid soup" (*QR* 54: 10). He obsessively returned to the topic in a subsequent review, referring to Franklin and his "companions ... devouring their own shoes and leather gun-cases" (*QR* 56: 278), as if to seal his account of Franklin's heroism. On their second expedition, Franklin and his men encounter murderous "Esquimaux" who "stole every thing they could lay their hands on" (*QR* 38: 344) and spend "a long dreary winter" (*QR* 38: 340), only to find "one of the most dreary, miserable, and uninteresting portions of sea-coast to be found in any part of the world" (*QR* 38: 348). As so often, Barrow's tone of pride seems misplaced. His next Arctic article, a review of Frederick Beechey's *Narrative of a Voyage to the Pacific and Beering's Straits* (1831) expresses his "very bitter regret" (*QR* 45: 61) that Beechey, heading east, failed to meet up, as planned, with Franklin.[37]

---

[37] This review also gives an account of the famous mutiny on the Bounty. Barrow anonymously published his authoritative book on this topic in the same year, 1831.

The Return of John Ross

Barrow's Providential narrative breaks down even more in his 16th *Quarterly* article on Arctic exploration, published in 1835, in which he takes on the return of the repressed—John Ross and Croker's Mountains. This review is an outpouring of venom that sounds distinctly more privately vindictive towards Ross, although Barrow's hatred can still be seen as both institutional and genre-based, the inevitable playing out of themes and narrative dynamics that had been developing for years, with the twist that Barrow himself takes over the role of persecutory villain.

Nine years before, Ross had responded to some of Barrow's earlier articles concerning Parry's expeditions, in an anonymous 45-page *Letter to John Barrow*, printed—according to the title page—"For private perusal only."[38] This angry pamphlet draws attention to Barrow's use of anonymous periodical discourse to disseminate his own prejudices and promote public approval of Arctic exploration. In this text, Ross, signing himself "ALMAN" (46) without apparent irony, disingenuously claims to "doubt" whether Barrow has contributed to the *Quarterly* (4), referring to "you and the Reviewer" (16) as if they are two separate claimants to Arctic expertise, the distinguished author of a book and a woefully misguided periodical writer. Ross's persona sarcastically observes that "incessantly occupied as your valuable time must be, you may not have had leisure to read even this distinguished Periodical with the attention it deserves" (5). Ross himself was of course all too well aware that the feeble "brains" of the "Quarterly Reviewer" (19) were those of the man he addresses with ostensible politeness. With thinly disguised personal animosity, "ALMAN" takes advantage of Barrow's anonymity, pretending to enlist him in his private campaign against the *Quarterly* with statements such as "But you know, Sir, as well as every rational man must, that the Reviewer is quite mistaken" (18). Ross even underscores Barrow's propensity for self-promotion by himself mentioning "the Strait which is *honoured* by your name" (43). He attacks the "absurdities, inconsistencies and self-contradictions" of the *Quarterly*'s "oracle on all matters of Arctic enquiry" (43–5), sardonically referring to the unnamed reviewer as "the chief Manager of the Arctic Exhibitions" (30). Ross's pamphlet is proof, were any needed, that Barrow's authorship of the *Quarterly*'s Arctic articles could be taken for granted, and thus his "magical management" of the "Arctic stage" (32).

The tone and word choices of this *Letter* echo those of a briefer pamphlet of 1819, *A Letter to John Barrow, Esq. on the Subject of the Polar Expeditions; or, The Reviewer Reviewed*, signed "A Friend to the Navy" but also probably written by Ross.[39] Attributing to Barrow "the almost entire management" of the current

---

[38] [John Ross], *A Letter to John Barrow, Esq. F.R.S. on the Late Extraordinary and Unexpected Hyperborean Discoveries* (London: W. Pople, 1826). Further references in parentheses.

[39] "A Friend to the Navy," *A Letter to John Barrow, Esq. on the Subject of the Polar Expeditions; or, The Reviewer Reviewed* (London: James Ridgway [sic]: 1819). References in parentheses.

search for the Northwest Passage (1), the anonymous author criticizes his 1818 book for discussing the Buchan and Ross expeditions before they have returned. This earlier *Letter* attacks Barrow for overstepping the boundaries of his role as an administrator in trying to orchestrate public opinion, sarcastically addressing him as "you ... who undertook to play so leading a character in this Arctic performance" (1). Accusing the Arctic expert of "vaunting self-conceit" (4) and "insolence" (7), the unfriendly author describes Barrow's book as resembling "the handbill of a conjuror, or the programme of a French spectacle" (10). The performance images are interesting in the light of the literary aspects of Barrow's prose. Whether or not Barrow actually read these pamphlets, however, is not known.

While Barrow's hostility to Ross clearly had multiple causes, his 1835 review shows signs that psychological motivations are uppermost. Until this article, the *Quarterly*'s Arctic expert has seemed deluded; here he begins to sound delusional. Blackballed by the Admiralty through Barrow's influence, Ross had finally found private funding for his second attempt to find the Northwest Passage. According to Janice Cavell, Barrow had "refused to accompany" Parry and Franklin on a visit to Ross's ship before it set out.[40] As mentioned earlier, Ross was trapped in the Arctic for four winters. Barrow had referred to Ross's long absence in his review of Beechey's book, an article in which he argues that in order to succeed, Arctic exploration must be sponsored by the government. He admits, "if Captain Ross, indeed, shall ever cast up again, either on this or on the other side of Beering's straits [sic], we shall be compelled to admit at least of one splendid exception; but until that officer reappears—as God send he soon may!—we must hold fast to the old doctrine" (*QR* 45: 60). Although presumably, as Fergus Fleming remarks, "It would be wrong to say he wished his old enemy dead,"[41] Barrow's "as God send he soon may!" smacks of insincerity. Ross and his crew eventually escaped after making their way overland to boats abandoned during Parry's third attempt to find the Passage. Ross returned to a hero's welcome.[42] Barrow however seems offended by the fact that Ross had come back despite not having been sent out by the government in the first place, and annoyed by the Admiralty's decision to compensate Ross financially after his return, even though he himself had suggested it.[43]

In addition to Ross's *Narrative*, Barrow's article reviews a journalistic work by Robert Huish that presents Ross in an unfavorable light, as well as the somewhat damaging Parliamentary Report on the expedition. The reviewer admits that Huish's book contains "crude opinions and unqualified abuse" (*QR* 54: 2), yet uses material from it as ammunition. Despite his continuing traditional reliance on the first person plural, Barrow implies that he is fighting one-on-one: "Captain

---

[40] Cavell, *Tracing the Connected Narrative*, 157.

[41] Fleming, *Barrow's Boys*, 280.

[42] On the aftermath of Ross's voyage, see M.J. Ross, *Polar Pioneers*, 165–91, and Ray Edinger, *Fury Beach: The Four-Year Odyssey of Captain John Ross and the Victory* (New York: Berkley Books, 2003), 215–63.

[43] See Cavell, *Tracing the Connected Narrative*, 158.

Ross having thought fit to throw down the gauntlet, he will find us prepared for the combat" (*QR* 54: 2). He adds that he "anticipat[es] ... an easy conquest over such an antagonist," mentioning "Mr. Barrow, the Secretary of the Admiralty" (*QR* 54: 2) in a footnote in what is by now a standard gesture of self-promotion. Barrow's "antagonist" is an old one, but he has a new potential hero—Ross's nephew and second-in-command James Clark Ross. Barrow accuses John Ross of "perversion of mind" (*QR* 54: 16), yet one could turn this accusation back against Barrow himself.

The comprehensiveness of his criticisms suggests a perverse desire to find no redeeming aspect of Ross's book. He describes it as a "strange narrative" (*QR* 54: 38), "ponderous" (*QR* 54: 3), "cumbersome" and "uninteresting" (*QR* 54: 4), written in a "cold and heartless manner" (*QR* 54: 25) and with a "very silly" introduction containing "trash" (*QR* 54: 37).[44] He calls the expedition "ill-prepared, ill-concerted" and "ill-executed" (*QR* 54: 23); Ross's steamship, the *Victory*, according to Barrow, was "the very worst description of vessel to navigate among ice," with engines "the most miserable that can be imagined" (*QR* 54: 5). He further argues that Ross had "no claim whatever on the public" (*QR* 54: 23) for monetary compensation.[45] Barrow accuses Ross of "lust of lucre" (*QR* 54: 3) for his method of publishing his book (he had not chosen to submit it to Murray, despite Barrow's efforts on Murray's behalf[46]), claiming that the explorer "hire[d] brazen-faced bagmen to beat up for private subscriptions" (*QR* 54: 38). He also deplores "the getting up of Vauxhall and panoramic exhibitions" (*QR* 54: 3)—a dismissive reference to the cultural sensation occasioned by the voyage. Barrow goes on to refer to Ross as a "vain and jealous man" (*QR* 54: 36) who has proved "utterly incompetent to conduct an arduous naval enterprise for discovery to a successful termination" (*QR* 54: 38).

As in his other Arctic reviews, discrepancies soon emerge between the material that Barrow summarizes and quotes at length, and the spin that he attempts to put on it. He carpingly recounts Ross's amazing story of survival, implying that it was Ross's own fault that he was frozen in, and asserting that "the results are next to nothing" (*QR* 54: 4). He refuses to concern himself with the "dismal savages" encountered by Ross (*QR* 54: 9), although he deigns to describe their igloos in some detail. He charges Ross with taking credit away from James Clark Ross (who discovered the magnetic North Pole on this expedition), insisting that the elder Ross's book "betrays an unworthy jealousy of what the young man had accomplished" (*QR* 54: 25–6). While the latter allegation has merit, it is weakened slightly by Barrow's mockery of John Ross's use of the first person plural (*QR* 54: 27).

---

[44] According to Cavell, Barrow, in a letter to Murray (December 3, 1835) had described Ross's book as "trashy" (*Tracing the Connected Narrative*, 158).

[45] In his official capacity, Barrow himself had had to write to Ross announcing the decision to award him funds (M.J. Ross, *Polar Pioneers*, 168). Barrow's implicit criticism of the Admiralty even as he quotes "their secretary" (*QR* 54: 23) is perhaps further evidence that his voice in this review is more individual than collective.

[46] See M.J. Ross, *Polar Pioneers*, 182, on Murray's eagerness to publish the book.

Barrow even accuses Ross of trying to "suppress everything that tends to the probability of a North-West Passage" (*QR* 54: 16). Playing up the conflict between uncle and nephew that is evident from the Parliamentary Report, he contrasts John Ross's assertion that the passage, if it existed, would be "utterly useless" with James Clark Ross's claim that this voyage "*has made it still more certain than it was before that a north-west passage must exist*" (*QR* 54: 28, his italics). This difference in views is made less clear-cut by Barrow's earlier quotation from the younger Ross, "where God had said No, it was for man to submit" (*QR* 54: 11), but for Barrow at any rate, submission is out of the question. In further attempted denigration of John Ross, he publicizes Huish's charge that the Captain, evidently "under the dominion of some fiend of hell" (*QR* 54: 20) during the land journey, wanted to leave behind a man who could not walk. With this detail Barrow demonizes Ross in the act of refusing to accuse him. By contrast, in an earlier article he had reported without comment the decision by Franklin's men to leave two sufferers behind on their overland trek (*QR* 28: 396).

In his 1835 article, Barrow also reflects self-consciously on the question of reprisals to personal attacks. He expresses surprise that Ross has not defended his character against the "numerous charges" of Huish (*QR* 54: 19), suggesting that "silent contempt ... is but too frequently resorted to when it may not be quite convenient to answer a charge of delinquency" (*QR* 54: 20). This statement implies that every attack should be answered, however far beneath "contempt." Barrow himself at one point in the review seems to be defending himself against the charge that "ill-natured reports ... circulated anonymously against" Ross (*QR* 54: 5). He comments that the accuser "seems to think ... that whatever is published anonymously cannot be true. God help us Reviewers if that were the case! We certainly are among those who published anonymously unfavourable reports, but not ill-natured nor unfaithful ones, on Captain Ross's former voyage" (*QR* 54: 5). Readers might be tempted to think that if this particular reviewer was not "ill-natured" in the past, then he is making up for it now.

Barrow most betrays a seemingly personal impulse to persecute in returning to his theme of mistaken perception. In the very first sentence of the review, he claims to feel "called upon to confute assertions which have no foundation in fact, and to expose misrepresentations which are adhered to, in spite of long by-gone correction, with a pertinacity that not only surprises, but almost confounds us" (*QR* 54: 1). Barrow is "almost confound[ed]," apparently because his earlier review proved inefficacious. His build-up to the question of "misrepresentations" is elaborate, as if he enjoys toying with his victim. He first mocks Ross's "most extraordinary discovery" of a "*wall* of water!" caused by the alleged "difference in altitude of the two seas east and west" of Boothia Peninsula. (Ross had named the peninsula after his wealthy patron Felix Booth.) Barrow sarcastically calls this wall "a miracle, for the sole purpose of stopping the Captain in his not otherwise supernatural career" (*QR* 54: 31). As in his 1818 review, he suggests that Ross invents fictitious obstructions out of cowardice. Barrow provides this detail apparently to foreshadow a greater "miracle." He continues,

> We are, indeed, utterly at a loss to comprehend what evil genius could have urged on the gallant Captain to stumble, once more, on those fatal mountains on which he suffered shipwreck in the year 1818. Had he no friend at his elbow? ... Nature might have made a range of mountains across Lancaster Sound, and Ross might have imagined that he saw them; but nature never exacts physical impossibilities from human beings: Ross, however, finds no difficulty in performing that which is physically impossible. (*QR* 54: 32)

Barrow of course never entertains the notion that the Northwest Passage itself might be a physical impossibility.

He next ridicules an attempt by Ross to resuscitate "*Croker's Mountain*" (*QR* 54: 32, his italics), lingering over its reduction from a mountain range to a single peak. After quoting Ross's 1818 description of the land around Lancaster Sound, Barrow comments: "Here this noble chain of mountains is shriveled up into *A mountain*; and, instead of its stretching *round the bottom of the bay* ... we now find IT perched at the extremity of the supposed north point of America, wholly out of the counterfeit bay" (*QR* 54: 33). He adds, "If Parry had not, in 1819, completely demolished this fine range of mountains, with Cape Rosamond in the centre of it—of whose castellated summit a splendid view illustrates Ross's book of 1818— Ross, in his volume of 1835, would have done the work for him" (*QR* 54: 34). Ross's misguidedness in reviving the controversy is made abundantly clear, but Barrow's humor rebounds upon himself because he cannot let Ross alone: "This said unfortunate *mountain* seems doomed to find no resting place" (*QR* 54: 34); "But we have not yet done with the new Croker's Mountain" (*QR* 54: 34), and so on. After several pages of heavy sarcasm, Barrow accuses Ross of "malicious feeling against Parry" (*QR* 54: 37). He asserts that "the real cause of grievance undoubtedly is, that the Parry of 1819 demolished the 'unsubstantial phantom'— the 'baseless fabric of a vision'" (*QR* 54: 36). Evidently, the "phantom" of Croker's Mountains (or Mountain) is not so easy to dispel after all.

Yet, despite foregrounding Ross's factual inaccuracies and incompetent mapmaking, Barrow as usual rejects all epistemological uncertainty. He claims that the "progressive discoveries" of Parry, Franklin, and others "have reduced [the Northwest Passage] almost to a practicable certainty" (*QR* 54: 38). "Sir John Ross" (he had been knighted after his return) may express doubts of the existence of a navigable waterway but "we have none whatever" (*QR* 54: 38). The review ends by proposing a new expedition to be headed by James Clark Ross. From Barrow's point of view, that is to say, the happy ending—a British ship sailing off into the sunset—is still just around the corner.[47] The implication is that Ross's

---

[47] The corresponding *Edinburgh* article on Ross's four-year voyage is, not surprisingly, far more favorable than the *Quarterly*'s, although it denounces Ross's (Tory) "political fanaticism" (*ER* 61: 444). The *Edinburgh* shared Ross's skepticism about the existence of a useful Northwest passage, questioning, in Ross's words, whether it was worth all this trouble to have a "BLACK LINE INSTEAD OF A BLANK" on the map (*ER* 61: 419, reviewer's emphasis).

second failure to find the Northwest Passage has somehow definitively proved its existence.[48] Although one might think that his articles had provided ample reasons to discourage further attempts, 10 years later, at Barrow's urging, the Royal Society would sponsor Franklin's final expedition to find the Northwest Passage, which resulted in the loss of all 129 men.

Shedding his anonymity, Barrow later continued his decades-long vendetta against Ross in his 1846 book, *Voyages of Discovery and Research Within the Arctic Regions*. The book devotes chapters to all the recent expeditions, starting with Ross's trip of 1818, which Barrow returns to reluctantly and refers to dismissively as "a few months voyage of pleasure, for so it may be called."[49] Taking the opportunity to attack afresh what he calls Ross's "strange conduct" (54), he denounces the contents of the explorer's first book as "not worth the paper on which it is printed" (32). The fiasco of Croker's Mountains is again dwelt on at length. Barrow mocks Ross for having "the courage—can it be called 'moral courage?'—to revisit, some years afterwards, this horrible spot in a miserable kind of ship, fitted out at the expense of a private individual for some purpose or other" (46). Although the book thus offers a particularly damning account of Ross's second voyage, Barrow refuses—much to Ross's subsequent indignation—to take sustained "notice" of this more recent expedition, "chiefly" on the grounds that it was "not authorized by any branch of the government" (508). Instead, Barrow renews his assault on Ross in a "miscellaneous" final chapter discussing the Parliamentary Report on the expedition, accusing its leader of uttering "unintelligible nonsense" during the parliamentary enquiry (516). As before, Barrow relies on labored humor at the expense of Ross's allegedly over-active imagination, accusing his foe of inventing "a water-built wall thirteen feet high, extending ... to the North Pole" (518). And as in his 1835 review, he pits Ross against his nephew, praising the latter's "talent and activity" at the expense of his uncle's allegedly defective leadership of their "ill-advised" expedition (523). As far as Barrow is concerned, with Ross's second voyage the epic quest for the Northwest Passage has clearly degenerated into farce.

Ross responded in a 62-page pamphlet entitled *Observations on a Work, entitled, "Voyages of Discovery and Research Within the Arctic Regions," by Sir John Barrow, Bart., Aetat. 82, Being a Refutation of the Numerous Misrepresentations Contained in that Volume* (1846).[50] In this text, Ross, as the self-proclaimed victim of "unscrupulous, personal, and slanderous attacks" (4),

---

[48] Fleming sees this "strange twist of reasoning" as a larger cultural phenomenon (*Barrow's Boys*, 318).

[49] Sir John Barrow, *Voyages of Discovery and Research Within the Arctic Regions, from the year 1818 to the present time* (London: John Murray, 1846), 513. Further references in parentheses. This description echoes that in his 1819 *Quarterly* attack on Ross (*QR* 21: 252).

[50] John Ross, *Observations on a Work, entitled, "Voyages of Discovery and Research Within the Arctic Regions," by Sir John Barrow, Bart.* (Edinburgh and London: William Blackwood, 1846). References in parentheses.

not only fulfills the cultural imperative to reply to alleged "personalities" (60), he also plays out the Gothic mechanism whereby the pursued turns upon his pursuer. The reference in the subtitle to Barrow's age echoes a similar reference on the title page of Barrow's book: Ross later remarks that advancing years have not softened his adversary's "long-cherished private animosity" (60). Ross uses as his epigraph the proverb, "Oh! that mine enemy would write a book!," suggesting from the start that he and Barrow are now newly locked into print combat.

His reprisal differs from others that I have discussed, however, in that it openly refuses to respond to anonymous attacks, even though Ross himself had anonymously berated the "Quarterly Reviewer" in his 1826 pamphlet (19). With a routine apology for stooping to a reprisal, he offers a pointed statement about Barrow's shift from ostensibly anonymous to signed expressions of "scurrility" (27): "I might fairly consider myself relieved from the necessity of giving importance to the work by any formal reply: still it deserves and shall obtain notice; for, however identical it may be in spirit with many similar *anonymous* productions, the authorship is *for once* avowed" (4). With this move, Ross attempts to claim the moral high ground. He contends however that he is refusing to answer certain charges such as "cowardice," because, as he puts it, "I am not reduced to so low an estimate of myself as to think it necessary to vindicate my character from such contemptible aspersions" (13). The assertion is unconvincing in that he predictably reiterates that in Lancaster Sound in 1818, he encountered "beyond the ice, to my eye, ... a continuous chain of mountainous land" (22). He even claims that part of his motive for undertaking the second expedition was because "for ten years I had suffered continual obloquy from malignant anonymous writers" and wanted to silence "the tongue of slander" (36).

Here and elsewhere in his self-vindication, Ross repudiates the role of villain and attempts to cast it back on Barrow, while claiming the role of hero for himself. He insists that the "main object" of Barrow's book is to "traduce" him (3), and accuses his opponent of "giving a "garbled and disingenuous account" of his 1818 voyage and of "wielding a very dull pen with a very rancorous spirit" (9). He paints Barrow as a figure of obsessive and implacable resentment: referring back to their "personal altercation" after his 1818 voyage, he charges, "Although twenty-seven years have elapsed Sir John Barrow still cherishes the feelings then excited, and either in his own person, or through those organs of the press over which he has any influence, incessantly seeks to depreciate my professional character" (9). In short, "Sir John Barrow," in Ross's words, is "malignant" (11) and scarcely "sane" (17). Perhaps even more damningly, unlike the Lords of the Admiralty, he cannot be classed among "GENTLEMEN" (31). By contrast, Ross paints himself as a dedicated naval officer who is beyond reproach, "one who, for upwards of fifty years, has laboured assiduously to serve his Sovereign and to maintain the glory of his country" (3). Disavowing "pecuniary motives" (38) for his second voyage, he self-aggrandizingly refers to the "honours" he has "received ... not only from my own sovereign, but from nearly every sovereign in Europe" (57). He also insists on sharing credit with his nephew for the main accomplishment of the expedition:

"I say *we* discovered the magnetic pole" (47). Ignoring the possibility that in this work he too could be accused of "personal imputations" (33), "scurrility" (27), "insinuation" (27), and "long-cherished animosity" (60), Ross concludes his reprisal with the lofty hope that in the future, "I shall not have to complain, as I have done of Sir John Barrow, that when I looked for an historian I found a calumniator" (62). Unfortunately, Ross's contributions to the feud help to preserve in print not only Barrow's "personal animosity" (4) but also his own.

The Arctic Sublime

At one point in the course of his Arctic reviews, Barrow defends the benefits of discovery even when "there is no story to tell; no romance in the narrative" (*QR* 34: 398). As we have seen, he certainly has a story to tell, and one that for him apparently remains charged with romance in the sense of glamour and adventure. But for the reader, romance in the sense of a heroic quest has been diluted by the protracted accounts of Parry's and Franklin's dubious triumphs on the way to an ever-deferred goal, while the dark undercurrent of the story—the relentless persecution of John Ross—becomes increasingly sordid. Cutting across that open-ended narrative, however, as I suggested earlier, are glimpses of a more traditionally Romantic scenario in which the perceiving mind finds—or half-creates—sublimity in the natural world. Franklin's glorious shoe leather soup and Ross's contemptible feast of mince pies are temporarily alike forgotten as Barrow provides his readers with food for feelings of awe.

It is fitting that such moments are at more than one remove. The *Edinburgh Review*'s article on Parry's fourth and Franklin's second expeditions comments that readers at home by the fire, rather than the explorers themselves, are more likely to attend to the wonders of the landscape:

> Our travellers, excellent nautical observers, do not seem to have felt much of those poetical impressions which sometimes give so brilliant a colouring to the narratives of voyages of discovery, and which may even arise in the minds of many readers, in musing on these dark and distant shores,—the solitary grandeur of the objects which border them,—and the dark mists through which they are descried. In truth, the severe realities which press on an Arctic navigator, and place life itself in almost hourly jeopardy, are not quite so favourable for this play of the fancy as the circumstances under which we peruse his narrative by our comfortable firesides. The rocks, headlands, and icy pinnacles, seen dimly through mist, are to him but sources of anxiety, remembrancers of peril, or calls to excessive toil; and, when forced to bear up among breakers, or to watch the drifting of the midnight ice, he is probably in the very worst of all possible moods for dwelling upon their picturesque appearance, or sublime effect. (*ER* 48: 435)[51]

---

[51] This *Edinburgh* article gives credit to "Mr Barrow" (*ER* 48: 429) for initiating recent polar exploration, but announces an "end to all hope" of a "practicable" Northwest Passage (*ER* 48: 431).

The "severe realities" of Arctic exploration preclude the appreciation of nature while on the spot. For a connoisseur of the sublime, imagined rather than real danger is of the essence. For many writers of the period, the Arctic exemplified the sublime as defined so influentially in 1757 by Edmund Burke, because of its extreme conditions and spectacular scenery. An earlier *Edinburgh* reviewer, like the one quoted above, had imagined the landscape in terms of one of Burke's staple ingredients, obscurity: "The darkness of a prolonged winter now broods impenetrably over the frozen continent, unless the moon chance at times to obtrude her faint rays, which only discover the horrors and wide desolation of the scene" (*ER* 30: 13). This writer's wording seems to evoke the "darkness visible" of that exemplary sublime location, Milton's hell (*Paradise Lost*, 1: 64).

Despite their distance from "comfortable firesides," Barrow reveals that his Arctic explorers experience some aesthetic pleasures for themselves, although in most of his *Quarterly* articles, a "sublime effect" is reserved for the "minds of ... readers." Parry's first expedition encounters "beautiful" tricks of the light: "parhelia, halos, parasclenae, prismatic arches, and other meteorological appearances" (*QR* 25: 198–9). At this point Barrow ascribes the cause of these "appearances" to "meteorological phenomena" (*QR* 25: 198), but his later treatment of optical illusions will be less scientific. Parry also describes a "chain" of icebergs "against which a heavy southerly swell, 'dashing the loose ice with tremendous force, sometimes raised a white spray over them to the height of more than one hundred feet, and, being accompanied with a loud noise, exactly resembling the roar of distant thunder, presented a scene at once sublime and terrific'" (*QR* 25: 178).[52] This passage draws on Burkean terms in emphasizing "greatness of dimension," "excessive loudness," and the reaction of fear.[53]

Perhaps more memorably, on their second voyage Parry and his men come across a solitary "spot of verdure" relieving the "dreary monotony of the surrounding wastes" (*QR* 30: 254). They hear the "'roaring of the mountain-cataract'" that "constitutes a principal feature of the sublime in scenery of this magnificent nature" (*QR* 30: 254). Parry's quotation is from *Madoc*, Robert Southey's epic poem about a medieval Welsh prince colonizing the New World, a choice of allusion that may reflect the imperialist anxiety underlying the account of the "strange people" encountered on the same expedition.[54] Enjoying the sight

---

[52] Compare Chauncey C. Loomis, "The Arctic Sublime," in U.C. Knoepflmacher and G.B. Tennyson, eds, *Nature and the Victorian Imagination* (Berkeley: University of California Press, 1977), 99–112, on how even the prosaic Parry evokes sublimity (102).

[53] Edmund Burke, *A Philosophical Enquiry into the Origin of our Ideas of the Sublime and Beautiful*, ed. J.T. Boulton (Notre Dame: University of Notre Dame Press, 1958), 72 and 82.

[54] On the "uneasy colonialist politics" of *Madoc*, see Bolton, *Writing the Empire*, 83. See also Tim Fulford, *Romantic Indians: Native Americans, British Literature, and Transatlantic Culture 1756–1830* (Oxford: Oxford University Press, 2006), 125–39, and Nigel Leask, "Southey's *Madoc*: Reimagining the Conquest of America," in Lynda Pratt, ed., *Robert Southey and the Contexts of English Romanticism* (Aldershot: Ashgate, 2006), 133–50.

of a stream "winding in the most romantic manner imaginable among the hills," Parry lingers over "the beauty of this picturesque river, which Captain Lyon and myself named after our mutual friend, Mr. Barrow" (*QR* 30: 255). Apparently the beleaguered explorers are not totally immune to "poetical impressions," though their choice of name domesticates the picturesque. By contrast, when attempting to travel to the Pole, Parry searches in vain for a "romantic" feeling: "nothing could well exceed the dreariness which such a view presented. The eye wearied itself in vain to find an object but ice and sky to rest upon; and even the latter was often hidden from our view by the dense and dismal fogs which so generally prevailed" (*QR* 37: 531). Antithetical to the delighted eye of the viewer of the picturesque or the affrighted eye of the viewer of the sublime, the eye here is "wearied" with no payoff. The "dismal fogs" seem to crowd out potentially poetical mists, and the blockage of the visual yields no recuperative sense of inner revelation.

Barrow's reviews of Parry and Franklin give more space than before to evoking the awe-inspiring aspects of the Arctic setting for the benefit of his readers, perhaps because he has more leisure for "play[s] of the fancy" once he becomes totally convinced of the existence of the Northwest Passage. As we have already seen, Barrow and his hero tend to rely on Burke for their sense of the sublime (just as they rely on William Gilpin and other eighteenth-century landscape experts for their notion of the picturesque). Barrow seems particularly impressed by Parry's Burkean evocations of visual "infinity."[55] In several of his articles he acknowledges the "immense fields of ice" (*QR* 30: 264) and staggering blankness of what Parry calls a "scene ... indescribably dreary in its appearance" (*QR* 25: 195). He also quotes Parry's references to "monotonous whiteness ... motionless torpor" (*QR* 34: 380) and "one unbroken surface of ice, uniform in its dazzling whiteness" (*QR* 25: 191). These examples accept Burke's contention that "Infinity has a tendency to fill the mind with that sort of delightful horror, which is the most genuine effect, and truest test of the sublime."[56]

Twentieth-century theorists, however, distinguished between the Burkean or "empirical" sublime and the Romantic or "idealist" sublime associated with Immanuel Kant.[57] While the Burkean sublime appeals to the instinct for self-preservation, the Kantian sublime involves a heightened consciousness of the self. In Kant's "dynamical" sublime, the encounter with the physical power of nature "discloses to us" our mental "superiority over nature,"[58] as in the Mount Snowdon passage of *The Prelude*. In his reviews Barrow occasionally conjures up Arctic

---

[55] Burke, *A Philosophical Enquiry*, 73.

[56] Ibid., 73.

[57] Frances Ferguson, however, in *Solitude and the Sublime: Romanticism and the Aesthetics of Individuation* (New York: Routledge, 1992), calls the Kantian sublime "formalist" (1).

[58] Ferguson, *Solitude and the Sublime*, 72.

scenery in terms of civilization, a move that recognizes the contribution of the perceiving mind to the experience of the sublime.[59]

The *Edinburgh Review* in 1818 had invoked the Burkean staple, vastness, in referring to "an immense rampart" of icebergs "present[ing] to the mariner a sublime spectacle, resembling at a distance, whole groups of churches, mantling castles, or fleets under full sail" (*ER* 30: 17).[60] A later *Edinburgh* article of 1843 on Buchan's 1818 abortive voyage to the North Pole—written by Barrow after he had stopped contributing to the *Quarterly*—quotes a passage that draws attention to the "deception" and "illusion" involved in perceiving an icy seascape in terms of manmade structures. The author of the book under review, Frederick Beechey, describes the "imposing grandeur" of the midnight sun illuminating the ice floes to reveal "architectural edifices, grottos, and caves here and there glittering as if with precious metals" (*ER* 78: 71). This passage seems to find in the Arctic what Wordsworth in *The Prelude* ambivalently calls "The attraction of a country in romance" (10: 696).[61] It also resembles what Duncan Wu calls the "Cloudscape New Jerusalem" passage from Book 2 of Wordsworth's *Excursion*, a set-piece description of heavenly architecture supposedly "wrought" by "earthly nature" (2: 881) but at the same time displaying the power of optical illusions, for better or worse. Shelley's "Mont Blanc," as Wu observes, alludes to the "Cloudscape" passage in describing glaciers in human-centered terms: "dome, pyramid, and pinnacle, / A city of death, distinct with many a tower / And wall impregnable of beaming ice" (ll. 104–6).[62] Both texts hark back to the sinister architecture of Milton's Pandemonium in Book 2 of *Paradise Lost*. To acknowledge implicitly the ability of the human mind to shape what it sees is to pose, like Shelley, the question of whether an icy wilderness can exist without "the human mind's imaginings" ("Mont Blanc," l. 143).[63]

---

[59] By contrast, for others, the distinctive scenery of the Arctic made it a site of unknowability. A later *Edinburgh* reviewer refused to admit that "Captain Ross" had captured the "splendour" of ice: "we are persuaded, that the ideas of visible objects, to which there is nothing analogous in ordinary experience, can never be communicated by mere description" (*ER* 31: 338). For this writer, the sense of nature's otherness is intensified in the Arctic.

[60] Hill claims that such Arctic optical illusions "brought into question the explorer's strategies for making sense of the world" (*White Horizon*, 19).

[61] Quotations from *The Prelude* are from the 1805 version in *Wordsworth: The Major Works*, ed. Stephen Gill (Oxford: Oxford University Press, 2000).

[62] Duncan Wu, *Romanticism: An Anthology*, second edition (Oxford: Blackwell, 1998), 848. Quotations from Coleridge's poetry are also from this edition.

[63] Quotations from Shelley are from *Shelley's Poetry and Prose*, ed. Donald Reiman and Neil Fraistat (New York: Norton, 2002). Although the reflections on nature in Barrow's Arctic reviews stress what Adam Potkay, in "Wordsworth and the Ethics of Things," *PMLA* 123 (2008): 390–404, calls the "mind's ascendancy over [nonhuman] things," Barrow's review in the *Edinburgh* also touches upon what Potkay calls "the leveling of human and nonhuman" (396) in emphasizing the "enjoyment and happiness" of Arctic animals and birds (*ER* 78: 74) and even their capacity for "compassionate conduct" (*ER* 78: 76), though for Barrow such behavior is Providential rather than showing any proto-ecological awareness.

More positively, though also potentially more frighteningly, in Kant's so-called mathematical sublime, the mind is checked in its encounter with apparent infinitude but then experiences what Neil Hertz calls "a gesture beyond blockage."[64] Such an understanding of the sublime may be even more relevant in the context of Arctic emptiness, or what is perceived to be emptiness. According to Thomas Weiskel, "We call an object sublime if the attempt to represent it determines the mind to regard its inability to grasp wholly the object as a symbol of the mind's relation to a transcendent order."[65] A sense of too much nature, in Hertz's words, confirms "the self's own integrity as an agent,"[66] and, at the risk of self-obliteration, points the perceiving mind towards transcendence. Although the examples quoted above make no "gesture beyond blockage," in his more detailed evocations of loneliness, mind-numbing silence and lack of life, Barrow gives his readers a chance to wonder what it would mean to look past nature.

Admittedly, Barrow never actually seeks transcendence. On one occasion he places fear safely and prosaically in the past, claiming that the heating equipment used on Parry's second voyage dispelled the "terrors of an Arctic winter"; he continues, "if, indeed, the former voyage had not produced the moral effects of divesting of its terrors that extremity of cold, and that long disappearance of the sun below the horizon, the bare contemplation of which had appeared so horrible" (*QR* 30: 235). But terror and horror do not prove so easy to leave behind. The same article refers to the ships' imprisonment in the ice as "a long, dreary, and helpless entanglement" in what Barrow calls, re-using his favorite Shakespeare quotation, "thrilling regions of thick-ribb'd ice" (*QR* 30: 362). The extremity of the isolation may work against the Christian orthodoxy of the *Quarterly*, if one remembers Coleridge's Ancient Mariner: "Oh wedding-guest! this soul hath been / Alone on a wide wide sea; / So lonely 'twas, that God himself / Scarce seemed there to be" (ll. 596–600). It might be objected that Barrow professedly believes in "Providence" (*QR* 28: 373). He would be more likely to agree with the speaker of Coleridge's "Chamouni; the Hour Before Sunrise, a Hymn" (1802) that "God" froze the torrents (l. 56). But Barrow's emphasis on isolation bears some resemblance to a skeptical version of the Romantic sublime, "Mont Blanc," the speaker of which, while conjuring up a transcendent "Power" (l. 127), imagines the mountain in terms of "Silence and solitude" (l. 144) and "vacancy" (l. 144).

Barrow comments repeatedly on what Parry calls the "inanimate stillness" of the Arctic (*QR* 34: 380), stressing its "almost total absence of animated beings" (*QR* 25: 199). At one point he quotes Parry's reference to "the silence which reigned around us, a silence far different from that peaceful composure which characterizes the landscape of a cultivated country; it was the death-like stillness

---

[64] Neil Hertz, *The End of the Line: Essays on Psychoanalysis and the Sublime* (New York: Columbia University Press, 1985), 43.

[65] Thomas Weiskel, *The Romantic Sublime: Studies in the Structure and Psychology of Transcendence* (Baltimore: The Johns Hopkins University Press, 1976), 23.

[66] Hertz, *The End of the Line*, 53.

of the most dreary desolation, and the total absence of animated existence" (*QR* 25: 191). The frozen immobility of the Arctic leads the contemplating mind to confront the prospect of its own disappearance.[67] Barrow later mentions, again quoting Parry, "In the very silence there is a deadness with which a human spectator appears *out of keeping*. The presence of man seems an intrusion on the dreary solitude of this wintry desert" (*QR* 34: 380). With this occasionally awe-struck response to the mediated landscape and the terrors of utter loneliness, the reviewer, like the speaker of "Mont Blanc," seems to hint at the question of what it means to be human—to be animated in this world without life.

In his account of Parry's journey to the Pole, even the "inanimate" disappears: Barrow resorts to the common trope of indescribability, claiming that the "reader" cannot "imagine to himself anything so dreary, desolate, and forlorn, as a sea covered with floating pieces of ice, unrelieved by a single object of animate or inanimate nature, and far from any land. If the plate ... be not exaggerated, it will express more than words can convey, the dark and dismal solitude where all nature seems still, and wrapt, as it were, in a death-like gloom" (*QR* 37: 530). The emphasis on darkness and gloom is rhetorical rather than realistic, given that Parry and his men were traveling during the summer when the sun never sets north of the Arctic Circle. Here Barrow falls back on the Burkean trope of obscurity as he and his readers confront the ultimate "solitude." Even more than the Alpine settings of key Romantic texts, the polar regions are a place where the human mind finds itself, like Wordsworth in *The Prelude*, "with infinitude,—and only there" (6: 539).

Even Barrow's final *Quarterly* attack on Ross offers touches both of Burkean sublimity and a more interiorized readerly sublimity. In the few quotations from Ross's book to which he apparently assents, Barrow once again indirectly evokes "indescribable" loudness (*QR* 54: 7), terrifying vastness and a horrifying infinitude. He quotes Ross's references to "mountains of crystal hurled through a narrow strait by a rapid tide; meeting, as mountains in motion would meet, with the noise of thunder, [and] breaking from each other's precipices huge fragments" (*QR* 54: 7). Ross's—and Barrow's—emphasis here is on the life-threatening dangers posed by "masses of ice" (*QR* 54: 6), but the only danger for the reader lies in not being able to "imagine" the "scene" (QR 54: 6–7). When Ross and his men are first frozen in, they encounter "nothing but one dazzling and monotonous, dull, and wearisome extent of snow" (*QR* 54: 7), a description that recalls Parry's Burkean preoccupation with vistas that appear infinite, except that Ross's repeated adjective "dull" (*QR* 54: 7, 21) sounds less poetic than the term "dreary." More Romantically, Barrow's review echoes his articles on Parry when he quotes a

---

[67] Eric G. Wilson, in *The Spiritual History of Ice: Romanticism, Science, and the Imagination* (New York: Palgrave Macmillan, 2003), distinguishes between a negative, "exoteric" view of ice "shared by orthodox forms of Christianity, political systems, and conventional sciences," and a positive "esoteric" view associated with "Romantic visionaries," although he finds the latter in Antarctic rather than Arctic texts (3). While I am proposing that Barrow improbably lines up with both orthodoxy and visionariness, I do not find any suggestion of ice as creative or life-giving in his reviews.

description by James Clark Ross of "the stillness of the night, amid this dreary waste of ice and snow, where there was not an object to remind us of life, and not a sound seemed ever to have been heard" (*QR* 54: 11). Again, the uncanniness of the lifeless "waste" takes the explorers, and the reader, momentarily past the boundaries of the knowable.

At a later point in the review, however, Barrow seems to agree with John Ross that the "tormenting, chilling, odious presence" of snow and ice is "disgust[ing]" (*QR* 54: 17) rather than sublime, Burkean or otherwise. Barrow approvingly provides the following long quotation from Ross:

> Who more than I has admired the glaciers of the extreme north; who more has loved to contemplate the icebergs sailing from the Pole before the tide and the gale, floating along the ocean, through calm and through storm, like castles and towers and mountains, gorgeous in colouring, and magnificent, if often capricious, in form?—and have I not too sought amid the crashing, and the splitting, and the thundering roarings of a sea of moving mountains, for the sublime, and felt that nature could do no more? In all this there has been beauty, horror, danger, everything that could excite; they would have excited a poet even to the verge of madness. But to see, to have seen, ice and snow, to have felt snow and ice for ever, and nothing for ever but snow and ice, during all the months of a year—to have seen and felt but uninterrupted and unceasing ice and snow during all the months of four years—this it is that has made the sight of those most chilling and wearisome objects an evil which is still one in recollection, as if the remembrance would never cease. (*QR* 54: 17)

The comparison with "castles and towers," like the references to manmade structures in other reviews, implicitly acknowledges the role of the human mind in helping to create sublime effects that seem the product of "nature." Thanks to the imagination, although this passage makes an explicit distinction between the sublime and the "unceasing" monotony of snow and ice, the monotony itself can be seen as sublime. The reader, vicariously contemplating the natural infinitude of year-round "snow and ice," may feel that even in this case or rather especially in this case, "nature could do no more." As the "four years" expand to "for ever," the mind's inability to take in the endlessness of the "evil" is suggested by the fact that Ross is still psychologically imprisoned by it even after having made his escape. (Ross's complaint has a Gothic tinge.) Visual infinity turns into a haunting internal infinity. Like Ross's memory, Barrow's mind is apparently checked, experiencing a powerful sense of blockage but without any breakthrough to a higher plane; the reader, by contrast, can move past the sublime otherness of the Arctic scenery to catch a glimpse of something "more."

Conclusion

As we have seen, transcending "personal" concerns takes place not only by way of the themes developed during my chosen feuds but also by way of the structures or trajectories of the feuds. We first encountered the profound idealized

Romantic self in the attacks, counterattacks and self-vindications inspired by the publication of *Wat Tyler*. The sublime version of Southey, though repeatedly demystified, would reappear throughout the controversy until trenchantly dismissed by Lord Byron's decision to leave the hapless Laureate floating on "his lake." The thematic opposition between the mired, disfigured, culturally enmeshed poet versus the transcendent genius, inhabitant of an ideal world, reemerged in the story of Coleridge's dealings with the *Edinburgh*. Meanwhile, in both the Southey-centered and the Coleridge–Jeffrey feuds, the multi-authored tapestry of "personalities," recriminations, and sideline commentaries unfurled in directions that pointed beyond partisan conflicts. While in the first case, particular opponents of Southey—Leigh Hunt and Byron—removed the feud to a more creative and entertaining plane, in the second case, the dynamics of the feud became unexpectedly diversified by the imaginative new voice of *Blackwood's Magazine* with its pseudonymous contributors. Both feuds show that "literary and political GOSSIPING," as Coleridge put it, are not always the same thing. In the three feuds explored in my third chapter, we saw Hunt, Hazlitt and Lady Morgan discovering idiosyncratic forms of Romantic selfhood from within the discourse of "personality." Each of these writers temporarily gestures outside the material constraints of print warfare, even though the skeptical Hazlitt is the only one who aspires to do so. As previously mentioned, like Hunt and Morgan, John Barrow does not seek transcendence whether as thematic preoccupation or rhetorical effect, but it finds him. In this final feud, transcendence as theme and as event are bound up, in that it is the sublime imagery in this sprawling text that points past the confines of "personality"-based discourse. Although during most of his articles on the Arctic, Barrow remains intent on his mutually validating private and public obsessions—hatred of John Ross and a nationalistic determination to find the Northwest Passage—at moments he and his mouthpiece, the *Quarterly Review*, seem to stumble upon the grand philosophical question of what lies—in Ross's phrase—"beyond the ice."

Bibliography

Allen, Michael. *Poe and the British Magazine Tradition*. New York: Oxford University Press, 1969.
Aske, Martin. "Critical Disfiguring: The 'Jealous Leer Malign' in Romantic Criticism." In John Beer, ed., *Questioning Romanticism*. Baltimore and London: The Johns Hopkins University Press, 1995. 49–70.
Barrow, Sir John. *An Auto-biographical Memoir*. London: John Murray, 1847.
———. *Voyages of Discovery and Research Within the Arctic Regions, from the year 1818 to the present time*. London: John Murray, 1846.
Beck, Rudolf. "'The Region of Beauty and Delight': Walton's Polar Fantasies in Mary Shelley's *Frankenstein*." *Keats-Shelley Journal* 49 (2000): 24–9.
Beer, John. "Coleridge, Hazlitt, and *Christabel*." *RES* n.s. 37 (1986): 40–54.
Beetham, Margaret. "Open and Closed: The Periodical as a Publishing Genre." *Victorian Periodicals Review* 22 (1989): 96–100.
Behrendt, Stephen C., ed. *Romanticism, Radicalism, and the Press*. Detroit: Wayne State University Press, 1997.
Belanger, Jacqueline E. *Critical Receptions: Sydney Owenson, Lady Morgan*. Bethesda: Academica Press, 2007.
Berton, Pierre. *The Arctic Grail: The Quest for the Northwest Passage and the North Pole 1818–1909*. New York: Lyons Press, 2000.
Blackwood's Magazine. Edinburgh: William Blackwood, 1817–24.
Blainey, Ann. *Immortal Boy: A Portrait of Leigh Hunt*. New York: St. Martin's Press, 1985.
Bloom, Lisa. *Gender on Ice: American Ideologies of Polar Expeditions*. Minneapolis: University of Minnesota Press, 1993.
Bolton, Carol. *Writing the Empire: Robert Southey and Romantic Colonialism*. London: Pickering & Chatto, 2007.
Bradley, Arthur and Alan Rawes, eds. *Romantic Biography*. Burlington: Ashgate, 2003.
Brandt, Anthony. *The Man Who Ate His Boots: The Tragic History of the Search for the Northwest Passage*. New York: Alfred A. Knopf, 2010.
The British Critic. London: F. and C. Rivington, 1793–1826.
"British History Online." Online at http://www.british–history.ac.uk/report.aspx?compid=45024. Accessed July 2, 2012.
Bromwich, David. *Hazlitt: The Mind of a Critic*. New Haven: Yale University Press, 1999.
Burke, Edmund. *A Philosophical Enquiry into the Origin of our Ideas of the Sublime and Beautiful*. Ed. J.T. Boulton. Notre Dame: University of Notre Dame Press, 1958.

Butler, Marilyn. "Culture's Medium: The Role of the Review." In Stuart Curran, ed., *The Cambridge Companion to British Romanticism*. Cambridge: Cambridge University Press, 1993. 120–47.

Byron, George Gordon, Lord. *Byron's Letters and Journals*. Ed. Leslie A. Marchand. 12 vols. Cambridge, Mass.: Belknap Press of Harvard University Press, 1973–82.

Cameron, J.M.R. "John Barrow, the *Quarterly Review*'s Imperial Reviewer." In Jonathan Cutmore, ed., *Conservatism and the* Quarterly Review*: A Critical Analysis*. London: Pickering & Chatto, 2007, 133–49.

Cameron, Kenneth Neill, and Donald H. Reiman and Doucet Devin Fischer, eds. *Shelley and His Circle*. 10 vols, ongoing. Cambridge, Mass.: Harvard University Press, 1961–70 and 1973–2002.

Cavell, Janice. *Tracing the Connected Narrative: Arctic Exploration in British Print Culture, 1818–1860*. Toronto: University of Toronto Press, 2008.

Christensen, Jerome. "The Detection of the Romantic Conspiracy in Britain." *South Atlantic Quarterly* 95 (1996): 603–27.

———. *Coleridge's Blessed Machine of Language*. Ithaca and London: Cornell University Press, 1981.

Christie, William. *The Edinburgh Review in the Literary Culture of Romantic Britain: Mammoth and Megalonyx*. London: Pickering & Chatto, 2009.

Clark, Roy Benjamin. *William Gifford: Tory Satirist, Critic, and Editor*. New York: Russell and Russell, 1930.

Clive, John. *Scotch Reviewers: The* Edinburgh Review *1802–1815*. Cambridge, Mass.: Harvard University Press, 1957.

Cockburn, Lord Henry. *Life of Lord Jeffrey, with a Selection from his Correspondence*. 2 vols. Philadelphia: Lippincott, Grambo & Co., 1852.

Coleman, Deirdre. "Jeffrey and Coleridge: Four Unpublished Letters." *The Wordsworth Circle* 18 (1987): 39–45.

Coleridge, Samuel Taylor. *Biographia Literaria*. Ed. James Engell and W. Jackson Bate. 2 vols. Princeton: Princeton University Press, 1983.

———. *Essays on His Times*. Ed. David V. Erdman. 3 vols. Princeton: Princeton University Press, 1978.

———. *Biographia Literaria*. Ed. George Watson. London: J.M. Dent, 1975.

———. *Collected Letters of Samuel Taylor Coleridge*. Ed. Earl Leslie Griggs. 6 vols. Oxford: Clarendon Press, 1956–1971.

———. *Collected Works: The Friend*. Ed. Barbara E. Rooke. 2 vols. Princeton: Princeton University Press, 1969.

Colley, Linda. *Britons: Forging the Nation, 1707–1837*. New Haven: Yale University Press, 1992.

Connolly, Claire. "'I accuse Miss Owenson': *The Wild Irish Girl* as Media Event." *Colby Quarterly* 36.2 (2000): 98–115.

Cox, Jeffrey N. "Leigh Hunt's Cockney School: The Lakers' 'Other.'" *Romanticism on the Net* 14 (May 1999). Online at http://www.erudit.org/revue/ron/1999/v/n14/005859ar.html. Accessed August 1, 2012.

———. *Poetry and Politics in the Cockney School*. Cambridge: Cambridge University Press, 1998.
Craciun, Adriana. "Writing the Disaster: Franklin and *Frankenstein*." *Nineteenth-Century Literature* 65.4 (March 2011): 433–80.
———. "The Frozen Ocean." *PMLA* 125 (2010): 693–702.
———. "The Scramble for the Arctic." *Interventions* 11.1 (2009): 103–14.
The Critical Review. London: Archibald Hamilton, 1756–1817.
Cronin, Richard. *Paper Pellets*. Oxford: Oxford University Press, 2011.
Curran, Stuart. *Poetic Form and British Romanticism*. New York: Oxford University Press, 1986.
Curry, Kenneth Curry and Robert Dedmon. "Southey's Contributions to the *Quarterly Review*." *The Wordsworth Circle* 6 (1975): 261–72.
Cutmore, Jonathan, ed. *Contributors to the Quarterly Review 1809–25: A History*. London: Pickering & Chatto, 2008.
———. *Conservatism and the* Quarterly Review: *A Critical Analysis*. London: Pickering & Chatto, 2007.
———. The *Quarterly Review* Archive. Online at http://www.rc.umd.edu/reference/qr/index.html. Accessed July 31, 2012.
———. *Writers and Readers of the Early* Quarterly Review. Unpublished manuscript.
de Montluzin, Emily Lorraine. "Killing the Cockneys: *Blackwood's*' Weapons of Choice Against Hunt, Hazlitt, and Keats." *Keats-Shelley Journal* 47 (1998): 87–107.
Demata, Massimiliano and Duncan Wu, eds. *British Romanticism and the* Edinburgh Review: *Bicentenary Essays*. New York: Palgrave Macmillan, 2002.
Donovan, Julie. *Sydney Owenson, Lady Morgan, and the Politics of Style*. Palo Alto: Academica Press, 2009.
Duff, David, ed. *Modern Genre Theory*. London: Longman, 1999.
Dyer, Gary. *British Satire and the Politics of Style 1789–1832*. Cambridge: Cambridge University Press, 1997.
Eagleton, Terry. *The Function of Criticism*. London: Verso, 1984.
Edgeworth, Maria. *Letters from England 1813–1844*. Ed. Christina Colvin. Oxford: Clarendon Press, 1971.
The Edinburgh Review. Edinburgh: Archibald Constable, 1802–1929.
Edinger, Ray. *Fury Beach: The Four-Year Odyssey of Captain John Ross and the Victory*. New York: Berkley Books, 2003.
Erdman, David, and Paul M. Zall. "Coleridge and Jeffrey in Controversy." *Studies in Romanticism* 14 (1975): 75–83.
The Examiner. London: John Hunt, 1808–28.
Ferguson, Frances. *Solitude and the Sublime: Romanticism and the Aesthetics of Individuation*. New York: Routledge, 1992.
Ferris, Ina. "The Irish Novel, 1800–1829." In Richard Maxwell and Katie Trumpener, eds, *The Cambridge Guide to Fiction in the Romantic Period*. Cambridge: Cambridge University Press, 2007: 235–49.

———. *The Romantic National Tale and the Question of Ireland*. Cambridge: Cambridge University Press, 2002.
Finkelstein, David, ed. *Print Culture and the Blackwood Tradition, 1805–1930*. Toronto: University of Toronto Press, 2006.
Fitzpatrick, W.J. *The Friends, Foes, and Adventures of Lady Morgan*. Dublin: W.B. Kelly, 1859.
Fleming, Fergus. *Barrow's Boys*. New York: Grove Press, 1998.
Flynn, Philip. "Beginning *Blackwood's*: The Right Mix of *Dulce* and *Utile*." *Victorian Periodicals Review* 39 (2006): 136–57.
———. "Blackwood's *Maga*, Lockhart's *Peter's Letters*, and the Politics of Publishing." *Studies in Romanticism* 45 (2006): 117–31.
Fontana, Biancamaria. *Rethinking the Politics of Commercial Society: The Edinburgh Review, 1802–1832*. Cambridge and New York: Cambridge University Press, 1985.
Franta, Andrew. *Romanticism and the Rise of the Mass Public*. Cambridge: Cambridge University Press, 2007.
"A Friend to the Navy." A Letter to John Barrow, Esq. on the Subject of the Polar Expeditions; or, The Reviewer Reviewed. London: James Ridgway [sic]: 1819.
Fulford, Tim. *Romantic Indians: Native Americans, British Literature, and Transatlantic Culture 1756–1830*. Oxford: Oxford University Press, 2006.
Fulford, Tim, Debbie Lee and Peter Kitson. *Literature, Science, and Exploration in the Romantic Era*. Cambridge: Cambridge University Press, 2004.
Fulford, Tim and Peter Kitson, eds. *Romanticism and Colonialism: Writing and Empire, 1780–1830*. Cambridge: Cambridge University Press, 1998.
Gilmartin, Kevin. *Writing Against Revolution: Literary Conservatism in Britain, 1790–1832*. Cambridge: Cambridge University Press, 2007.
———. *Print Politics: The Press and Radical Opposition in Early Nineteenth-Century England*. Cambridge: Cambridge University Press, 1996.
Goldberg, Brian. *The Lake Poets and Professional Identity*. Cambridge: Cambridge University Press, 2007.
Graham, Walter. *English Literary Periodicals*. New York: Octagon Books, 1966.
Grayling, A.C. *The Quarrel of the Age: The Life and Times of William Hazlitt*. London: Weidenfeld and Nicolson, 2000.
Hay, Daisy. "Liberals, *Liberales* and *The Liberal*: A Reassessment." *European Romantic Review* 19.4 (2008): 307–20.
Hayden, John O. *The Romantic Reviewers 1802–1824*. Chicago: University of Chicago Press, 1968.
Hazlitt, William. *Selected Writings*. Ed. Duncan Wu. 9 vols. London: Pickering & Chatto, 1998.
———. *Works*. Ed. P.P. Howe. 21 vols. London and Toronto: J.M. Dent and Sons, 1930–34.
Hertz, Neil. *The End of the Line: Essays on Psychoanalysis and the Sublime*. New York: Columbia University Press, 1985.
Higgins, David. *Romantic Genius and the Literary Magazine: Biography, Celebrity, and Politics*. London: Routledge, 2005.

Hill, Jen. *White Horizon: The Arctic in the Nineteenth-Century Imagination*. Albany: State University of New York Press, 2007.

Hoadley, Frank Taliaferro. "The Controversy over Southey's *Wat Tyler*." *Studies in Philology* 38 (1941): 81–96.

Hofkosh, Sonia. *Sexual Politics and the Romantic Author*. Cambridge: Cambridge University Press, 1998.

Houghton, Walter Edwards, ed. *The Wellesley Index to Victorian Periodicals, 1824–1900; Tables of Contents and Identification of Contributors*. 5 vols. Toronto: University of Toronto Press, 1966–89.

Hunt, Leigh. *The Autobiography of Leigh Hunt, with Reminiscences of Friends and Contemporaries*. 2 vols. New York: Harper and Brothers, 1850.

———. *Lord Byron and Some of his Contemporaries*. London: Henry Colburn, 1828.

———. *Ultra-Crepidarius: A Satire on William Gifford*. London: John Hunt, 1823.

———. *The Feast of the Poets*. London: James Cawthorn, 1814.

Jackson, J.R. de J. ed. *Coleridge: The Critical Heritage*. London: Routledge and Kegan Paul, 1970.

Jones, A.G.E. "Sir John Ross and Sir John Barrow." *Polar Portraits: Collected Papers*. Whitby: Caedmon, 1992: 219–28.

Jones, Elizabeth. "Keats in the Suburbs." *Keats-Shelley Journal* 45 (1996): 23–43.

Jones, Steven, ed. *The Satiric Eye: Forms of Satire in the Romantic Period*. New York: Palgrave Macmillan, 2003.

———. *Satire and Romanticism*. New York: St. Martin's Press, 2000.

Keach, William. "Cockney Couplets: Keats and the Politics of Style." *Studies in Romanticism* 25 (1986): 182–96.

Kearns, Sheila M. *Coleridge, Wordsworth, and Romantic Autobiography*. London: Associated University Presses, 1995.

Keats, John. *The Letters of John Keats*. Ed. H.E. Rollins. 2 vols. Cambridge, Mass.: Harvard University Press, 1958.

Keen, Paul. *The Crisis of Literature in the 1790s: Print Culture and the Public Sphere*. Cambridge: Cambridge University Press, 1999.

Khalip, Jacques. *Anonymous Life: Romanticism and Dispossession*. Stanford: Stanford University Press, 2009.

Kitson, Peter J., ed. *Travels, Explorations and Empires: Writings from the Era of Imperial Expansion*. Volume 3: *North and South Poles*. London: Pickering & Chatto, 2001.

Klancher, Jon. *The Making of English Reading Audiences 1790–1832*. Madison: University of Wisconsin Press, 1987.

Knox, Julian. "Coleridge's 'Cousin-German': *Blackwood's*, Alter-Egos, and the Making of a Man of Letters." *European Romantic Review* 21.4 (August 2010): 425–46.

Kucich, Greg. "Romance." In Nicholas Roe, ed., *Romanticism: An Oxford Guide*. Oxford: Oxford University Press, 2005: 463–81.

Lapp, Robert. *Contest for Cultural Authority: Hazlitt, Coleridge, and the Distresses of the Regency.* Detroit: Wayne State University Press, 1999.

Latane, David. "The Birth of the Author in the Victorian Archive." *Victorian Periodicals Review* 22 (1989): 110–17.

Leask, Nigel. "Southey's *Madoc*: Reimagining the Conquest of America." In Lynda Pratt, ed., *Robert Southey and the Contexts of English Romanticism.* Aldershot: Ashgate, 2006, 133–50.

Levinson, Marjorie. *Keats's Life of Allegory: The Origins of a Style.* Oxford: Basil Blackwell, 1988.

The Liberal: Verse and Prose from the South. London: John Hunt, 1822–23.

Lockhart, John Gibson. *Peter's Letters to his Kinsfolk.* 3 vols. Edinburgh: Blackwood, 1819.

The London Magazine. London: Baldwin, Cradock, & Joy, 1820–29.

Loomis, Chauncey C. "The Arctic Sublime." In U.C. Knoepflmacher and G.B. Tennyson, eds, *Nature and the Victorian Imagination.* Berkeley: University of California Press, 1977. 99–112.

McGann, Jerome. *The Romantic Ideology: A Critical Investigation.* Chicago: University of Chicago Press, 1983.

Madden, Lionel, ed. *Robert Southey: The Critical Heritage.* London and Boston: Routledge & Kegan Paul, 1972.

Magnuson, Paul. *Reading Public Romanticism.* Princeton: Princeton University Press, 1998.

Maniquis, Robert. "Poetry and Barrel-Organs: The Text in the Book of the *Biographia Literaria*." In Frederick Burwick, ed., *Coleridge's Biographia: Text and Meaning.* Columbus: Ohio State University Press, 1989: 255–309.

Manning, Peter. "Detaching Lamb's Thoughts." In Kim Wheatley, ed., *Romantic Periodicals and Print Culture.* London: Frank Cass, 2003. 137–46.

Marshall, William H. *Byron, Shelley, Hunt, and "The Liberal."* Philadelphia: University of Pennsylvania, 1960.

Martin, Constance. "William Scoresby Jr. and the Open Polar Sea—Myth and Reality." *Arctic* 41 (1988): 39–47.

Mason, Nicholas. "'The Quack has become God': Puffery, Print, and the 'Death' of Literature in Romantic-Era Britain." *Nineteenth-Century Literature* 60 (2005): 1–31.

Mason, Nicholas, et al., eds. *Blackwood's Magazine, 1817–25: Selections from Maga's Infancy.* 6 vols. London: Pickering & Chatto, 2006.

Milnes, Tim. "Seeing in the Dark: Hazlitt's Immanent Idealism." *Studies in Romanticism* 39.1 (2000): 3–26.

Milton, John. *Complete Poems and Major Prose.* Ed. Merritt Y. Hughes. Indianapolis: Bobbs-Merrill, 1957.

Mole, Tom. *Byron's Romantic Celebrity: Industrial Culture and the Hermeneutic of Intimacy.* New York: Palgrave Macmillan, 2007.

[Morgan, Sir Charles, and Lady Morgan.] *The Mohawks; a Satirical Poem with Notes.* London: Henry Colburn, 1822.

Morrison, Robert. "*Blackwood's* Berserker: John Wilson and the Language of Extremity." *Romanticism on the Net* 20 (November 2000). Online at http://www.erudit.org/revue/ron/2000/v/n20/005951ar.html. Accessed July 31, 2012.

Moskal, Jeanne. "Gender, Nationality and Textual Authority in Lady Morgan's Travel Books." In Paula Feldman and Theresa M. Kelley, eds, *Romantic Women Writers: Voices and Countervoices*. Hanover: University Press of New England, 1995: 171–93.

Murphy, Peter. *Poetry as an Occupation and an Art in Britain, 1760–1830*. Cambridge: Cambridge University Press, 1993.

———. "Impersonation and Authorship in Romantic Britain." *ELH* 59 (1992): 625–49.

Natarajan, Uttara. *Hazlitt and the Reach of Sense*. Oxford: Clarendon Press, 1998.

Natarajan, Uttara, Tom Paulin and Duncan Wu, eds. *Metaphysical Hazlitt: Bicentenary Essays*. London: Routledge, 2005.

Newcomer, James. *Lady Morgan the Novelist*. Lewisburg: Bucknell University Press, 1990.

Newlyn, Lucy, ed. *The Cambridge Companion to Coleridge*. Cambridge: Cambridge University Press, 2002.

Noble, Andrew. "John Wilson (Christopher North) and the Tory Hegemony." In Douglas Gifford, ed., *The History of Scottish Literature*. Volume 3: *The Nineteenth Century*. Aberdeen: Aberdeen University Press, 1987: 125–52.

Owenson, Sydney (Lady Morgan). *Florence Macarthy: An Irish Tale*. Ed. Jenny McAuley. London: Pickering & Chatto, 2012.

———. *Letter to the Reviewers of "Italy."* Paris: A. and W. Galignani, 1821.

Parker, Mark. *Literary Magazines and British Romanticism*. Cambridge: Cambridge University Press, 2000.

Parker, Patricia. *Inescapable Romance*. Princeton: Princeton University Press, 1979.

Parker, Reeve. *Coleridge's Meditative Art* (Ithaca: Cornell University Press, 1975)

The Parliamentary Debates from the Year 1803 to the Present Time. Volume 35. London: Hansard, 1817.

Peacock, Thomas Love. *Works*. 10 vols. London: Constable, 1924–34.

Poovey, Mary. *The Proper Lady and the Woman Writer*. Chicago: University of Chicago Press, 1984.

Porden, Eleanor Anne. *The Arctic Expeditions*. London: John Murray, 1818.

Potkay, Adam. "Wordsworth and the Ethics of Things." *PMLA* 123 (2008): 390–404.

Potter, Russell A. *Arctic Spectacles: The Frozen North in Visual Culture, 1818–1875*. Seattle: University of Washington Press, 2007.

Pottinger, George. *Heirs of the Enlightenment: Edinburgh Reviewers and Writers 1800–1830*. Edinburgh: Scottish Academic Press, 1992.

Pykett, Lyn. "Reading the Periodical Press: Text and Context." *Victorian Periodicals Review* 22 (1989): 100–108.

The Quarterly Review. London: John Murray, 1809–1967.

Reiman, Donald H. "Coleridge and the Art of Equivocation." *Studies in Romanticism* 25 (1986): 325–50.

———. *The Romantics Reviewed: Contemporary Reviews of British Romantic Writers.* 9 vols. New York and London: Garland Publishing, 1972.

Richard, Jessica. "'A Paradise of My Own Creation': *Frankenstein* and the Improbable Romance of Polar Exploration." *Nineteenth-Century Contexts* 25.4 (2003): 295–314.

Robinson, Henry Crabb. *Henry Crabb Robinson on Books and Their Writers.* Ed. Edith J. Morley. 3 vols. London: J.M. Dent & Sons, 1938.

———. *Diary, Reminiscences, and Correspondence of Henry Crabb Robinson.* Ed. Thomas Sadler. 2 vols. London and New York: Macmillan, 1872.

Roe, Nicholas. *Fiery Heart: The First Life of Leigh Hunt.* London: Pimlico, 2005.

———. ed. *Leigh Hunt: Life, Poetics, Politics.* London: Routledge, 2003.

———. *John Keats and the Culture of Dissent.* Oxford: Clarendon Press, 1997.

Ross, John. *Observations on a Work, entitled, "Voyages of Discovery and Research Within the Arctic Regions," by Sir John Barrow, Bart.* Edinburgh and London: William Blackwood, 1846.

[Ross, John]. *A Letter to John Barrow, Esq. F.R.S. on the Late Extraordinary and Unexpected Hyperborean Discoveries.* London: W. Pople, 1826.

Ross, M.J. *Polar Pioneers: John Ross and James Clark Ross.* Montreal: McGill-Queen's University Press, 1994.

Russett, Margaret. *Fictions and Fakes: Forging Romantic Authenticity, 1760–1845.* Cambridge: Cambridge University Press, 2006.

———. *De Quincey's Romanticism: Canonical Minority and the Forms of Transmission.* Cambridge: Cambridge University Press, 1997.

Savours, Ann. *The Search for the North West Passage.* New York: St. Martin's Press, 1999.

Schneider, Elisabeth. "The Unknown Reviewer of *Christabel*." *PMLA* 20 (1955): 417–32.

Schoenfield, Mark. *British Periodicals and Romantic Identity: The "Literary Lower Empire."* New York: Palgrave Macmillan, 2009.

———. "Regulating Standards: The *Edinburgh Review* and the Circulations of Judgment." *The Wordsworth Circle* 24 (1993): 148–51.

———. "Voices Together: Lamb, Hazlitt, and the *London*." *Studies in Romanticism* 29 (1990), 257–72.

Scott, Sir Walter. *Letters.* Ed. H.J.C. Grierson. 12 vols. London: Constable, 1932.

Sedgwick, Eve. "The Character in the Veil: Imagery of the Surface in the Gothic Novel." *PMLA* 96.2 (March 1981): 255–70.

Shattock, Joanne. *Politics and Reviewers: The* Edinburgh *and the* Quarterly *in the Early Victorian Age.* Leicester: Leicester University Press, 1989.

Shelley, Mary. *Frankenstein: The 1818 Text.* Ed. Marilyn Butler. Oxford: Oxford World's Classics, 1994.

Shelley, Percy Bysshe. *Shelley's Poetry and Prose: A Norton Critical Edition.* Ed. Donald H. Reiman and Neil Fraistat. Second edition. New York: Norton, 2002.

Simpson, David. "Romantic Indians: Robert Southey's Distinctions." *The Wordsworth Circle* 38 (2007): 20–25.

Smiles, Samuel. *A Publisher and His Friends*. 2 vols. London: John Murray, 1891.

Smith, Sydney. *Letters of Sydney Smith*. Ed. Nowell C. Smith. 2 vols. Oxford: Clarendon Press, 1953.

Southey, Robert. *New Letters of Robert Southey*. Ed. Kenneth Curry. 2 vols. New York: Columbia University Press, 1965.

———. *The Life and Correspondence of Robert Southey*. Ed. Charles Cuthbert Southey. 6 vols. London: Longman, Brown, Green and Longmans, 1850.

———. *A Letter to William Smith, Esq., M.P.* London: John Murray, 1817.

Spufford, Francis. *I May Be Some Time: Ice and the English Imagination*. New York: St. Martin's Press, 1997.

Stauffer, Andrew M. *Anger, Revolution, and Romanticism*. Cambridge: Cambridge University Press, 2005.

St. Clair, William. *The Reading Nation in the Romantic Period*. Cambridge: Cambridge University Press, 2004.

Stevenson, Lionel. *The Wild Irish Girl: The Life of Sydney Owenson, Lady Morgan (1776–1859)*. New York: Russell and Russell, 1969 (first published 1936).

Stewart, David G. *Romantic Magazines and Metropolitan Literary Culture*. Basingstoke: Palgrave Macmillan, 2011.

———. "*The Examiner*, Robert Southey's Print Celebrity and the Marketing of the *Quarterly Review*." *Prose Studies* 31 (April 2009): 22–39.

———."P.G. Patmore's Rejected Articles and the Image of the Magazine Market." *Romanticism* 12.3 (2006), 200–211.

Storey, Mark. "Romantic Biography: The Case of Robert Southey." In Arthur Bradley and Alan Rawes, eds, *Romantic Biography*. Aldershot: Ashgate, 2003. 33–47.

———. *Robert Southey: A Life*. Oxford: Oxford University Press, 1997.

Strout, Alan Lang. *A Bibliography of Articles in* Blackwood's Magazine *1817–1825*. Lubbock, Texas: Texas Technological College, 1959.

———. "Samuel Taylor Coleridge and John Wilson of *Blackwood's Magazine*." *PMLA* 48 (1933): 100–128.

Swaim, Barton. "'Edinburgh is a Talking Town': Scottish Periodical-Writing and the Competitive Conversation." *Prose Studies* 28.3 (2006): 245–57.

Swann, Karen. "Literary Gentlemen and Lovely Ladies: The Debate on the Character of *Christabel*." *ELH* 52 (1985): 394–418.

Sweet, Nanora. "The *New Monthly Magazine* and the Liberalism of the 1820s." In Kim Wheatley, ed., *Romantic Periodicals and Print Culture*. London: Frank Cass, 2003. 147–62.

Thompson, James R. *Leigh Hunt*. Boston: Twayne, 1977.

Treadwell, James. *Autobiographical Writing and British Literature 1783–1834*. Oxford: Oxford University Press, 2005.

Vine, Steven. "To 'Make a Bull': Autobiography, Idealism, and Writing in Coleridge's *Biographia Literaria*." In Peter J. Kitson and Thomas N. Corns, eds, *Coleridge and the Armoury of the Human Mind*. London: Frank Cass, 1991. 99–114.

Ward, William S. *British Periodicals and Newspapers, 1789–1832: A Bibliography of Secondary Sources.* Lexington: University Press of Kentucky, 1972.

Webb, Timothy. "Correcting the Irritability of his Temper: The Evolution of Leigh Hunt's *Autobiography*." In Robert Brinkley and Keith Hanley, eds, *Romantic Revisions*. Cambridge: Cambridge University Press, 1992: 268–90.

Weiskel, Thomas. *The Romantic Sublime: Studies in the Structure and Psychology of Transcendence.* Baltimore: The Johns Hopkins University Press, 1976.

Wheatley, Kim, ed. *Romantic Periodicals and Print Culture.* London: Frank Cass, 2003.

———. *Shelley and His Readers: Beyond Paranoid Politics.* Columbus: University of Missouri Press, 1999.

———. "The *Blackwood's* Attacks on Leigh Hunt." *Nineteenth-Century Literature* 47 (June 1992): 1–31.

Wheeler, Kathleen M. *Sources, Processes and Methods in Coleridge's* Biographia Literaria. Cambridge: Cambridge University Press, 1980.

White, Deborah Elise. *Romantic Returns: Superstition, Imagination, History.* Stanford: Stanford University Press, 2000.

Williams, Glyn. *Voyages of Delusion.* New Haven: Yale University Press, 2003.

Wilson, Eric G. *The Spiritual History of Ice: Romanticism, Science, and the Imagination.* New York: Palgrave Macmillan, 2003.

Wilson, James D. "A Note on Coleridge and the *Quarterly Review*." *The Wordsworth Circle* 6 (1975): 51–3.

Wolfson, Susan. *Formal Charges: The Shaping of Poetry in British Romanticism.* Stanford: Stanford University Press, 1997.

Wordsworth, Jonathan. *Francis Jeffrey: On the Lake Poets.* Poole: Woodstock Books, 1998.

Wordsworth, William. *The Major Works.* Ed. Stephen Gill. Oxford: Oxford University Press, 2000.

Wordsworth, William, and Dorothy Wordsworth. *The Letters of William and Dorothy Wordsworth.* Ed. Ernest de Selincourt. 8 vols. Second edition. Oxford: Clarendon Press, 1967.

Wu, Duncan. *William Hazlitt: The First Modern Man.* Oxford: Oxford University Press, 2008.

———. *Romanticism: An Anthology.* Second edition. Oxford: Blackwell, 1998.

Index

Admiralty 18, 139, 142, 160–61, 161n45
African exploration 140n3
"age of personality" 1, 2, 3–4, 11, 16, 22, 44, 57, 58, 95, 98, 120
Allen, Michael 3n9
anonymity 75, 89, 108, 110, 120, 129, 149n26, 162, 165
    convention of 6–11, 14, 18, 57, 61–2, 77, 80, 98, 102n12, 119, 140–41
anonymous discourse 22, 23, 35, 37, 38, 46, 51, 64, 132–3, 159–60
Anti-Jacobin 102, 126, 136
    attack on Coleridge 60, 66–7, 75, 85, 86
anti-Jacobinism 32
apostasy 22, 23n6, 74
    Coleridge's 126
    Southey's 16, 24, 40, 53, 75
    Wordsworth's 27
Arctic exploration 18–19, 20, 139–73
Aske, Martin 100n7
audiences, *see* mass audience; reading public
Aurora Borealis 148
autobiography 2, 17, 23, 41, 44n37, 87, 135
    Barrow's 148,
    in *Biographia Literaria* 58–9, 75
    Hunt's 100, 105, 119
    in Jeffrey's footnote in the *Edinburgh* 77–8, 93
    reluctant 42, 80

Back, George 142
Baillie, Joanna 63, 79
Banks, Joseph 149
Barbauld, Anna Laetitia 97
Barrow, John 141–2
    and anonymity 9, 18–19
    feud with John Ross 10, 18, 20, 139–73
        on Ross's first expedition 150–53
        on Ross's second expedition 159–64, 171–2

    works
        An Auto-biographical Memoir 141n6, 148
        A Chronological History of Voyages 141
        Voyages of Discovery and Research 140, 142, 164
Bate, W. Jackson 61n12
Beck, Rudolf 143n14
Beechey, Frederick 145n19, 158, 169
Beer, John 70n25
Bering Strait 146, 148, 150, 160
Berton, Pierre 139, 151
Blackwood's Magazine 3, 4, 58; *see also* Lockhart; John Wilson
    on Arctic exploration 142n11, 149n26, 151
    on *Biographia Literaria* 19, 81, 84–90
    and collaborative discourse 93, 173
    on Hazlitt 99; *see also* Cockney School
    on Hunt 16, 39, 49, 98, 99, 107, 108n21, 109–10; *see also* Cockney School
    on *Ultra-Crepidarius* 116–8
    on Keats 99 *see also* Cockney School
    on Jeffrey 17, 61, 90–95; *see also* Timothy Tickler
    on Lady Morgan 99n6
    and personal attacks 85, 90, 124
    playfulness of 50, 87, 92
Blackwood, William 109n22
Blainey, Ann 112n27
Bloom, Lisa 143n14
Bolton, Carol 142n9, 167n54
Bonaparte, Napoleon 43
Booth, Felix 162
Bradley, Arthur 45n38
Brandt, Anthony 139n3
The British Critic 104n14
    on *Biographia Literaria* 81–4
    on *Ultra-Crepidarius* 115, 117

Bromwich, David 121, 126
Brougham, Henry 26, 30, 46
"Brutus Billy" 25–6
Buchan, David 149, 150, 151, 160, 169
Burke, Edmund 34
    Hazlitt on 106, 121
    on the sublime 167–69, 171
Byron, Lord George Gordon 19, 87, 109, 118
    in the *Illiberal!* 110
    on Southey 53–6
    works
        Childe Harold's Pilgrimage 144n17
        The Vision of Judgment 16, 21n3, 23, 53–6, 173
Byronic hero 133

Cameron, J.M.R. 145n18
Campbell, Thomas 87
Canada 146, 150, 155, 156
cannibalism 155
Canning, George 24, 51
Cavell, Janice 140n4, 142n11, 143n15, 151n29, 160, 161n44
"Chaldee Manuscript" 84
childhood 27–9, 32
Christensen, Jerome 1n4, 23n6, 59n6
Christie, Jonathan 94n53
Christie, William 3n10, 60n11, 61n12, 90n46
Clark, Roy 118n34
Clarkson, Catherine 35
Clarkson, Thomas 64
class prejudice 99, 104, 105, 107, 113, 155n34
class status 32, 52, 68, 107, 113
Cockburn, Henry 63n14
Cockney School 90, 95, 99–100, 105, 107, 109, 110, 116–18, 127
    Blackwood's attacks on 15, 39, 49, 84, 86, 91–2, 99, 105, 107, 114
    Cockney classicism 102, 107, 111–14, 118, 127
    Cockney diction 106, 115
    Cockney manners 106–7
    Cockney rhymes 103, 114
    Cockney versification 111, 115
Colburn, Henry 10, 136
Coleman, Deirdre 64, 65
Coleridge, John Taylor 8n26, 106, 107–8

Coleridge, Samuel Taylor 1–4, 5–10, 19, 24, 57–95, 97
    attack on Hazlitt 69–71
    attack on Jeffrey 17, 57, 61–3, 68–9, 73, 78, 82
    correspondence with Jeffrey 63–5
    defense of Southey 22, 30, 39, 42, 53, 66, 75
    and Lake School 27n17, 64, 66, 79
    on "personality" 1, 7, 11–14, 58, 65–7, 70, 72–3
    private meeting with Jeffrey 61, 68, 77, 78–9, 80, 89, 92
    private relationship with Hazlitt 72
    response to *Wat Tyler* 23, 33–8, 43; *see also Courier*
    satirized 39, 51, 88
    works
        Biographia Literaria 7, 11–14, 17, 42, 57–63, 65–73, 95
        reception of 73–90, 94
        reviewed by *Blackwood's* 19, 84–90
        reviewed by *British Critic* 81–4
        reviewed by the *Edinburgh* 36, 61, 73–80, 126
        "Chamouni" 170
        Christabel 19, 69–70, 72, 73, 78, 79, 88, 93, 95
        "Dejection: An Ode" 76
        The Friend 7, 11, 14, 59
        Kubla Khan 48
        Remorse 12
        "Rime of the Ancient Mariner" 19, 68n21, 79, 91, 93, 95, 142, 170
        Statesman's Manual 59n7, 69, 70, 71, 72, 74n28, 78–80
    collaborative writing 2, 6, 7, 16, 58, 65, 80, 140
    in *Blackwood's* 84, 90, 93, 99
Colley, Linda 142n13
colonialism 142, 154n33; *see also* imperialism
comedy 2, 17, 18, 22, 23, 25, 39–40, 50–53, 132–6, 151
    in *Blackwood's* 58, 61, 85, 95
Connolly, Claire 128n52
Courier 9, 26, 31–8, 39, 43, 45, 51
Cox, Jeffery 63n13, 99n4

Craciun, Adriana 143n13, 144n16
Croker, John Wilson 8n26, 18, 19, 51, 98, 105–6, 114, 115, 139n1
  feud with Lady Morgan 127–36
Croker's Mountains 152, 153, 159, 163, 164
Cronin, Richard 3n9, 8n25, 10n34, 15, 16
Curry, Kenneth 9n28
Cutmore, Jonathan 4, 6n23, 141

Davy, Humphry 65
Dedmon, Robert 9n28
de Montluzin, Emily 107n19
De Quincey, Thomas 90
Donovan, Julie 135n68
duels 10, 94n53, 132
Dyer, Gary 25n11, 102n11, 112n29

Edgeworth, Maria 132
Edinburgh Magazine 131–2, 136
Edinburgh Review 1–20, 57–95; *see also* Jeffrey
  on Arctic exploration 145n19, 149n26, 153, 163n47, 166–7, 169
  on the *Biographia* 36, 73–80
  and *Blackwood's* 3n10, 90–95
  on *Christabel* 69–70, 78, 79, 81, 93
  on Humphry Davy 65
  on Lady Morgan 10
  on the Lake School 27, 57, 59, 64, 79, 82
  and "personality" 1, 11, 67, 94
  on *The Statesman's Manual* 69, 71, 74n28, 78, 79, 80
  on *Wat Tyler* 22, 49–50
Edinger, Ray 160n42
editors, role of 6, 8, 65, 70, 72–3, 102, 119, 120; *see also* Gifford; Jeffrey
Eldon, Lord 21, 33
Engell, James 58n6, 61n12, 66n20
Erdman, David 5, 12n37, 31n24, 33n26, 57n2, 61n12, 65n19, 68, 85n39, 86n43, 94n53, 95
Examiner 3, 9, 98, 100, 101, 128–9; *see also* Hunt
  attacks on Gifford 108, 109, 119, 120, 124
  attacks on Southey 22, 26–30, 36–40, 46–9, 50–53
  on *The Statesman's Manual* 70, 80

face-to-face encounters 9–10, 61, 68, 77, 78–9, 80, 89, 92
fame 22, 43, 44, 66, 78, 107, 116, 120, 126, 128, 133–4
Ferguson, Frances 28n20, 168n57
Ferris, Ina 135
Fitzpatrick, W.J. 128, 129n53
Fleming, Fergus 139n3, 145, 149n26, 150n28, 152n30, 153n31, 160, 164n48
Flynn, Philip 84n37, 94n52
Fonte, Bartolomeo de 154–5
Foot, Michael 34
Franklin, John 139, 168
  final expedition 147, 164
  land expeditions 147, 154, 155–6, 158, 162, 166
Franta, Andrew 18n49
French Revolution 31, 44, 52
Fulford, Tim 142n12, 148n25, 167n54

"*game, the*" 14, 60, 63, 69, 70, 73, 86, 94, 99, 128; *see also* "personality"
genius 11, 22, 25, 173
genres 5, 18, 32, 81, 97, 144; *see also* autobiography; romance; satire
  comedy of manners 95
  Gothic 2, 88, 89, 93, 133, 136, 144, 146, 165
  lyric 2, 15, 27, 41, 46, 74, 144
Gifford, William 10, 24; *see also* Hazlitt; Hunt
  on the *Edinburgh* 4, 8
  as editor of the *Quarterly* 7, 8, 140, 141n5
  feud with Hazlitt 17, 97–8, 119–27, 132
  feud with Hunt 17, 19, 40, 51, 98–119, 128
  on Lady Morgan 129, 130–31
  works
    The Baviad 101, 104, 121, 134
    The Maeviad 102, 134
Gilmartin, Kevin 1n3, 14–15, 30n22
Goldberg, Brian 1n2
gossip 1, 7, 9, 12, 15, 17, 58, 61, 75, 89, 94, 95, 173
Greenland 148, 150, 153
Griggs, Earl Leslie 80n35

"*habit* of malignity" 3, 12, 13, 14; *see also* personal attacks
Hay, Daisy 109n23
Hayden, John 61n12
Hazlitt, William 1, 7, 9, 72
    attacks on Coleridge 69, 70–73, 74, 78, 80, 93
    review of the *Biographia* 17, 53, 57, 61, 66, 73–7, 81
    attacks on Southey 17, 22–4, 25, 26–30, 35–8, 46–9
    and *Blackwood's* 93, 122, 99
    "disinterested imagination" 18, 120, 122–7
    feud with Gifford and the *Quarterly* 8, 18, 97–8, 119–27, 132
    "Keswick escapade" 72
    on Lady Morgan 10
    works
        Essay on the Principles of Human Action 122–3
        Lectures on the English Poets 120, 121
        Letter to William Gifford, Esq. 111, 112, 117, 123–7, 132
        "Mr. Gifford" 101, 120, 124, 127n49
        "Mr. Jeffrey" 124
        "My First Acquaintance with Poets" 48, 72
        Political Essays 121, 127
        The Round Table 106, 130
        Table-Talk 108, 122 120, 121
Hertz, Neil 170
Higgins, David 22n4, 85n39, 86n41, 90
Hill, Jen 142, 156
Hofkosh, Sonia 72n27
Hogg, James 90
Hone, William 25–6, 35, 38–9, 108, 155
hospitality 17, 57, 72, 74, 78, 81, 82, 88, 89, 93
House of Commons 21, 30, 34, 36, 41, 42
Huish, Robert 160, 162
Hunt, Leigh 1, 9, 36, 97–119, 126, 155, 173; *see also* Cockney School
    attacks on Southey 22, 23, 34, 39–40, 50–53
    and *Blackwood's* 16, 49, 84, 86, 90, 91n48, 92, 105
    feud with Gifford 8, 10, 17–18, 97–119
    works
        Autobiography 10, 99, 100, 102, 105, 119
        Feast of the Poets 102, 103–5, 109, 111, 112, 122n42
        Foliage 102, 107, 108, 110, 111, 112, 114
        The Round Table 8, 98, 106, 108, 120, 121, 130
        "To a Spider Running across a Room" 110, 111, 132
        The Story of Rimini 102, 105, 114, 115
        Ultra-Crepidarius 18, 19, 98, 102, 110–16, 122n42
        reception of 116–19

ideal self 18, 34, 74, 119, 123–4, 172–3
The Illiberal! 109–10
imperialism 18, 140, 142, 143n14, 145, 154, 167

Jackson, J.R. de J. 61n12
Jacobinism 32, 33, 34, 52, 130
Jeffrey, Francis 4, 8, 14, 61–3, 74, 80–84
    on anonymity 8–9,
    attack on Southey 22, 49–50
    attacks on Wordsworth 13, 15, 27
    in the *Biographia* 65–71, 73
    in *Blackwood's* 85–95
    feud with Coleridge 17, 26, 57–95, 173
        correspondence with Coleridge 63–5
        footnote to review of the *Biographia* 77–80, 85n39
        private meeting with Coleridge 10, 78–9, 91
Jones, Elizabeth 99n4
Jones, Steven 102, 105n16

Kant, Immanuel 168, 170
Keach, William 105n17
Keats, John 2, 128; *see also* Cockney School
    attacked by the *Quarterly* 8n26, 15, 97, 102, 105, 110, 132, 144
    on Hazlitt 127n48
Khalip, Jacques 6n19, 123
Kitson, Peter 140n3, 142n12, 146, 150

Klancher, Jon 6
Knox, Julian 86n43
Kucich, Greg 144n17

Lake District 10, 56, 57, 61, 63, 68, 72, 77, 79, 80
Lamb, Charles 16, 66, 75, 97, 112n29, 122
Lancaster Sound 152, 153, 154, 155, 163, 165
Lapp, Robert 22, 23, 24n10, 34n27, 37, 53, 60n9, 69n24, 74, 75, 79, 80
Leask, Nigel 167n54
Lessing, Gotthold Ephraim 12–13
Levinson, Marjorie 1n2, 99n4
libel 86, 106
The Liberal 53, 109, 110, 112
Literary Examiner 116–7
Literary Gazette 74
Lockhart, John Gibson 84, 92n49, 93, 94, 108n21, 118
London Magazine 16, 94, 97, 132
Loomis, Chauncey 167n52

McAuley, Jenny 135n67
McGann, Jerome 17
Magnuson, Paul 1n2
Maldonado, Lorenzo 146, 154
malignity 11, 13, 33, 38, 57, 63, 69, 70, 71, 73, 112, 117; *see also* "habit of malignity"
Manning, Peter 16, 59, 97, 125
masculinity 34, 105, 113, 143, 156
Mason, Nicholas 131n60
mass audience 5n18, 10–11, 21n3
Milnes, Tim 120n38
Milton, John 167, 169
misogyny 18, 29, 47, 51, 100
The Mohawks 132
Mole, Tom 10, 11n35
Monthly Review 9, 53
Moore, Thomas 70n25, 87, 118, 119
Morgan, Lady (Sydney Owenson) 1, 10, 97, 139, 173
and *Blackwood's* 99n6
feud with the *Quarterly* 8n26, 18, 98, 100, 127–37
self-portraits 7, 134–6
works
Florence Macarthy: An Irish Tale 16, 18, 19, 98, 128, 132–7, 148n25
France 129–30, 134
Italy 131–2
Letter to the Reviewers of "Italy" 5n16, 101n10, 131
O'Donnel: A National Tale 130n58
The Wild Irish Girl 129
Woman; or, Ida of Athens 129
Morgan, Sir Charles 130, 131
Morning Chronicle 25, 35, 36, 37, 98n3
Morrison, Robert 85n39
Moskal, Jeanne 130n57
Murphy, Peter 15n42, 85, 86n41, 124
Murray, John 2n8, 10, 41, 50, 51, 73, 88, 95, 101, 105, 109, 112, 113, 119, 141, 161
mutiny on the Bounty 158n37

Natarajan, Uttara 120n38
nationalism 7, 18, 100, 140, 142, 148, 173
Native Americans 142, 144, 155, 156, 157
Navy 140, 143n13, 150
New Monthly Magazine 45, 122, 136
Newcomer, James 132n64, 137n76
North Pole 139, 143, 148n25, 149, 150, 151, 158, 168, 169, 171
Northwest Passage 18, 139, 141, 146, 147, 149–57, 160, 163–4, 168, 173

O'Reilly, Bernard 149–51
Owenson, Sydney, *see* Lady Morgan

Parker, Mark 8n25
Parker, Patricia 143n16
parliamentary debates 21, 23, 26, 30, 41
Parry, William Edward 139, 144, 147, 150, 153–8, 160, 163, 166–8, 170–71
Peacock, Thomas Love 56
works
"Essay on Fashionable Literature" 7
Melincourt 24–5, 39, 51
persecution-by-association 5, 65
personal attacks 3, 11–14, 17, 22, 77, 84, 108; *see also* reprisals
allegations of 23, 26, 57, 63, 129, 133
motives for
economics 13, 14
entertainment 10, 13, 85, 131
misogyny 18, 100
nationalism 18, 100

personal ill will 11, 13, 69, 70, 71, 82, 100, 159, 166
political partisanship 13, 18
"personalities" 3, 15, 16, 18, 19, 51, 73, 85, 97, 124; see also "personality"
"personality" 4, 14, 31, 59, 60, 81, 84, 94, 119, 127, 140, 147; see also "personalities"
   in the *Biographia* 7, 65–72
   in Coleridge's letters 72–3
physical appearance 15n42, 55, 71, 121, 133
pirate publishing 21, 25, 33, 35
Polar Sea 143, 149, 150, 151, 155
Poovey, Mary 143n14
Pope, Alexander 47, 102, 116, 132
   works
      The Dunciad 111
      "Epistle to Dr. Arbuthnot" 115
Porden, Eleanor Anne 148n25
Potkay, Adam 169n63
Potter, Russell 153
Pottinger, George 6n21
Prince of Wales (Prince Regent) 101, 104, 106n18, 112, 115
puffing 131
Pykett, Lyn 2n7

Quarterly Review 1–20, 97–137, 139–73; see also Arctic exploration; Barrow; Gifford
   and anonymity 6–9, 141–2, 164–5
   and Coleridge 12, 73
   on Franklin 147, 154, 155, 156, 158, 162, 166, 168
   and Hazlitt 18, 19, 97, 119–27
   and Hunt 17–18, 19, 50–51, 99–119
   on Keats 2, 8n26, 15, 97, 102, 105, 132, 144n17
   and Lady Morgan 18, 19, 127–137
   on parliamentary reform 16, 21, 26, 30
   on Parry 153–8, 167–8
   on political reformers 24, 106
   its rhetoric 2–4, 85
   on Ross 150–53, 155, 159–65, 171–3
   and Shelley 2, 8, 97, 102, 106, 108, 110
   and Southey 21–51
   and the sublime 166–73

Rawes, Alan 45n38

reading public 11, 13–14
reception 14, 16, 17, 105, 109, 110, 139
   and *Biographia Literaria* 59, 60, 73–90, 94
   of *Florence Macarthy* 136–7
   of the *Letter to William Gifford* 126–7
   of the *Letter to William Smith* 45–53
   and sales 18n49, 73, 128
   of *Ultra-Crepidarius* 116–19
   of *Wat Tyler* 22–31, 35–40, 54
Reiman, Donald 58n4, 64, 70n25, 106
reprisals 4–5, 8, 22, 42, 57, 97, 100, 101, 129–32, 162, 165
republicanism 21, 32, 52
Richard, Jessica 143, 144n16, 145
Robinson, Henry Crabb 4, 17, 45, 68, 81, 88
Robinson, Mary 40, 101, 104, 105, 109, 112, 113, 115, 117, 119, 122
Roe, Nicholas 99n4, 107n20, 108n21
romance 2, 18, 87, 88, 92, 95, 136, 143, 144, 166
Romantic ideology 17, 23, 34n27, 61, 122–3
Romantic themes 2, 172
   exploring the "deep" self 7, 17, 28, 48, 74, 87, 135, 172–3
   idealistic poet 11, 23, 25, 34, 39, 74, 136
   power of the supernatural 2, 17, 50–1, 95, 140
   quest for transcendence 46, 48, 119, 123, 124, 135, 140, 168
Ross, James Clark 161, 162, 163, 172
Ross, John 1, 4, 10, 18, 139–73; see also Barrow
   as Munchausen 153
   responses to Barrow's attacks 19, 159–60, 164
   works
      A Letter to John Barrow 19n51, 159–60
      Narrative of a Second Voyage 139, 160
      Observations 4n14, 10n32, 18n50, 164
      Voyage of Discovery 139, 150
Ross, M.J. 10n32, 139n3, 160n42, 161n46
Rousseau, Jean-Jacques 87
Russett, Margaret 10n34, 85n40, 86, 146n23

St. Clair, William 2n5, 6, 18n49, 19, 21n3

satire 2, 25n11, 38–40, 49, 50–56, 97, 102–5, 115–6, 119, 133
Schoenfield, Mark 1n4, 5n18, 6
Scoresby, William 149, 150
Scott, John 10n34, 94, 98, 132
Scott, Walter 2n8, 4, 19, 92, 95
Sedgwick, Eve 136n71
self-defense-by-association 5, 65
self-vindication 5, 17, 60
    Hazlitt's 121, 125–6
    Jeffrey's 74, 77–8, 93
    Morgan's 132
    Ross's 165
    Southey's 22–3, 31, 41–6
Shakespeare, William 29, 170
Shelley, Mary 54, 111, 142, 143, 145, 149
Shelley, Percy Bysshe 2, 8n26, 19, 54, 97, 101, 108, 109
    works
        Adonais 8n26, 97, 132
        "Mont Blanc" (Shelley) 144, 169
Simpson, David 142n12
Smith, Sydney 80, 153
Smith, William 9, 21, 30, 31, 34, 40–50
Southey, Robert 1, 8–10, 16–17, 21–56, 59, 60–7, 75, 78–84, 89–92, 173
    works
        Letter to William Smith 8, 16, 19, 22, 23, 40–53
        Madoc 19, 167
        "Parliamentary Reform" 16, 19, 21, 24, 25, 26–31, 36, 40, 42, 46
        A Vision of Judgment 53–6
        Wat Tyler 16, 21–56, 59
Spufford, Francis 143n13, 147n24
spurious authorship 145, 146, 149
Stauffer, Andrew 5n17, 71n26
Stewart, David 3n10, 5n18, 9, 16, 22n5, 27n16
Storey, Mark 27n17, 52
Strachan, John 3n9, 85n38
Strout, Alan Lang 90
sublime, the 2, 19, 46, 76, 140, 143, 166–73
Swaim, Barton 3n9
Swann, Karen 88
Sweet, Nanora 8n25

Thompson, James 116n32

Tickler, Timothy 90–95; *see also* *Blackwood's*
The Times 51, 121n41
Toby, the Sapient Pig 43
transcendence 1, 2, 22, 48, 76, 98, 122–7, 136, 144, 170; *see also* the sublime
Treadwell, James 58n3

vituperation 1, 3n9, 5, 13, 30, 40, 63, 94; *see also* "the game"

Walpole, Horace 146
Webb, Timothy 100n8
Weiskel, Thomas 170
Wheatley, Kim 2n6
White, Deborah Elise 122–3
Wilson, Eric 171
Wilson, James 12n38
Wilson, John 17, 61, 84–93, 117; *see also* *Blackwood's*
Winterbottam (Winterbotham), William 21n3
Wordsworth, Dorothy 35
Wordsworth, Jonathan
Wordsworth, William 27–9, 37, 45, 63
    and *Blackwood's* 85
    and the *Edinburgh* 2, 13, 14, 15, 57n2, 59, 67, 68–9, 89
    and the Lake School 62–4, 65–6, 79
    works
        "Complaint of a Forsaken Indian Woman" 156n35, 157
        The Excursion 13, 60, 76, 169
        Lyrical Ballads 60, 68, 69, 70, 76–7, 78, 80, 82
        "My Heart Leaps Up" 19, 27, 28
        "Ode" 27, 28, 44
        The Prelude 31, 32, 43–4, 123, 169, 171
        "Tintern Abbey" 19, 41, 46, 48, 126
Wynn, Charles 30–31
Wu, Duncan 8n25, 10n30, 70n25, 119n36, 120n38, 121, 169

Zall, Paul 5, 57n2, 61n12, 65n19
"Z" 93n50; *see also* Lockhart
    and Hazlitt 122
    on Hunt 91n48